Palgrave Studies in Financial Services Technology

Series Editor
Bernardo Nicoletti
Rome, Italy

The Palgrave Studies in Financial Services Technology series features original research from leading and emerging scholars on contemporary issues and developments in financial services technology. Falling into 4 broad categories: channels, payments, credit, and governance; topics covered include payments, mobile payments, trading and foreign transactions, big data, risk, compliance, and business intelligence to support consumer and commercial financial services. Covering all topics within the life cycle of financial services, from channels to risk management, from security to advanced applications, from information systems to automation, the series also covers the full range of sectors: retail banking, private banking, corporate banking, custody and brokerage, wholesale banking, and insurance companies. Titles within the series will be of value to both academics and those working in the management of financial services.

More information about this series at
http://www.springer.com/series/14627

Bernardo Nicoletti

The Future of FinTech

Integrating Finance and Technology in Financial Services

palgrave
macmillan

Bernardo Nicoletti
Rome, Italy

Palgrave Studies in Financial Services Technology
ISBN 978-3-319-51414-7 ISBN 978-3-319-51415-4 (eBook)
DOI 10.1007/978-3-319-51415-4

Library of Congress Control Number: 2017932557

Cover design by Samantha Johnson

Printed on acid-free paper

This Palgrave Macmillan imprint is published by Springer Nature
The registered company is Springer International Publishing AG
The registered company address is: Gewerbestrasse 11, 6330 Cham, Switzerland

Acknowledgments

This book is the result of the last several years of research on financial services, where several people are worthy to be acknowledged for their support, useful comments, and cooperation.

A special mention should be made of Prof. Gustavo Piga, Prof. Corrado Cerruti, and Prof. Andrea Appoloni at the Universita' di Tor Vergata a Roma. Moreover, I acknowledge the support from Dr. Gian Marco Balletti in collecting and evaluating some basic materials during his thesis at the same university.

A special thanks also to Aimee Dibbens from Palgrave Macmillan for her continuous support and encouragement. This series started with mobile banking, continued with digital insurance, and now analyzes fin-tech initiatives.

I acknowledge my family, whose constant support and patience made this book happen.

Bernardo Nicoletti

Contents

List of Abbreviations and Acronyms

ABI	Associazione Bancaria Italiana
ACH	Automated Clearing House
ADAS	Advanced Driver Assistance Systems
AFI	Alliance for Financial Inclusion
AI	Artificial Intelligence
AML	Anti-Money Laundering
API	Application Programming Interface
App	Application (mostly for mobile)
ATM	Automated Teller Machine
B2B	Business to Business
B2C	Business to Consumer
BaFin	Bundesanstalt für Finanzdienstleistungsaufsicht
BCBS	Basel Committee on Banking Supervision
BI	Business Intelligence
BMC	Business Model Canvas
BMI	Business Model Innovation
BPM	Business Process Management
BTC	Bitcoin
C2B	Customer to Business
CA	Controlling Authority
CB	Commerzbank
CBA	Commercial Bank of Africa

CD	Compact Disk
CFO	Chief Financial Officer
CIB	Corporate and Investment Banking
CIO	Chief Information Officer
CKM	Customer Knowledge Management
CLV	Customer Lifetime Value
CPU	Central Processing Unit
CRM	Customer Relationship Management or Credit Risk Management
CSR	Customer Service Representative
DLT	Distributed Ledger Technology (aka Blockchain)
ECB	European Central Bank
ECM	Enterprise Content Management
ECN	Electronic Communication Network
EMV	Europay, MasterCard, and VISA
ERP	Enterprise Resource Planning
ESA	European Space Agency
EU	European Union
EY	Ernst & Young
FCA	Financial Conduct Authority
FINMA (Swiss)	Financial Market Supervisory Authority
Fintech	Financial Technology
FINTRAC	Financial Transactions and Reports Analysis Centre of Canada
FMA	First Mover Advantage
FTE	Full-Time Equivalent
FX	Foreign Exchange
GPU	Graphics Processing Unit
HR	Human Resource
GSM	General System for Mobile Communication
ICAAP	Internal Capital Adequacy Assessment Process
ICR	Intelligent Character Recognition
ICT	Information and Communications Technology
ID	Identification Data
IIN	Issuer Identification Number
IMSI	International Mobile Subscriber Identity

ING	ING-Diba
IOU	I Owe You
IPO	Initial Public Offering
IxD	Interaction Design
KBA	Knowledge-Based Authentication
KPI	Key Performance Indicator
KYC	Know Your Customer
LAN	Local Area Network
MFI	Microfinance Institution
MNO	Mobile Network Operator
MVP	Minimum Viable Product
NASA	National Aeronautics and Space Administration
NFC	Near-Field Communication
NIST	National Institute of Standards and Technology
NLP	Natural Language Processing
OCR	Optical Character Recognition
OEM	Original Equipment Manufacturer
OTC	Over the Counter
P2P	Person to Person or Peer to Peer
PC	Personal Computer
PCI DSS	Payment Card Industry Data Security Standard
PDCA	Plan-Do-Check-Act
PED	Project Entropia Dollars
PFM	Personal Finance Management
PII	Personal Identifying Information
POS	Point of Sale
PPC	Pay per Click
PSE	(EU) Payment Services Directive
PwC	PricewaterhouseCoopers
ROI	Return on Investment
S2S	Service to Sale
SDK	Software Development Kit
SDM	Secure Domain Manager
SEO	Search Engine Optimization
SEPA	Single European Payment Area
SG&A	Selling, General, and Administrative Expenses

SIFIs	Systematically Important Financial Institutions
SIM	Subscriber Identity Module
SMEs	Small- and Medium-Sized Enterprises or Subject Matter Experts
SMS	Short Message Service
STP	Straight-Through Processing
TAM	Technology Acceptance Model
TCO	Total Cost of Ownership
TSM	Telecommunication Management System
UBI	Usage-Based Insurance
UI	User Interface
UICC	Universal Integrated Circuit Card
UN	United Nations.
UPC	Universal Product Code
USC	Utility Settlement Coin
VC	Venture Capital or Virtual Currency
VoC	Voice of the Customer
VoIP	Voice over Internet Protocol

List of Figures

List of Tables

1
Introduction

Financial technology, commonly called "fintech", is now a highly used buzzword. Startups competing with traditional financial services, offering customer-centric services capable of combining speed and flexibility, are spreading throughout the world. They are radically changing the expectations and the engagement of customers. Customers enjoy more and more a digital perspective, characterized by a nearly complete immediacy and availability of the information, enabled by technological devices such as smartphones and tablets, and by other trends such as the Internet of Things (IoT).

Traditional financial organizations, such as banks and insurance companies, are changing, with the aim of narrowing the technological gap between them and the fintech startups. Nevertheless, their paths toward change and innovation are full of hurdles. Old routines never overhauled and rigid business models are one of their primary issues to tackle.

Fintech companies are involved in a process of "disintermediation through innovation"[1]: Big Data, blockchain, robo-advisors, Internet of

[1] https://twitter.com/dslotnik/status/735897993447104512, Accessed 1 August 2016.

B. Nicoletti, *The Future of FinTech*,
DOI 10.1007/978-3-319-51415-4_1

Everything (IoE), contextually with a by far more effective exploitation of digital channels and mobile devices, are levers that are allowing them to reshape the financial services industry. These solutions provide the market with innovative adding-value solutions, backed by forward-looking strategies and cutting-edge business models.

This book has a twofold aim: on one hand, it aims to provide the big picture of the fintech initiatives, not only by giving insights on their evolution, their status, the main delivered innovations, but also by presenting business cases of successful companies. On the other hand, it aims also to provide organizations with guiding principles, lumped together and centralized in a business model presented and applied throughout all the chapters. The model has its most comprehensive application in Chap. 8, which analyzes an Italian business-to-business (B2B) fintech company.

2

Financial Services and Fintech

Introduction

Fintech organizations, mainly startups, are reshaping the financial services industry, offering customer-centric services capable of combining speed and flexibility, backed by forward-looking strategies, and cutting-edge business models.

This chapter aims to provide the big picture of this fragmented universe. It starts with the history of fintech initiatives, dealing with the different waves that have characterized their paths. The rise of fintech initiatives depends on many factors. They include supply-side factors, with the onset of the digital transformation, and demand-side factors, with the emergence of new life models. The 2008 financial crisis also played an important role by prompting tighter regulation of traditional players and a growing sense of mistrust among customers toward traditional financial institutions.

This chapter provides some insights about the financial services industry altogether, identifying the "breaches" where fintech companies

B. Nicoletti, *The Future of FinTech*,
DOI 10.1007/978-3-319-51415-4_2

are leveraging with the aim of disintermediating traditional financial organizations.

Eventually, this chapter provides an analysis of the most relevant fintech regions and ecosystems from a worldwide perspective, presenting the possible developments and evolutions of the whole sector.

Changing Environment

In the last few years, there have been substantial changes in the banking and financial sectors. The reasons are several, such as the impact of the 2008 financial and economic crisis, the increasing regulation of incumbent players, and the social and behavioral changes in the customers. In the last few years, the digital transformation is the most important catalyst behind the fintech phenomenon.

The Financial Crisis, Regulation, and Trust

The 2008 financial and economic crisis triggered a series of major upheavals in the financial services sector. The first was the realization that the activities of the major financial institutions can generate systemic risk. This led to the development of different measures designed to quantify that risk. Regulation gave directions and forced actions to mitigate them. In particular, the notion of a financial entity's contribution to systemic risk led to the definition of systematically important financial institutions (SIFIs). The Basel Committee on Banking Supervision (BCBS) increased banks' regulatory reserve requirement in order to take account of individual contributions to global risk (Benoit et al. 2016). Similarly, regulators asked many companies to verify and improve their solvency. This regulatory tightening placed a dual burden on financial institutions: directly, by forcing them to set aside greater reserves and therefore scale back their activities and, indirectly, in that the public opinion considered them the main culprits behind the financial crisis.

As the global economy emerged from the crisis, it became clear that many customers, and especially the younger generations, the so-called millennials, had lost faith in the traditional financial services. From their point of view, financial institutions were the root cause of the financial and economic crisis. To make matters worse, those agents had only managed to avoid bankruptcy thanks to continuing massive injections or support of public money (Sorkin 2010). If the banks themselves were incapable of managing the risks they took, why should anyone take their advice or trust them with their savings? Old and new generations of customers are willing to turn their backs on the traditional players. They are keen to see new companies emerge that played no part in the recent crisis and could offer innovative solutions to financial services.

From Customers to Users of Financial Services

As well as taking a dimmer view of the financial services, younger generations have developed very different consumer habits from their elders. They have grown up used to having access to personalized solutions, tailored to their needs. This is in stark contrast with the mass marketing approach of the banks and other traditional financial institutions. The conventional model of the customer is somebody who consumes whatever is the offer. The new customer is more and more the "user" of financial services of his choice (Cui and Wu 2016). The old customers were passive. They were satisfied with choosing from a finite selection of products or pre-defined services. Today, customers are active. They expect to receive solutions, customized to their personal needs. The example of asset management is a case in point. A banking network offers the same savings products to a maximum number of customers in order to generate economies of scale. The user-customer expects a flexible solution that can be adapted to his/her individual needs and investment objectives. Matching products and services to the expectations of the user require close mass interaction. This is only possible via a digitized platform.

From the outset, many fintech companies have targeted younger generations that are used to digital, interactive, customized solutions. This strategy is not without risks. On average, younger generations own fewer assets than the rest of the population. The gap is particularly wide with respect to the oldest generations who tend to have substantial financial wealth and capability of savings. In order to be economically viable, fintech companies quickly need to attract large quantities of assets. There are two pivotal factors for this: the number of customers and the average amount of assets per customer. Even if they attract large numbers of young customers, fintech initiatives will still struggle to reach a profit as long as younger generations' wealth remains low. It is possible that fintech companies have time to grow in parallel with younger generations' assets, and eventually become profitable. There is no guarantee that they will be able to retain these customers. As younger generations age, they will face increasingly complex savings challenges. Solutions such as the robo-advisors currently offer only basic solutions that are not always suited to these demands. Robo-advisors are ideal for customers with few assets who mainly want to avoid high bank charges, while traditional institutions aim toward customers that tend to have more assets and require much greater expertise. Fintech companies will struggle to make money if they lose their customers as soon as they become profitable.

Conversely, if the traditional players are to attract profitable customers, they will have to evolve and offer the same or higher levels of interactivity and profitability as their fintech rivals.

Today's fintech solutions such as the robo-advisors are just one example of the way incumbent companies are innovating in order to transform their customer relationships and offer new approaches in financial services. For the time being, private banking customers receive this type of service. However, in the near future, thanks to fintech initiatives, a broader range of customers will receive this type of services. This is the only way the sector giants can survive the transition from consumers to users.

Financial Services: Problems and Challenges

European financial services have accumulated very large losses in the last decades. The Italian government is working on plans to set up a €50 billion bad bank bailout.[1] From the spread crisis of 2011, the overall Italian

[1] http://seekingalpha.com/news/3193629-italy-tasks-jpmorgan-50b-bank-bailout, Accessed 20 August 2016.

universe of banks has produced nearly €50 billion of net losses. The Royal Bank of Scotland, since the beginning of the crisis, has accumulated £48 billion of losses.[2] Deutsche Bank, for instance, suffered a heavy and continuous contraction of the profitability. It registered in 2015 its own record amount of a €6.8 billion loss.[3] Other large banks, such as Commerzbank, and, unexpectedly, Credit Suisse had similar financial problems.[4] More specifically, the accounts of the Swiss institution for 2015 closed with a net loss of €2.6 billion, where the heavy depreciation (€3.5 billion) of the investment bank Donaldson, Lufkin, and Jenrette, acquired in 2000, has turned out to be a heavy toll to pay.

Stability in the financial services sector is critical for a smooth functioning of the real economy due to the magnitude of the impact that negative externalities could have on it. The recent global crisis has largely shown the negative effects of a bad functioning of the financial services system and, most importantly, of its failures. Small businesses, overtopped by information asymmetries, might not be able to get the funds to pursue their initiatives. Customers with deposited savings might postpone their investments, and even the payment system, as the Greek case clearly shows, might be at risk.

Following these events, regulators have moved toward a new direction[5]:

(1) New solvency regulation
(2) Upgraded capital regulation
(3) Focus on structural reforms in the financial services

The rationale behind this trend is the concern on the stability in the financial services sector, even in times of crisis or of stressing situations. A large amount of losses has, in a certain number of cases, been covered by

[2] http://www.telegraph.co.uk/finance/newsbysector/banksandfinance/10664372/RBS-has-lost-all-the-46bn-pumped-in-by-the-taxpayer.html, Accessed 26 July 2016.

[3] http://www.investing.businessweek.wallst.com/research/stocks/financials/financials.asp?ticker=DBK:GR, Accessed 26 July 2016.

[4] http://www.streetinsider.com/Credit+Ratings/S%26P+Takes+Ratings+Actions+on+Several+U.K.,+German,+Swiss,+and+Austrian+Banks+(BCS)+(DB)+(CS)+(LYG)+(RBS)/10222021.html, Accessed 26 July 2016.

[5] file:///C:/Users/Nicoletti/Downloads/PwC%20study%20impact%20of%20bank%20structural%20reform%20(3).pdf, Accessed 20 August 2016.

governments or by central banks, including the European Central Bank (ECB).[6] Without the support of the public finances, the amount of losses undergone by these financial institutions would have been disastrously high and the real economy would have had a critical hit. Notwithstanding this support, most of the financial institutions have not reached the levels of profitability registered before the crisis. New and changing hurdles have quickly turned into losses, whereas the actions put in place did not seem to be highly effective.

New challenges are more and more appearing:

- the continuously increasing relevance of fintech initiatives; and
- a new stability-focused regulation

Therefore, traditional financial services are taking drastic measures. Cost-cutting policies are the traditional countermeasures to fight the reduction in the levels of profitability. By reducing head count, a number of physical branches, selling, general, and administrative expenses (SG&A), and operative expenses, traditional financial institutions expect to achieve a sustainable comeback to the pre-crisis levels of profitability.

Some figures from three financial giants show an example of what institutions are doing to aim to achieve a sustainable growth by means of cost-cutting policies. Deutsche Bank has announced a slash in its workforce of 9000 permanent staff and 6000 contractors, in addition to other 20,000 workers in the process of selling and outsourcing businesses and assets.[7] According to John Cryan, the chief executive, this will allow savings for €3.8 billion by 2018. Unicredit, as part of a more general overhaul, will eliminate about 18,200 jobs, allowing savings for €1.6 billion, by 2018.[8] Barclays, on the other hand, will cut about 1000 jobs in investment banking worldwide.[9]

---

[6] http://ec.europa.eu/economy_finance/publications/publication15887_en.pdf, Accessed 20 August 2016.

[7] https://global.handelsblatt.com/edition/296/ressort/finance/article/deutsche-banks-late-start, Accessed 26 July 2016.

[8] http://www.nytimes.com/2015/11/12/business/dealbook/unicredit-of-italy-to-cut-18200-jobs-as-part-of-overhaul.html?_r=0, Accessed 26 July 2016.

[9] http://www.reuters.com/article/us-barclays-employment-asia-idUSKCN0UZ0UP, Accessed 26 July 2016.

Customer Centricity

The business model is one of the main causes of the huge amount of losses recently undergone by traditional financial services institutions. These organizations often have obsolete, non-updated business models, designed for old-style markets and customers that in the meantime have changed their needs. Although financial services tried to develop closer relationships with their customers, financial services have not managed to give the right priority to their needs. The majority of their products and services still lack customizations. The complaints about the inefficiencies regarding service, such as the one provided in the branches and call centers, and advice are common issues. On the other side, these financial institutions are still charging high costs for overdrafts or other common and more and more non-difficult operations.

Financial institutions are aware that customers take a primary role in their business. They are recognizing more and more the need of radical changes in order to face a new and quickly changing environment. This process, once started, is full of challenges. Old routines, consolidates cultures, resistance to change, agency costs, and information asymmetries make this path more difficult than it really is. There is also the danger that the process overshadows the main objective (today more than ever): the achievement of a sustainable growth and an above-average level of profitability by embarking on a customer-centric transformation (Sieljacks 2014).

To listen to the voice of the customer is important. According to a TransferWise survey, the five main factors that prompt consumers to choose technology providers over banks are as follows: a more secure service than banks (34%), a lower cost than banks (29%), a more convenient service than banks (26%), a quicker service than banks (18%), and a better customer service than banks (18%).[10]

New approaches have been playing a critical role in the definition of a new environment. The development of new financial products, together

[10] https://transferwise.com/gb/blog/how-technology-is-democratising-the-financial-services-sector, Accessed 24 August 2016.

with an updated regulation, has radically changed not only the needs and desires of customers but also the ways to engage them.

McKinsey and Company developed a process to manage the transformation to a customer-centric organization (Auerbach et al. 2012):

- Vision and positioning: "Create an institution that customers want to bank with and employees feel proud of."
- Customer engagement model: "Design a bank that delivers exceptional customer service where customers expect it, and excites them where they do not."
- Development agenda: "Define an integrated development agenda to drive short-term gains and long-term growth."
- Organization, capabilities, and insights: "Build the insights engine, organizational capabilities, and governance needed to sustain momentum."

Digital Transformation

One powerful way to meet today's challenges is to move toward a digital transformation. The financial services sector is a laggard in this respect. There are some exceptions. High-frequency trading and related arbitrage strategies are good examples of the impact new technologies have already made.[11] It has become common practice to monitor changes in market prices over tiny fractions of a second, construct arbitrage strategies based on statistical rules, and move in and out of positions at high speed to profit from very short-term fluctuations in prices. In this case, the most important aspect of the digital transformation is the ability to process a sequence of repetitive tasks at speeds previously unknown in trading. For a long time, the high cost of implementing, in a systematic way, these approaches prevented their widespread use. The acquisition and processing of information were not commonly available. They were expensive, raising a barrier to entry for new players. In addition, in the asset management sector, in particular, this first digital transformation

---

[11] http://www.bis.org/publ/mktc07.pdf, Accessed 20 August 2016.

only really affected the production side of the business and not distribution. Investors who purchased a share in an investment fund from their financial services network continued to receive standard quarterly reports on the performance of their savings. These reports took very limited account of their specific investment objectives (retirement funding, investment for a future real-estate purchase), or of any other holdings in their portfolio.

The second stage in the digital transformation, linked to the emergence of fintech initiatives, has been more far-reaching. It began with the increased availability of solutions that could improve at the same time the entire value chain. Recent information and communications technology (ICT) developments have brought solutions both for the production side (databases, decision-making tools) and for distribution (digital channels, knowledge of customers, good customer experience, and flexibility of customer offerings). These advances are enabling new entrants to find a place in the industry. They allow occupying market niche offerings based on the interactivity and customization sought by younger generations, at a much lower cost than the ones offered by traditional institutions.

On the production side, investment managers increasingly use sophisticated Big Data Analytics and risk management tools to create new products. The biggest change has been in distribution, with customers, or service users as mentioned in this book, receiving offerings personalized to their needs. To achieve this, distributors need to know as much as possible about their customers, hence the widespread use of metrics, quantitative information that distributors collect by closely analyzing their customers' overall lifestyles. In financial services, customer relationship management was for a long time thought to be the preserve of the large institutions due to the high cost of customer information acquisition. Now, both newcomers and other non-financial entities (telecoms operators, retail chains, and especially e-commerce operators) can use emerging technologies to offer new services to their prospect and customer base. They can also build up new customer bases more easily, as customers are eager to buy personalized services rather than ready-made products. In the asset management industry, this second digital transformation has affected both production and distribution at the same time. By statistically inferring the level of a customer's income, for example, as well as his/her monthly outgoings, an asset operator can compute the monthly saving capacity and offer suitable investment strategies. These analytical approaches are particularly effective with large customer bases, where it is possible to simulate the behavior of new customers based on the past behavior of existing customers in the same segment. It is also possible to forecast the future behavior of a customer based on his/her particular characteristics. The financial institution can use this information to provide a personalized approach and an excellent customer experience.

Definition of Fintech

The word fintech derives from the coupling of two complementary areas: financial services and solutions based on advanced technology. The economic literature does not agree on a single definition of fintech due to the overall diversity of the business. The word "fintech" has made its way into the *Oxford Dictionary* as: "Computer programs and other technology used to support or enable banking and financial services."[12] Wikipedia defines "FinTech" as: "Financial technology, also known as Fintech, is a line of business based on using software to provide financial services. fintech companies are generally startups founded with the purpose of disrupting incumbent financial systems and corporations that rely less on software."[13]

It is possible to set out a broad working definition of the term that perfectly fits with the aim of this book. In particular, it is possible to define fintech as initiatives, with an innovative and disruptive business model, which leverage on ICT in the area of financial services. A simpler definition of fintech is as an industry made up of organizations using novel financial technology to support or enable financial services.[14]

There are two main aspects to consider—the subject and the scope of the definition:

---

[12] http://www.oxforddictionaries.com/it/definizione/inglese/fintech, Accessed 20 August 2016.

[13] https://en.wikipedia.org/wiki/Financial_technology, Accessed 20 August 2016.

[14] https://www.linkedin.com/pulse/what-fintech-attempting-definition-patrick-schueffel, Accessed 25 July 2016.

- It is important not to consider fintech initiatives as an ecosystem populated only by startups. The term is often associated with startups, mainly because the use of advanced digital solutions in financial services is a relatively modern trend. Even mature and maturing companies have started to transform their businesses with advanced financial technology solutions, for instance, by making use of online or mobile services.
- The scope of the fintech definition requires more details. This book presents a typical fintech business model. The model helps to understand the reasons why some initiatives are more successful than others. It is important to understand that financial technology solutions are a very complex and regulated subject, where several and different stakeholders place their interests.

Fintech initiatives cover a wide range of financial areas. Lending Club, one of the world's largest peer-to-peer lending platform (Schumpeter 2013), directly connects borrowers and investors by making credit more affordable and investing more rewarding, and promoting a completely new loan program.

Kickstarter, a very large funding platform for creative projects, has strongly lowered the level of accessibility of funds for startups or simple projects.[15] Wealthfront embodies a fusion between finance and automation, allowing the management of assets through complex algorithms.[16] CommonBond is a marketplace lender that refinances graduate and undergraduate student loans. It has lowered the cost of student loans and allowed saving an average of 14,000 dollars over the lifetime of the loan (Mulhere 2015). These examples depict a clear situation. Fintech companies are threatening traditional financial services. The former can provide more innovative and customer-centric business models. These disruptive organizations are gradually gaining market share and profits against traditional financial services, which are in serious need of reviewing their business models and changing strategy in order to be more competitive in the market.

[15] https://www.kickstarter.com/, Accessed 20 August 2016.

[16] https://www.wealthfront.com/, Accessed 20 August 2016.

Things have never been easy for fintech startups. Houman Shadab, a law professor at New York Law School, states: "Fintech is different from many other startup sectors because the financial world is heavily regulated and mostly consists of a relatively few numbers of large, well-established companies" (Desai 2015). He points out the difficulties that the modern economic scenario is putting in place to threaten fintech initiatives. Later chapters deal with this topic by discussing the main obstacles and bottlenecks that fintech startups face since their very beginning.

History of Fintech

Fintech is a relatively modern concept. It can be dated back to the first half of the nineteenth century (Douglas et al. 2015), with the introduction of the telegraph (1838) and later with the successful construction of the first transatlantic cable in 1866. Together, these two technological innovations put the basis for the financial globalization of the late 1800s. Nowadays, in the era of Internet of Things, it can be difficult to think about an unlinked world, where information flows with great difficulties over regions and continents. Before the transatlantic cable was successfully completed, communications between Europe and the Americas took place only by ship. Apart from the duration of the trips, there was a considerable risk of having delays due to possible storms and shipwrecks. The significance and the scope of that innovation, even for financial uses, are clear.

Banking as an industry was one of the early adopters of computers. The first mainframe for commercial use was built for a bank. Banks themselves used computers to enhance and speed up legacy processes that already existed.

What has been widely recognized as one of the greatest financial technology innovations of the last century is the automatic teller machine (ATM). In 2009, Paul Volcker, former chairperson of the US Federal Reserve, said: "The most important financial innovation that I have seen in the past 20 years is the automatic teller machine ('ATM'), that really helps people and prevents visits to the bank and it is a real convenience."[17]

---

[17] Volcker, P. (2009), The only thing useful banks have invented in 20 years is the ATM, *The New York Post*, available at http://nypost.com/2009/12/13/the-only-thing-useful-banks-have-invented-in-20-years-is-the-atm/, Accessed 1 August 2016.

Barclays Bank installed the first ATM in the city of Enfield, UK, on 27 June 1967. It actually allowed people to perform financial transactions through an electronic telecommunication device. The ATM is one of the initial applications of technology to the financial area, allowing important economic savings to financial institutions by introducing automation rather than a person's labor in the relationships between the customers and the financial institutions.

The ATM innovation is interesting. It has marked the start of a new fintech era. The relationships between financial services and technology, since that date, have faded. The ATM was the first innovation that clearly showed the deep potential interlinkage between finance and technology. The way to the digitalization of the financial services industry was open. Until the end of the 1980s, this industry remained, at least from a consumer perspective, largely an industry based on analog technologies.

Arner et al. (2015) have identified 1987 as the turning point for the fintech industry, referring to two facts:

(1) The iconic image from Oliver Stone's movie *Wall Street*, picturing an investment banker handling an early mobile phone.
(2) The "Black Monday" stock market crash. One of the recognized causes of the crash, started in Hong Kong and immediately spread through Europe and the United States, was the so-called program trading: a computerized type of trading that involves the execution of a basket of stocks at pre-determined conditions. In short, a computer application buys and sells shares once the prices reach certain thresholds.

The Black Monday stock market crash highlighted the strict interlinkage and risks between finance and technology, bringing this fact to the attention of the regulators. In particular, regulators developed new rules and reviewed compensation protocols in order to bring uniformity to the most relevant financial products. With the aim of controlling the pace of price variations, the New York Stock Exchange introduced circuit breakers, together with program trading curbs. Furthermore, there were continued efforts to foster cooperation.

The 1990s saw the start of a shift from analog to digital technologies for the financial services industry. The development of the World Wide Web and the first experiments of Internet banking from Well Fargo in the USA and ING in Europe marked this decade. In addition, the replacement of the telegraph first with the fax and later with the email/instant messages enhanced communications throughout the world, setting the stage for stronger financial relationships.

Starting from the twenty-first century, the internal and external processes related to the financial services industry have moved to full digitization. The significance of the investments in the ICT sector shows the relevance that this area has in the financial services industry.

Traditional financial institutions have direct competition from fintech startups. The mobile phone has radically changed the way many customers choose to do their banking. In fact, in some parts of the world, it has allowed people to have a bank account or sort of.

Fintech initiatives are spreading very rapidly, affecting new areas and branches. In 2009, Satoshi Nakamoto (a pseudonym) introduced a new type of money called Bitcoin (Skinner 2016). It is a form of digital currency to perform transactions without the involvement of central banks or other intermediaries.

The future is more uncertain than ever. The rate of innovation in the financial industry is very high. Not necessarily the reactions of traditional financial institutions will be successful. What currently seems to be most likely is that, considering what experts, scholars, and practitioners say, fintech initiatives will continue to grow in the future.

In the 1990s, Citicorp (later Citigroup, the result of the merger between Citicorp and Travelers Group) initiated a project with the aim of promoting and fostering technological collaboration with outsiders. Its official name was "Financial Services Technology Consortium" and Fintech was its synthetic name. Nowadays, this term has changed its scope. It does not anymore identify a specific initiative or organization. It is a big box comprising also startups delivering technology-based proposition values, capable of enabling, enhancing, and even, in some cases, disrupting financial services. So, the fintech terminology includes:

- Startups
- Use of advanced financial technologies in traditional financial institutions
- Collaboration of startups and traditional companies, be them financial institutions or technological firms

Fintech Stages

It is important to distinguish three main eras of the fintech evolution (Arner et al. 2015). From around 1866 to 1967, the financial services industry, while heavily interlinked with technology, remained largely an analog industry, at least in its public image. This is the period of fintech 1.0.

From 1967, the development of digital technology for communications and processing of transactions increasingly transformed finance from an analog to a digital industry. By 1987 at the latest, financial services, at least in developed countries, had become not only highly globalized, but also digitized. This period of fintech 2.0 continued until 2008. During this period, the traditional regulated financial services industry dominated the financial technology initiatives. It used technology to provide financial products and services.

Since 2008, a new stage has started (fintech 3.0). New startups and established technology companies have begun to deliver financial products and services directly to businesses and consumers.

Nowadays, industry 4.0 is a vision of an increased connection between physical and virtual industrial machines (Schlechtendahl et al. 2015). This computerization of manufacturing brings many benefits, allowing data gathering, integration, and analysis on a scale not seen earlier. Similarly, it is possible to imagine a fintech 4.0 stage. This stage will see fintech companies and fintech initiatives in traditional financial institutions more intensively connected. That would be

- from a technical point of view, a systematization of technological solutions; and

- from an industry point of view, the integration of fintech initiatives in the established financial system.

In a fintech 4.0 scenario, there might be also threats. As fintech start-ups grow in number and sophistication, they will establish an increasing number of links with traditional providers. Interfaces between systems are a common source of cyber vulnerabilities. To help guard against this, interfaces between digital financial systems should be subject to particularly stringent scrutiny, including penetration testing, during the product development process, including by people who can take a clean slate, holistic view of the aggregated system.

An Overview of Fintech Initiatives Around the World

An important point is the overall situation of fintech initiatives from a rate-of-growth point of view. The fintech market has experienced an increase in two critical aspects: investments and market size. There is a correlation in the two aspects. If banks and financial institutions invest more in advanced technology, the market size will most likely increase. What is not obvious and must be analyzed is the final result or, in other words, the long-term payback and the ROI (return on investment) of those investments.

In 2014, investments in fintech business ventures tripled to $12.21 billion. Taking into consideration the previous year, the result is a global growth of 201%. According to Venture Scanner, at the end of 2015, there were 1379 fintech companies with a total funding amount of $33 billion.[18] These figures do not include fintech initiatives in traditional financial institutions.

These figures clearly identify fintech as a "hot ticket", showing a relevant growth in investments, revenues, and employment: "the sector has now grown from its disruptive roots into an industry in its own right."[19]

---

[18] Venture Scanner, 2016. Fintech Q1 Update, [online] Available at: http://insights.venturescanner.com/category/financial-technology/, Accessed 27 July 2016.

[19] EY (2016), UK FinTech: on the cutting edge, EY Report.

The size of the investments and the outstanding rate of growth of the sector imply some insights about its phase of the life cycle: fintech initiatives are still far from mature, varying by different degrees in different parts of the world.

Ecosystems

The consultancy company Ernst & Young (EY) ranked the most relevant fintech ecosystems from a worldwide perspective. It identified four core ecosystem attributes,[20] to which it is necessary to add "solutions" as the fifth one:

(1) Demand: the customer demand across consumers, corporates, and financial institutions
(2) Talent: the availability of technological, financial services, and entrepreneurial talents
(3) Capital: the availability of financial resources for startups and internal initiatives
(4) Policy: the government policies on regulations, taxes, and innovation initiatives
(5) Solutions: the introduction of new technology, products, services, and processes

From a broad perspective, a business ecosystem is "an economic community supported by a foundation of interacting organizations and individuals—the organisms of the business world. The economic community produces goods and services of value to customers, who are themselves members of the ecosystem. The member organizations also include vendors, lead producers, competitors, and other stakeholders. Over time, they co-evolve their capabilities and roles. They tend to align themselves with the directions set by one or more central companies. Those companies holding leadership roles may change over time, but the function of the ecosystem leader is valued by the community because it enables

[20] EY (2016), UK Fintech: on the cutting edge, EY Report.

members to move toward shared visions to align their investments, and to find mutually supportive roles" (Moore 1996).

It is important to understand the composition of a fintech ecosystem, starting from the subsystems connected to the stakeholders and linked to the five core ecosystems' attributes (see Fig. 2.1):

(1) The demand attribute is the result of the synergies built between customers, financial institutions, corporates, and governments.
(2) The talent attribute depends on universities and other educational institutions, technology and financial institutions, and entrepreneurs operating their businesses in sectors with a high level of correlation with financial technology.
(3) The solutions attribute depends on the technological companies, the academia, and, potentially, on crowdsourcing.
(4) The capital attribute depends on three main categories of investors:

- angel investors, or business angels, who usually invest during the early stage/startup phase of the venture's life cycle in exchange for an equity ownership interest

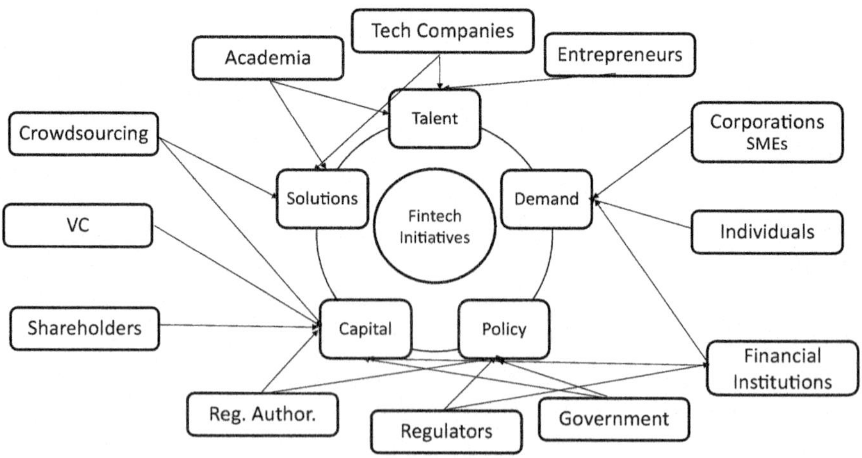

Fig. 2.1 The Fintech ecosystem (adapted by the author from EY 2016)

- venture capital investors (called VC investors), who finance/capitalize growth by providing capital and general support to growing companies that do not have access to equities market
- IPO (initial public offering) investors, who basically provide capital to private companies publicly selling their shares for the first time.

(5) The policy attribute refers not only to the specific policy environment but also to the effectiveness of the tax incentives and government programs: the ordinary stakeholders belonging to this area are regulators and governments.

At the center of the ecosystem, there are the fintech companies, which may benefit from the system or not depending not only on the specific structure, competencies, and capabilities of the company to profit from the environment, but also on the effectiveness of the channels that link the different components of the whole ecosystem.

Ranking National Ecosystems

Based on the attributes that constitute the basis for the benchmarking activity, it is possible to move to take a snapshot of the regions in the world that currently occupy a position of leadership in the fintech scenario.

The insights provided in Tables 2.1 and 2.2 are taken from analyses conducted by EY, which, together with CB Insights, analyzed a certain number of regions from a fintech point of view.[21] The tables show some of the results of those analyses.

The market size and the investments are different in the different areas of the United States, implying an internal (regional) differentiation. The United Kingdom has shown a facilitating regulatory framework that has

[21] http://www.ey.com/Publication/vwLUAssets/EY-UK-FinTech-On-the-cutting-edge-Executive-summary/$FILE/EY-UK-FinTech-On-the-cutting-edge-exec-summary.pdf, Accessed 20 August 2016.

Table 2.1 Market size and investments of some regions

	Market size (Billions)	Investment (Billions)	Fintech staff
UK	$6.6	0.5	61,000
New York	$5.6	1.4	57,000
California	$4.7	3.6	74,000
Germany	$1.8	0.4	13,000
Australia	$0.7	0.2	10,000
Hong Kong	$0.6	0.05	8000
Singapore	$0.6	0.04	7000

Table 2.2 Fintech evaluation of some regions

	Talent	Solutions	Capital	Policy	Demand	Total
UK	4	3	3	4	4	18
California	4	4	4	2	3	17
New York	3	2	4	1	4	14
Singapore	2	1	1	4	2	10
Germany	2	3	3	2	2	12
Australia	2	2	2	3	1	10
Hong Kong	1	2	2	3	3	11

enabled a fast growth without the involvement of large amounts of capital. One example is the Project Innovate (2014). The Financial Conduct Authority (FCA) launched the project to support innovative businesses. Its main task is "to foster competition and growth in financial services by supporting both small and large businesses that are developing new products and services that could genuinely benefit consumers".[22] In addition to the key differentiation provided by policy management, the United Kingdom seems to have a leading position also for what concerns tax initiatives, immediately followed by Singapore. The United States, instead, seems to benefit from a concentration of large venture capital funds with experience in fintech investing, especially in the area of the Silicon Valley. New York is still behind the Silicon Valley, even though the gap is narrowing and the consolidated growth registered in the last years is beyond the best forecasted estimates. Taking into consideration fintech

[22] Financial Conduct Authority's Project Innovate celebrates the first anniversary with plans for "regulatory sandbox", www.fca.org.uk, 2015, Accessed 20 August 2016.

investments, in 2014, Accenture forecasted that the United States could reach $4.7 billion annually only by 2018: as of December 2015, $7.13 billion were invested only in the regions of New York and Florida.[23]

By analyzing the report developed by EY, "UK Fintech: On the Cutting Edge" (2016), with some adjustments by the author, it is possible to define the status of the different regions (see Table 2.2).

The United Kingdom currently occupies a position of marginal leadership, immediately followed by California and New York that act as autonomous fintech hubs.

Furthermore, by building a radar graph of the three main competitive ecosystems, the global fintech scenario becomes clearer (see Fig. 2.2). The United Kingdom is actually balancing the five attributes mentioned before. At the same time, this ecosystem has been able to optimize the interfaces between all the involved stakeholders, with a powerful policy management and innovative government initiatives. New York and California regions have been able to maximize their points of strength.

Asia-Pacific is systematically gaining importance, attracting large amounts of capital due to it being the world's largest unbanked population, having a strong private wealth market, and its economies still growing strongly. The rapid development of ICT in this region is transforming the entire industry landscape, heralding a new era of convergence services.

The Asia-Pacific region is very diverse and includes both developing and developed countries.[24] The key regions are mainland China, East Asia, Oceania, South East Asia, and South Asia.

As one of the emerging countries in the financial sector, China is experiencing an unprecedented level of convergence between finance and technology (Shim and Shin 2016). There are estimations that China is the largest fintech market in the world.[25] This is due in part to the fact that China has a population of more than 1.3 billion and economically is first

[23] Accenture (2014), The Rise of Fintech: New York's Opportunity for Tech Leadership, *Accenture Report.*

[24] https://avpn.asia/wp-content/uploads/2016/03/The-2015-Asia-Pacific-Alternative-Finance-Benchmarking-Report.pdf, Accessed 01 August 2016.

[25] https://www.crowdfundinsider.com/2016/08/88693-china-winning-fintech-revolution/, Accessed 04 August 2016.

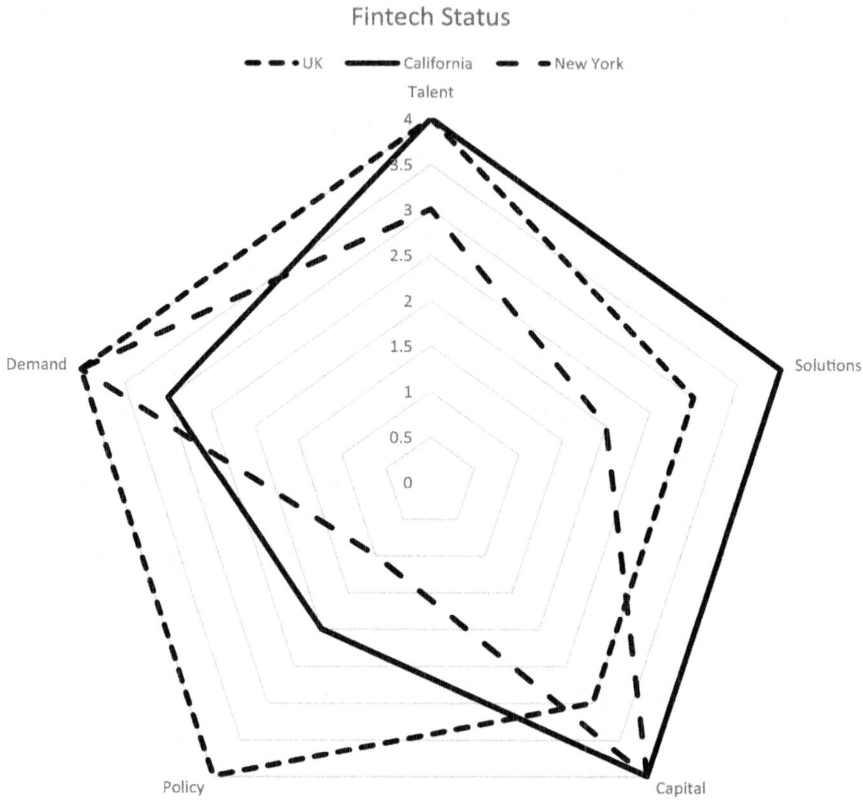

Fig. 2.2 Status of Fintech in different regions

in GDP (PPP) at over $20 trillion.[26] It is also due to necessity. Traditional Chinese state-based financial institutions have been unable to keep up with the demand for access to capital for both consumers and businesses.

The total volume of online alternative finance transactions in China was $101.69 billion in 2015. This was over 90 times the volume of the rest of the Asia-Pacific region combined. Outside of mainland China, Oceania—which includes Australia and New Zealand—accounts for

[26] GDP is the gross domestic product, which is the value of all final goods and services produced within a state in a given year. The GDP can be adjusted for purchasing power parity (PPP) calculations.

both the largest combined share and fastest growth in the volume of online alternative finance transactions in the Asia-Pacific region, totaling more than $621 million in 2015. The volume of alternative finance across East Asia (Japan, South Korea, Taiwan, and Hong Kong) has also grown rapidly, from $123 million in 2014 to $412 million in 2015. South East Asia (including Singapore, Malaysia, Thailand, and Indonesia) accounted for $47 million in transactions in 2015. Across the South Asian countries (India, Sri Lanka, and Pakistan)—online alternative finance transaction volume totaled $40 million in 2015.

Unfortunately, mainland Europe and the Middle East are still lagging.

Downsides of Disruptive Fintech Initiatives

Notwithstanding the benefits of fintech initiatives, there are a certain number of potential issues.[27] Often, disruptive technologies have some downsides due to the ways they are used (Gilbert and Bower 2002). In the case of fintech initiatives, the environment makes potential downsides even bigger:

- There are new risk exposures with fintech initiatives. Financial services and market providers generally consider themselves fortresses. Fintech initiatives can open the virtual door to similar activities. As the technologies advance, so too do hackers' abilities and resources.[28] The nature of attackers has grown. They are highly organized. In some cases, they might even be nation-states.[29] There are substantial risks for the industry. Fintech initiatives might suffer from the risks involved with them.

---

[27] http://www.PwC.co.nz/PWC.NZ/media/pdf-documents/industries/financial-services/PwC-global-fintech-report-2016-blurred-lines-how-fintech-is-shaping-financial-services.pdf, Accessed 20 August 2016.

[28] For an example, see: https://www.finextra.com/newsarticle/29255/bitcoin-tumbles-as-hackers-steal-65-million-from-hong-kong-exchange, Accessed 20 August 2016.

[29] https://www.fireeye.com/content/dam/fireeye-www/global/en/current-threats/pdfs/fireeye-wwc-report.pdf, Accessed 20 August 2016.

- Fintech initiatives have deep risks connected with regulations (Wehinger 2012). Technology generally helps to go beyond traditional national borders. In the case of fintech initiatives, national borders are less relevant from a technology point of view, but regulatory agencies on all sides are keeping a close watch. This is true especially for international sovereignty aspects, legal jurisdiction, customer data protection, and taxation. While regulators with risk management on their agenda currently are a perceived barrier to fintech initiatives, the expectation is to see a higher level of coordination among the financial services, fintech companies, and regulatory officials. This is not easy to do. It might even be a disaster to stifle such a promising industry change at this stage of development.
- There is a cultural challenge on how traditional financial institutions accept technology (Nolan 2009). Without fintech innovation, there is a risk of technology complacency and eventual obsolescence relative to other countries. Without taking some steps to advance their financial technologies, financial institutions in some countries risk losing competitive advantage by allowing their financial environment to become non-competitive in the global marketplace. For example, the South Korean government realizes that fintech initiatives are changing the nature of financial services.[30] The industry there is highly regulated, and the government worries about the viability of its existing banking infrastructure going forward.

Conclusions

In the last few years, the financial services industry has been experiencing a drastic change. The technological gap between traditional organizations and fintech companies is getting more difficult to narrow. Contextually, startup companies are taking center stage by leveraging on technology with the aim of achieving a competitive advantage. The definition of fintech encompasses any company operating in the financial services

[30] http://www.kpmg.com/FR/fr/activite/Advisory/RiskConsulting/Documents/KPMG-Frontiers-In-Finance-June-2015.pdf, Accessed 20 August 2016.

industry that has embraced innovative approaches in its business, and not just startups.

Fintech is a disruption force in the financial services system, essentially for the following reasons[31]:

- Unbundling: Historically, large financial institutions served as one-stop shops and could count on their loyal customers to turn to them for all of their financial needs. More and more customers are eager to shop around and are comfortable using multiple providers to fulfill their financial services' needs.
- Creating better, more innovative products and services: Thanks in part to the unbundling trend, fintech startups often have the opportunity to create better products and services than their entrenched competitors.
- Improving customer experience: Traditional financial institutions did not have to worry about customer experience because of the historical lock-in they held. Fintech companies use customer experience as a key point of differentiation. This gives them a real edge in customer acquisition and retention.
- Offering better pricing: Fintech upstarts are exploiting increased consumer sophistication and decreased trust of large financial services providers to create offerings that have more compelling pricing.
- Targeting underserved markets: Many fintech startups hope not only to build a business serving underserved markets but also to leverage them as footholds for later expansion into other markets or upselling to their initial market.
- Using innovative solutions: Thanks to the use of advanced technologies and lean processes, fintech companies can provide very interesting services to different segments of the market.

Fintech is growing at a stunning pace. A study by Accenture found that global investment in fintech initiatives in the first quarter of 2016 reached $5.3 billion, a 67% increase over the same period last year, and

[31] https://econsultancy.com/blog/68159-five-ways-fintech-upstarts-are-disrupting-established-financial-institutions/, Accessed 10 August 2016.

the percentage of investments going to fintech companies in Europe and Asia-Pacific nearly doubled to 62%.[32] These figures depict a clear situation: from a global perspective, this area is a "hot ticket".

Nevertheless, not all the nation-states, or regions, offer the same conditions to new business ventures. The United Kingdom and the United States are currently leading the way. Asia-Pacific is growing fast, attracting large amounts of capital from all over the world.

Fintech companies operate in a breeding ground. However, before going to analyze what they should do to better perform their business, it is important to consider their nature and the fragmented universe that comprises them all. This is the objective of the following chapter.

References

Accenture. (2014). *The rise of Fintech: New York's opportunity for tech leadership*. Retrieved July 31, 2016, from http://pfnyc.org/wp-content/uploads/2014/06/NY-fintech-Report-2014.pdf

Arner, D.W., Barberis, J., Buckley, R.P. (2015). The evolution of FinTech: A new post-crisis paradigm? Retrieved July 27, 2016, from http://hollandfintech.com/wp-content/uploads/2015/10/SSRN-id2676553.pdf

Arner, D. W., Barberis, J. N., & Buckley, R. P. (2015, October 1). *The evolution of Fintech: A new post-crisis paradigm?* University of Hong Kong Faculty of Law Research Paper No. 2015/047, 1–44.

Auerbach, P., Argimon, R. F., Roland, C., & Teschke, B. (2012). Banking on customer centricity: Transforming banks into customer-centric organizations. *McKinsey & Company Review*, 3–14

Benoit, S., Colliard, J. E., Hurlin, C., & Pérignon, C. (2016). Where the risks lie: A survey on systemic risk. *Review of Finance*, 1–59. doi:10.1093/rof/rfw026.

Cui, A. S., & Wu, F. (2016). Utilizing customer knowledge in innovation: Antecedents and impact of customer involvement on new product performance. *Journal of the Academy of Marketing Science, 44*(4), 516–538.

[32] https://newsroom.accenture.com/news/global-fintech-investment-growth-continues-in-2016-driven-by-europe-and-asia-accenture-study-finds.htm, Accessed 26 July 2016.

Desai, F. (2015, December 14). The Fintech boom and bank innovation. *Forbes*. Retrieved August 24, 2016, from http://www.forbes.com/sites/falgunidesai/2015/12/14/the-fintech-revolution/#68a3879036da

Ernst and Young. (2016). *UK Fintech: On the cutting edge, Ernst and Young Report*. Retrieved July 31, 2016, from http://www.ey.com/Publication/vwLUAssets/EY-UK-FinTech-On-the-cutting-edge/$FILE/EY-UK-FinTech-On-the-cutting-edge.pdf

Gilbert, C., & Bower, J. L. (2002). Disruptive change when trying harder is part of the problem. *Harvard Business Review, 80*(5), 95.

Moore, J. F. (1996). *The death of competition: Leadership and strategy in the age of business ecosystems*. New York, NY: Harper Business.

Mulhere, K. (2015). Why now might be the best time to refinance your student loans. *Money Magazine*. Retrieved August 25, 2016, from http://time.com/money/4045088/student-loan-refinancing-growth-and-risks/

Nolan, S. (2009). Kick-starting a customer-centric revolution. *Manager: British Journal of Administrative Management, 65*, 28–30.

Schlechtendahl, J., Keinert, M., Kretschmer, F., Lechler, A., & Verl, A. (2015). Making existing production systems Industry 4.0-ready. *Production Engineering, 9*(1), 143–148.

Schumpeter, J. (2013, January 5). Lending club: Peer review. *The Economist*.

Shim, Y., & Shin, D. H. (2016). Analyzing China's Fintech industry from the perspective of Actor–Network theory. *Telecommunications Policy, 40*(2), 168–181.

Sieljacks, K. H. (2014). *Building customer centricity in the banking industry*. Master Thesis Aarhus University, Aarhus, Denmark.

Skinner, C. (2016). *How Fintech firms are using bitcoin blockchain and mobile technologies to create the Internet of value*. Singapore: Marshall Cavendish International (Asia) Pte Ltd.

Sorkin, A. R. (2010). *Too big to fail: The inside story of how Wall Street and Washington fought to save the financial system and themselves*. London, UK: Penguin.

Venture Scanner. (2016). Fintech Q1 update. Retrieved July 27, 2016, from http://insights.venturescanner.com/category/financial-technology/

Volcker, P. (2009). The only thing useful banks have invented in 20 years is the ATM. *The New York Post*. Retrieved July 27, 2016, from http://nypost.com/2009/12/13/the-only-thing-useful-banks-have-invented-in-20-years-is-the-atm

Wehinger, G. (2012). The financial industry in the new regulatory landscape. *OECD Journal: Financial Market Trends, 2011*(2), 225–249.

3

Model and Classifications

Introduction

The financial services industry is significantly changing, also due to the digital transformation. The latter has forced new and old organizations to innovate their value propositions, their internal processes, and especially the engagement with their customers.

The fintech world is a galaxy. It is interesting to analyze some possible classifications. It is possible to classify fintech initiatives based on a series of criteria, which in turn are based on the following questions: Why was fintech born? For whom was it born? Which service does it aim to provide? Where and when does it intend to perform its business? How do fintech initiatives work? This chapter provides an answer to these questions, supporting the statements with business cases and examples.

Having cleared the nature of fintech companies and the structure of their ecosystem, this chapter presents a business model to interpret how a fintech company should organize its business model, where to focus and how to create a leading proactive mindset in this complex sector. The following chapters use this model to help in the interpretation of different aspects of fintech initiatives.

B. Nicoletti, *The Future of FinTech*,
DOI 10.1007/978-3-319-51415-4_3

Classifications

In order to develop detailed classifications of fintech initiatives, it is interesting to refer to the so-called five Ws. They are based on the following sentence by Rudyard Kipling in his book *The Little Elephant*[1]:

> I keep six honest serving-men
> (They taught me all I knew);
> Their names are What and Why and When
> And How and Where and Who.[2]

The questions to consider are as follows:

1. Who did that?
2. What happened?
3. Where did it take place?
4. When did it take place?
5. Why did that happen?

Furthermore, some other authors added the sixth question, "how":

6. How does it work?

As far as fintech initiatives are concerned, these questions may necessitate a slight adaptation:

1. Why a fintech initiative was born?
2. For whom was it born?
3. Which are the services it aims to provide?
4. Where does it aim to perform its business?
5. When does it aim to operate, within the framework of the financial cycle?
6. How is fintech working?

It is necessary to take into account that classifications are always simplifications of the reality. Very often, items can be classified in

[1] Kipling R. (2013), Just So Stories, CreateSpace Independent Publishing Platform.
[2] Kipling, R, ibid.

more than one class. On the other side, classifications are useful since they allow discovering gaps or over-/under-representations. Hence, classifications can underline potential opportunities.

Why

Several organizations are still stuck in rigid, old business models and routines. The overall innovation process, together with the implementation of new knowledge and skills, is not easy to implement (Koen et al. 2011; Teece 2010).

In traditional financial institutions, there is a combination of a widespread difficulty of financial services to innovate with the internal resistance to change, typical of any organization. The result is a growing gap that new entrants are ready to fill. In the financial services industry, these new entrants are the fintech startups.

At a first glance, it may seem that these disruptive organizations have been capable exploiting only the inefficiencies within the banking processes by delivering a better service to the final customer. Some people may identify this as their only raison d'être. This is not completely wrong. Still, it does not cover the overall universe of financial technology.

Kantox

"Banks still own 99 percent of the market, which is the main challenge of Kantox, and 99% of fintech startups besides, is the education of its customers."—Philippe Gelis, Chief Executive Officer (CEO) and co-founder.[3]

An example of a company that has exploited the inefficiencies generated in the interbank processes is Kantox. This company was born in 2011. It aims to provide foreign currency exchange and international payment solutions for corporate customers. Kantox has managed to leverage on the unfairness of the banking system—where large companies are able to negotiate by far greater conditions compared with the ones offered to mid-caps and smaller ones—by providing customers with a clear, transparent peer-to-peer (P2P) marketplace. In this way, it enables corporate businesses to get significantly better exchange rates.

---

[3] https://www.linkedin.com/pulse/why-fintech-banks-rule-world-philippe-gelis, Accessed 10 August 2016.

The Kantox case leads into two directions:

1. The first one focuses on fintech companies, stressing their great potential due to their knowledge, flexibility, and overall proposition value.
2. The second one focuses on financial institutions, stressing their still largely dominant customer base and economic strength.

This relationship will most likely affect the future of the financial services industry.

The main raison d'être of startups operating in the financial technology field may be identified in the inefficiencies of the traditional organizations. Kickstarter, for instance, is a global crowdfunding platform where the public can fund creative projects. This makes for a great example of a company that aims to aid and serve those customers who are completely ignored by financial institutions. This usually happens for several reasons, the main ones being:

- The low appeal of some financial services due to their overall low profitability
- The inefficiencies and the general lack of skills, capabilities, and will of financial institutions to recognize and pursue new opportunities

Another classification considers that Fintech companies were born to provide services. The classification criteria can be the objectives of these services. Fairview Capital (2009) has developed a classification model of fintech initiatives based on the applications and services they provide. The model has four groups: customer service, financial services, compliance, and business processes:

1. Customer service: processes and services that deal with the customer at the user interface level as well as at the backend database level:

    - Customer relationship management (CRM)
    - Call center software

- Electronic billing and payment technology
- Electronic trading and banking

2. Financial services: applications and processes for portfolio management and risk management:

    - Portfolio management
    - Asset management
    - Risk management solutions
    - Exchanges

PayPal

"The very first company I started failed with a great bang. The second one failed a little bit less, but still failed. The third one, you know, proper failed, but it was kind of okay. I recovered quickly. Number four almost didn't fail. It still didn't really feel great, but it did okay. Number five was PayPal."—Max Levcin, former Chief Information Officer (CIO) of PayPal.[4]

PayPal is a company that offers an online payment system. PayPal represents a clear example of a company that directly deals with customers by providing them with a service, which is a better alternative to those offered by financial institutions.[5] The company was established in 1998, a time when electronic payments were not so common. E-commerce became a common practice just a few years later; therefore, PayPal managed to build its business on the existing infrastructure of financial institutions. This turned out to be (apparently, at least) a win-win relationship. Customers, traditional financial institutions, and fintech companies, all benefitted from this, not to mention that the ability of PayPal, and of the fintech startups, is the attempt to disintermediate traditional financial institutions in the area of financial services. This has constituted—and still does—a serious threat for traditional organizations operating their businesses in this industry.

[4] http://startupquotes.startupvitamins.com/post/35746044155/the-very-first-company-i-started-failed-with-a, Accessed 26 August 2016.

[5] https://www.paypal.com/uk/webapps/mpp/ua/servicedescription-full, Accessed 09 August 2016.

Wealthfront

"Wealthfront is built as a software company and designed for a new generation of investors. Over 60% of our clients are under 35. We have focused on providing a completely automated investment service, eliminating the cost of retail locations and sales teams."—Adam Nash, CEO of Wealthfront.[6]

Wealthfront is an American company that offers investment services fully based on complex algorithms.[7] The company's investment strategy is formulated by identifying the risk tolerance, the investment goals, and the budget of the investors through a streamlined questionnaire, subsequently automating the process through a software designed to automatically adjust their portfolios, keeping them diversified and tax efficient while maintaining the target allocation.

3. Compliance: methods for a company to comply with external and internal regulations:

   - Financial statement reporting and analysis
   - Trade clearing
   - Compliance with regulations in one or more nations

Droit

"We saw a glaring gap in the marketplace. How do you come to compliant and optimal pre-trade decisions, and how do you make sure post-trade that you have always done the right thing? We unify pre-trade decision making with post-trade compliance reporting by using the same infrastructure, data, and logic."—Satya Pemmaraju, founding partner and CEO of Droit.[8]

Droit Financial Technologies LLC is an American company born in 2012 that aims to deliver comprehensive and adaptable solutions in dealing with the large new market structure and regulatory requirements that affect the over-the-counter (OTC) derivatives space.[9] By using these solutions, a customer company is able to focus its efforts toward its core business, with consistent savings of time and money. Briefly, Droit manages to address three main questions (three Ws) related to the trading process: what to trade, when to trade, and where to trade.

[6] http://fortune.com/2015/08/06/wealthfront-investing-qa/, Accessed 26 August 2016.

[7] https://www.wealthfront.com/, Accessed 09 August 2016.

[8] http://www.wallstreetandtech.com/compliance/droit-taps-industry-veterans-as-advisors-to-its-derivatives-compliance-platform/d/d-id/1316887, Accessed 26 August 2016.

[9] https://www.linkedin.com/company/droit-financial-technologies-llc, Accessed 20 August 2016.

Xero

"If I'd done this five years ago, I might have been happy with a $5 million exit, and now I won't be happy unless it's at least a $100 million exit."—Rod Drury, CEO and founder of Xero.[10]

Xero is a New Zealand company, with offices worldwide, established in 2006 with the aim of providing businesses with an easy-to-use, powerful online accounting software.[11] The company provides an online accounting software to small- and medium-sized enterprises (SMEs), thus facilitating organizations in focusing their efforts in the core areas of their business.[12] It is a typical example of a company with an innovative product that brings changes in the processes of its customers. Currently, several companies reach the market with solutions that find their target in the internal processes of other companies, not necessarily performing their businesses in the financial services industry.

The main point of strenght of Xero solutions is in their intuitiveness: although the platform is powerful in terms of the offer (audit controls, parallel business intelligence engine, etc.), Xero developers have been capable of keeping it simple and fun.[13]

4. Business processes: Collections of linked activities with the objective to deliver a specific result:

- Application service providers
- Data warehousing and analytics
- Data quality
- Document management
- Imaging software
- Knowledge management
- System integration
- Security
- ICT infrastructure and outsourcing

[10] https://pando.com/2013/05/01/xero-a-billion-dollar-software-company-that-had-five-years-in-stealth-at-the-bottom-of-the-planet/, Accessed 26 August 2016.

[11] https://www.xero.com/media/4681900/reviewers-guide-us-version.pdf, Accessed 09 August 2016.

[12] https://www.xero.com/media/4681900/reviewers-guide-us-version.pdf, Accessed 09 August. 2016.

[13] http://www.forbes.com/sites/groupthink/2013/03/14/kiwi-startup-does-impossible-makes-accounting-fun/#1126f1266dfe, Accessed 26 July 2016.

In this list, security is an important item. It has always been a critical point for organizations that build their business online (and especially for their customers). Using several tools, it is possible to steal credentials. At the same time, hackers have developed malicious software products that leverage on the huge increase in the computational power of chips (central processing unit [CPU], graphics processing unit [GPU]) with the aim of illegally taking hold of sensitive credentials. For this reason, security issues have always been a limit for the diffusion of e-commerce and overall online solutions. Recently, multiple solutions have been developed to facilitate payments and the storage of information online (cloud computing).

SecureKey

"The responsibility for providing a secure and convenient online experience is a challenge faced by every market in today's always-on world. Coming on the heels of our SecureKey Concierge service launch earlier this month, we are excited to offer our platform capabilities as a private label service to other leading organizations in vertical market communities where privacy and security are both a necessity and a challenge, ensuring a more secure online experience for users."—Charles Walton, CEO of SecureKey[14]

SecureKey is a Canadian authentication and identity provider for those businesses that deliver online customer services.[15] Linking the identity of the consumer ID to a trusted device and with a security customer, SecureKey makes it possible to deliver an easy solution for all the organizations and institutions (as well as financial ones) where security issues are very important.

This type of classification has taken into consideration the very first reason why fintech startups were born, which is: to provide customers with services that respond to a general lack of innovation in financial institutions. These initiatives should also be able to exploit the pre-existing infrastructures and/or aim to serve customers not considered before by traditional financial institutions.

[14] http://www.skconcierge.us/2015/09/, Accessed 26 August 2016.

[15] http://securekey.com/about-securekey/, Accessed 09 August 2016.

Who

At the center of the business model of fintech initiatives, there is a service. The subsequent business relationship established through the service may have different forms depending on the nature of the subjects that are making use of it:

1. P2P—person-to-person services
2. B2P—business-to-person services
3. P2B—person-to-business services
4. B2B—business-to-business services

An important form of a new relationship established in the financial technology industry is P2P, meaning person-to-person or peer-to-peer. Companies following a P2P business model act as facilitators or as match-making entities. They provide customers with a platform that matches or facilitates the match between demand and supply, with defined rules, guidelines, and regulations, eventually with some remuneration and payment mechanisms. P2P stresses the centricity of the customers, who are able to both offer and buy products/services by means of the intermediation offered by a company.

A typical example of P2P is online lending. Marketplace lenders continue to evolve as P2P scales beyond what retail investors can support, pushing platforms to solicit increasingly institutional capital. These companies match buyers and sellers while minimizing their own balance sheet risk. Revenue comes from the collection of an upfront origination fee, as well as a servicing fee throughout the duration of the loan.

Lending Club uses an online platform to facilitate the match between investors and borrowers: the former and the latter are both interested in having access to more favorable financial conditions in a safe, transparent, and simple environment, that is, where Lending Club leverages on. For clarifying how a P2P business model works, with reference to Lending Club and other credit companies, it is possible to consider the following simplified process[16]:

---

[16] http://uk.businessinsider.com/peer-to-peer-lending-how-digital-lending-marketplaces-are-disrupting-the-predominant-banking-model-2015-5?r=US&IR=T, Accessed 09 August 2016.

1. Borrower applies for a loan to the lending platform.
2. The lending platform commits to the borrower.
3. The lending platform informs the partner bank that the borrower is verified and investors have committed.
4. The partner bank issues the actual loan to the borrower.
5. The borrower sends a loan note to the partner bank.
6. The lender/investor gives cash to the lending platform.
7. The lending platform purchases the loan note using the lender's/investor's cash from the partner bank.
8. The partner bank sends the loan note to the lending platform.
9. The lending platform sends the loan note to the lender/investor.
10. When the due time is reached, the borrower pays back the lending platform, which then pays back the lender/investor.

There are parallel processes dealing with the revenue sources and the situations where there are issues in the repayments.

Some considerations regarding the process used by Lending Club are as follows:

- The financial institutions are not completely excluded from the process, but they act as partners of the lending company.
- The work of intermediation carried on by the fintechs is very important. It allows to lower burdens (mainly regulatory ones) and consequently lower fees and roles.

Pingit[17]

"Barclays' Pingit could revolutionise the way people send and receive money."—Antony Jenkins, former CEO of Barclays

Barclays introduced Pingit in the United Kingdom in February 2012. Since then, Barclays has steadily added new functionalities. As of 2013, Pingit had 1.5 million customers (Nicoletti 2014). It is a P2P payment system for sending and receiving payments. Pingit is a system for the mobile transfer of money. Initially, it was only available to customers in the United Kingdom with a Barclays current account, a UK smartphone, and older than 18 years.

[17] https://www.theguardian.com/money/2012/feb/16/barclays-pingit-money-sending-smartphone, Accessed 26 August 2016.

Pingit (continued)

The benefits connected with Barclays Pingit are substantial. There are no charges for both senders and recipients of the service. Pingit transactions arrive almost immediately in the recipient's account; The Pingit service works on the Faster Payment Scheme, so payments are effectively instantaneous, even between Barclays and non-Barclays customers. Finally, there is a limitation on the number of transactions per day. In the wake of the success of Pingit, VocaLink has launched a similar service called Zapp.[18]

Lending Club

"Over time, the platforms in finance—marketplace lending or otherwise—that serve the customer better than others, offer investors solid risk-adjusted returns transparently, and demonstrate strong unit economics will win."—David Klein, CEO and co-founder of CommonBond[19]

An example of a startup that follows the P2P business model is Lending Club, with headquarters in San Francisco, CA. The estimation is that it is the world's largest P2P lending platform.[20] The company raised $1 billion in what became the largest technology IPO of 2014 in the United States. It was the first P2P lender to register its offerings as securities with the Securities and Exchange Commission (SEC), and to offer loan trading on a secondary market. Lending Club operates an online lending platform that enables borrowers to obtain a loan and investors to purchase notes backed by payments made on loans.

The company claims that it originated $15.98 billion in loans through its platform up to 31 December 2015. Lending Club enables borrowers to create unsecured personal loans between $1000 and $35,000. The standard loan period is three years. Investors can search and browse the loan listings on the Lending Club website. They can select loans that they want to invest in based on the information supplied about the borrower, amount of loan, loan grade, and loan purpose. Investors make money from interests. Lending Club makes money by charging borrowers an origination fee and investors a service fee.

(continued)

[18] http://www.zapp.co.uk/, Accessed 20 August 2016.

[19] http://www.cnbc.com/2016/05/10/why-you-shouldnt-panic-about-the-lending-club-scandal-commentary.html, Accessed 20 August 2016.

[20] Schumpeter (2013), Peer review, The Economist, 5 January.

Lending Club (continued)

Though viewed as a pioneer in the fintech industry and one of the largest such firms, Lending Club experienced problems in early 2016, with difficulties in attracting investors, a scandal over some of the firm's loans, and concerns by the board over CEO Renaud Laplanche's disclosures. The result was a large drop in its share price and Laplanche's resignation.[21] This is an example of how a market leader could create problems that would affect the entire marketplace. In the immediate term, there will probably be some more cases of the same type. Ultimately, the fundamentals of the model will win. If you believe in efficient markets—even semi-efficient markets—that is what could happen.

The ATM is the typical example of B2P: the customer can easily access an ATM, withdraw money, and make a variety of financial transactions while consistently saving time and resources (for the provider and the customer alike). Apart from the innovation itself, the focus is on the participants of the relationship. On one side, there is a financial institution, which gives the customer the possibility to perform simple transactions. On the other side, there is a person in need of doing such transactions at any time.

In the case of online lending, B2P is characterized by balance sheet lenders that originate loans from their own capital or raise funds (for instance, from an industrial loan company in the United States[22]).

Following the classification already provided, the second type of financial services are P2B ones. Although the areas where fintech companies operate using this specific approach are several, the success of very recent companies and technologies (as Kickstarter or Bitcoin technology) helps us in their clear identification:

- Trading
- Crowdfunding

---

[21] http://www.cnbc.com/2016/05/10/why-you-shouldnt-panic-about-the-lending-club-scandal-commentary.html, Accessed 05 August 2016.

[22] http://citeseerx.ist.psu.edu/viewdoc/download?doi=10.1.1.365.7515&rep=rep1&type=pdf, Accessed 20 August 2016.

- Deposit
- Virtual currencies
- Insurance

Kickstarter and Indiegogo are two companies that offer crowdfunding services to their users.[23] In particular, by means of their online platforms, these companies allow projects to be funded by raising contributions from the internet population. There are different variations of crowdfunding. A rather general definition is that crowdfunding involves an open call, essentially through the internet, for the provision of financial resources either in the form of donation or in exchange for some form of reward and/or voting rights (Belleflamme et al. 2010). The following chapter provides further details and additional insights about crowdfunding and virtual currencies, with reference to business ventures and individuals that have built their success on these practices.

B2B services refer to the existing economic transactions between two or more companies. Companies that are willing to establish business relationships with other companies with the aim of maximizing opportunities for both partners follow a B2B model. Relationships between companies are complex and difficult to manage, but they are one of the best catalysts for innovation.

Fintech initiatives that follow a B2B business model offer financial services to other businesses. In short, the proposition value is delivered to different entities other than B2P, implying a series of consequences on the structure of the business and on fintechs' strategical approach.

McKinsey examined more than 3000 companies in the McKinsey Panorama fintech database and found that the share of fintech companies with B2B offerings has increased, from 34% of those launched in 2011 to 47% of last year's startups (Dietz et al. 2016). (These companies may maintain B2C products as well.) Only 21% are seeking to disintermediate the client relationship, for example, by offering treasury services to corporate banking clients. Less than 12% are truly trying to disrupt

[23] http://www.crowdcrux.com/30-people-to-promote-your-kickstarter-or-indiegogo-campaign-to-on-twitter/, Accessed 20 August 2016.

existing business models, with sophisticated systems based on blockchain (encrypted) transactions technology, for instance.

B2B fintech companies collaborate with and provide services to established banks that continue to own the relationship with the end customer. Corporate and investment banking (CIB) is different. The trend toward B2B is especially evident in CIB, which accounts for 15% of all fintech activity across markets.

Some examples may be useful to understand the rationale behind the B2B approach. Kantox is one of the companies that has been able to exploit the inefficiencies of traditional banks with the aim of offering better foreign currency exchange and international payments services to businesses. This is a clear example of B2B: the proposition value is delivered to corporate customers and no individuals are involved.

Fundbox

"Fundbox is a very cool simple and elegant financing solution. It took less than a few minutes to obtain short-term funding. I would recommend it to any business seeking to finance."—Edwin Warfield, CEO of Citybizlist

Fundbox is an American company that operates in the area of invoice financing. In more detail, Fundbox is able to turn unpaid invoices into needed funds.[24] This operation technically is not a loan. Companies such as Fundbox or Bluevine earn money by buying the invoices in exchange of a lower (compared to the face value of the invoices) amount of money. The subsequent difference between the value of the invoice and the value paid for the invoice by these companies represent their potential margins.

Apart from the specific businesses of these startups, the focus should be on the actors. The customers are not individuals, but only corporations or SMEs which may benefit from their services.

The largest part of fintech initiatives that follow a B2B model operates in the following areas:

- Money transfer
- Credit for SMEs

[24] https://fundbox.com/, Accessed 09 August 2016.

- Provision of advanced services and packages to financial institutions
- Support for the internationalization of the businesses
- Other professional services to the businesses

Apart from the four different approaches to the business examined, there are other potential approaches. Although several forms could be identified depending on the degree of detail utilized—when dealing with governments, for instance, there may be a B2G (business-to-government) and vice versa or B2E (business-to-employees).

An interesting development is instant payments, which generalizes the concept of P2P. It allows for 24/7 real-time P2P, P2B, P2G payments for small businesses and organizations as well for e-commerce and m-commerce. The payments are interbank transfers settled individually in real time. The solution is flexible and open for additional financial institutions to join. New types of payment services can be added over time. The payment solution relies on two components: a smartphone application for initiating and reporting payments and a real-time payment and settlement system among the financial services participating in the scheme. The subscribers associate their bank account with their mobile phone number (businesses and organizations have proxy numbers). The payer enters the payee's mobile number (or proxy) and authorizes the payment through the mobile bank ID application. The payer's account is debited and the payment instruction is settled in the clearing systems (automated clearing house [ACH] in the United States). The payee's bank receives the payment information and credits the payee's account. The application notifies both the payer and the payee.

What

The base of another classification is on "what" fintech companies provide the market with. The research[25] developed by H2 Ventures, KPMG, and

[25] H2 Ventures, KPMG and Matchi, "Fintech 100, Leading Global Fintech innovators, Report 2015", 2016. https://www.kpmg.com/FR/fr/IssuesAndInsights/ArticlesPublications/Documents/Etude-Fintech100-2015.pdf, Accessed 26 July 2016.

Matchi (2016) may be instrumental in defining "what" fintech initiatives are delivering. It provides also some insights about the most innovative and disruptive companies from a global perspective.

The research has taken into consideration the 50 leading fintech and emerging stars companies, chosen based on their overall potential from a long-term perspective.

From a broader perspective, the classification based on "what" coincides with the area of specialization of the company, leading to this further classification:

- Insurance
- Wealth management
- Payments
- Credit
- Crowdfunding
- Retail banking
- Security
- Currency and forex (foreign exchanges and remittances)
- Other

Figure 3.1 shows what the 100 leading global fintech innovators are providing to the market in 2015. This is not the current share of the overall universe of fintech, but reflects just one part of it. Most likely, it reflects the part that combines the highest potential with a solid and efficient internal structure, able to deliver an effective value proposition based on a successful business model.

Where

A classification based on "where" the fintech initiative intends to operate may be interpreted in different ways. A first classification takes into account the different regions where fintech companies have developed their businesses. Chapter 1 covers this subject. This classification takes into consideration only a geographical parameter, being instrumental to a general ranking between different states, regions, or cities.

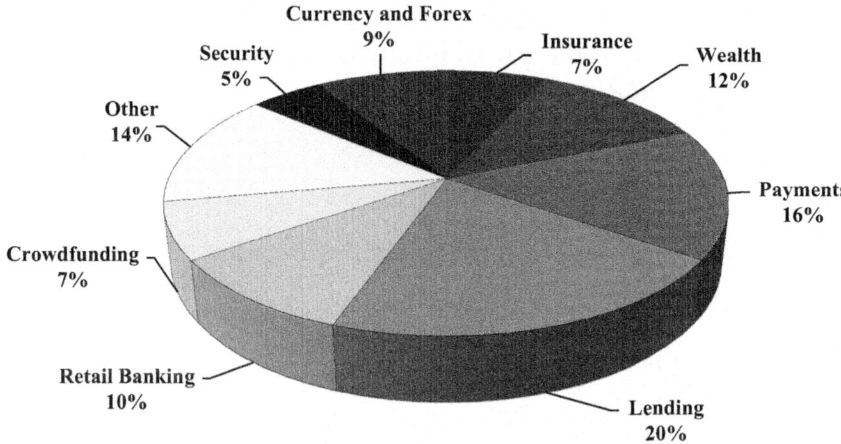

Fig. 3.1 Fintech specialization share (elaboration from "Fintech 100, Leading Global Fintech innovators, Report" 2015)

Another classification is on "where" is the business ownership and, in particular, the relationship between the business idea and its development.

The consultancy company EY stated that the overall financial technology sector is globally growing in terms of employment, investment, and a number of fintech companies, but it is still far from mature. Following this line of reasoning, most fintech initiatives fall into one of the following classes:

1. Startups
2. Traditional financial institutions, such as banks or insurance companies
3. Technological or retail companies moving into financial services
4. Advanced startups with a mixed ownership

Boundaries between these categories are not so clear due to the several initiatives and financial operations pursued by financial institutions in order to acquire shares of startups with higher potential. In the very first phases of a firm's life cycle, seed funding is sometimes allowed only in exchange equity, implying that a certain number of fintech startups have traditional financial institutions in their ownership structure.

A later chapter deals in detail with the topic of the financial relationship between traditional financial institutions and fintech startups, contextually giving some insights about its implications.

When

Fintech may be classified into two categories according to "when" companies provide their services:

1. Traditional fintech
2. Emergent fintech

A research developed by EY and commissioned by the UK Trade and Investment[26] helps in clarifying the differences between these two categories.

According to EY, the perception is that companies that follow a traditional model are "facilitators". They are typically large, incumbent technology vendors that perform their businesses in the financial services sector.[27] On the other hand, companies that follow an emergent model are disruptors or innovators, with a focus on disintermediating the incumbent financial institutions.[28]

Because of different cultures, the business models in these two classes are quite different (see Table 3.1). Emergent companies cover multiple and diverse areas. It turns out to be difficult to summarize their business models. Eventually, different types of revenue streams are possible.

Companies following a traditional model operate under an established revenue model that tends to use cost per transaction, cost per click, a percentage of assets, or license fees.[29]

One critical point for fintechs is infrastructure replacement. Emergent fintech companies are putting their efforts in trying to cope with the need for infrastructure, including P2P networks and Bitcoin technologies.

[26] Ernst & Young (2014), Landscaping UK Fintech, commissioned by UK Trade and Investment.

[27] Ernst & Young, ibid.

[28] Ernst & Young, ibid.

[29] Ernst & Young, ibid.

Table 3.1 Traditional versus emergent fintech (elaboration of the author on Ernst & Young (EY) 2014)

Traditional	Emergent
Market players are generally perceived as facilitators, which are typically large, incumbent technology vendors supporting the financial services sector. For example, Fiserv, Accenture, SunGard, TCS, FirstData.	Market players are disruptors and innovators by nature. They are disintermediating traditional financial institutions or provide new technology and different processes solutions to service existing needs. For example: Zopa, Fidor Bank, TransferWise.
Companies focus on the support, maintenance, and delivery of the existing infrastructure, which in some cases is outsourced.	Two operating models have emerged: of either using the existing infrastructure, which tends to be controlled by established players, or replacing it completely or using solutions in the cloud.The replacement of infrastructure is a high-risk strategy; however, it produces better results if successful.
Operate under established revenue models that tend to use cost per transaction, a percentage of assets, or license fees.	Emerging revenue models are broad and tend to function using multiple different types of revenue streams, including advertisement and data monetization. Fees are different among providers and consumers (the latter ones with no payment in some cases).

The traditional infrastructure is a limit and an opportunity at the same time. PayPal, for instance, has built its business on the existing infrastructure, but at the same time, has delivered additional services to its customers. Other companies, such as the already mentioned Kantox, use instead a completely different approach to the business, circumventing the old and established infrastructures (for instance, with a P2P business model).

How

It is interesting to analyze and clarify how fintech initiatives are innovating and how are they planning to deliver their services. This section considers answers to these questions. It takes into consideration the fact that most of the innovations through which fintech initiatives deliver their services will be clarified in the following chapter.

Another classification takes into account "how" fintech initiatives provide their services:

- Mobility (for instance, mobile banking)
- Big Data Analytics
- IoT
- Cloud computing
- Artificial intelligence (AI)
- Robotics
- Social networks, etc.

The world is changing at a pace that only some decades ago was impossible to foresee and to anticipate. Contextually, new technologies and innovations are setting the stage for new ways to provide services. This classification aims to stress the importance of carefully taking into consideration the future of the current business of fintech initiatives. It is important to keep in mind that some financial institutions have already implemented most of these technologies (mobile banking, Big Data, AI, and so forth). Fintech initiatives further develop or use them with a different business model.

A more important classification aims to explain and classify how fintech companies innovate. Two classes are possible (see Fig. 3.2):

- Enablers
- Disruptors

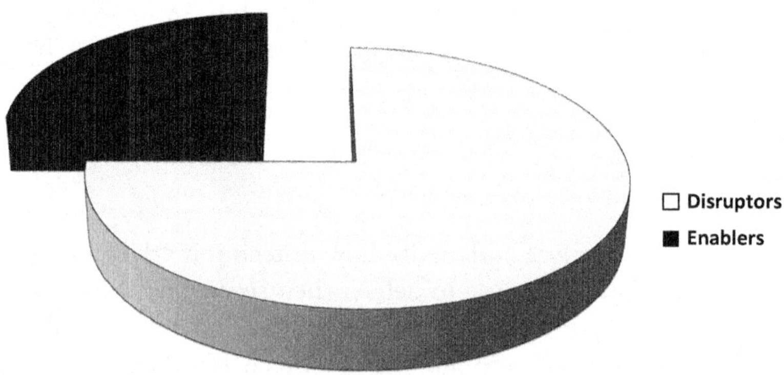

Fig. 3.2 Percentage of enablers and disruptors (elaboration from "Fintech 100, Leading Global Fintech innovators, Report" 2015)

By elaborating the report developed by H2 Ventures and KPMG[30]—dealing with the leading 50 fintech companies across the globe and the "most intriguing" emerging stars[31]—it is possible to state that the most important fintech companies, which have proven themselves as successful at least in the first stages of their life cycles, aim to disrupt their target market. The results of an analysis on such a limited amount of companies cannot be broadened to the overall universe of fintech initiatives. Several professionals (Pollari 2016)[32] have highlighted how fintech initiatives are moving beyond disruption, with a growing percentage of companies that are now addressing their efforts toward supporting incumbent financial institutions in order to narrow their technological gap.

The overall universe of fintech initiatives is intrinsically related to the concept of innovation. Disruptors or not, each of the fintech initiatives addresses its efforts in somehow changing the market. It is also possible to classify fintech initiatives from how they innovate based on:

- Product or service innovations
- Process innovations
- Organizational innovations
- Business model innovations

By taking into account the ecosystems described in Chap. 1, the link between these four different forms of innovation becomes clear. The definition of a product innovation is "the development of new products, changes in the design of established products, or use of new materials or components in the manufacture of established products".[33] Most financial technology initiatives are actually delivering innovative services or products to the market. Innovations may cover either changes to products that already exist or changes that are more extensive.

---

[30] Fintech 100, Leading Global Fintech innovators, Report 2015.

[31] Fintech 100, ibid.

[32] http://fintechinnovators.com/about-list, Accessed 01 August 2016.

[33] http://www.psi.org.uk/publications/archivepdfs/Small%20companies/SF1.pdf, Accessed 20 August 2016.

Product innovations, mainly brought by fintech startups, are radically changing the way financial services work, most likely giving rise to process innovations. When a value proposition changes in its core areas, companies may start adapting their businesses to it, thus overhauling their organizations. Eventually, fintech companies may find a completely new environment, where both customers and organizations have radically changed their identity, their needs, and their *modus operandi.* New ways of being profitable may develop, setting the stage for new business models that are able to convert these possibilities into a rewarding business.

This is just a way of explaining the linkages between different forms of innovation. This is one of many possible interpretations to explain the intricate developments of the financial services industry. Something external, for example new international regulations, can also foster innovations. Sometimes, by contrast, the process simply follows another direction: process innovations could foster product innovations that successively may spring something else.

It is necessary to consider two main elements when dealing with the past and future developments of fintech initiatives:

- The strong links existing between different forms of innovation
- The fact that the process through which innovations spread through an industry is not deterministic

It is interesting to consider how innovations may find their target not only in the products but also in the internal processes of a company. In order to understand the rationale, it is important to understand the borderline between process innovations and the implications of product innovations onto the internal processes of a company. The difference stands in the target and in the magnitude of the change.

From a macroscopic view of the financial services industry, more so than in the past, marginal and drastic innovations are being introduced in the market. Whenever a large financial organization or a little startup is delivering an innovation, this has somehow an implication on its internal structure: the job characteristics, the hierarchies, the management systems, and the processes may be affected.

Nevertheless, when a relevant number of disrupting startups start delivering product innovations to the market, it will likely generate a decrease in the profitability levels of the incumbent organizations or, at least, they might fear or be concerned with the very first and sheer signals of this development. Incumbent organizations could decide to apply some changes to the way they actually work, by re-engineering their processes, making them leaner and more efficient. This can be done by implementing specific solutions that manage the flow of information, by reducing waste, by completely embracing the digital innovation, or by radically changing the way through which a specific product is produced and/or delivered. That is called "process innovation".

Square and Square Capital

"Square can monetize [Capital] very efficiently. It allows them to build up a high-margin revenue stream to complement the traditional lines of business."—Roger Lee, general partner of Battery Ventures[34]

Another American company that is delivering process innovations to the market is Square, a venture that provides businesses with varied tools that support them in very different areas.[35] The company helps in accepting credit cards, tracking sales and inventory, financing small businesses, and so forth. Furthermore, Square offers hardware, payments products and devices, with the aim of building an efficient and effective ecosystem in support of their customer companies. Square's subsidiary, Square Capital, was founded in May 2014 and offers cash advances to small businesses.[36] Square Capital has already advanced $225 million in business financing to more than 20,000 businesses in 2015. In April 2015, Square Capital advanced nearly $25 million in capital, at the time a run rate of $300–$400 million in business lending per year.

Process innovations are not simple restructures inspired by efficiency and effectiveness principles. They especially leverage on specific tools and products that aim to overhaul critical processes along the value chain of the business organization. Sometimes, these products are provided externally, sometimes they are developed internally. Nevertheless,

[34] http://uk.businessinsider.com/square-capitals-big-upside-2015-11?r=US&IR=T, Accessed 26 August 2016.

[35] https://squareup.com/global/en/pos, Accessed 20 August 2016.

[36] Square Capital (2015): We've Now Extended $225 M in Business Financing. Available online at https://squareup.com/townsquare/weve-now-extended-225m-in-business-financing/, Accessed 20 August 2016.

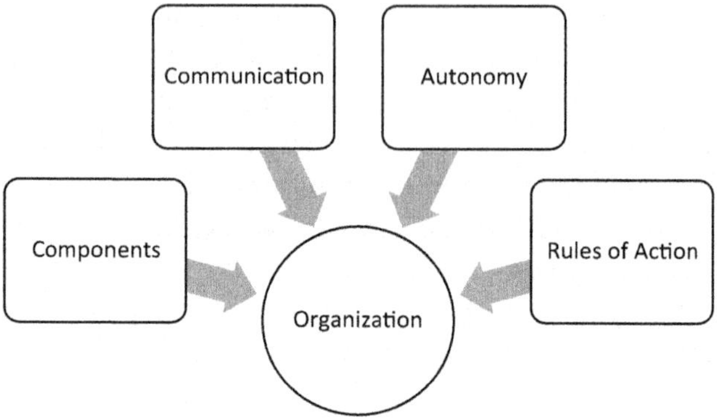

Fig. 3.3 The organization and its elements

the classification in this section comprises financial technology startups that are actually providing businesses with tools that are able to overhaul significantly the structure of their processes. Xero and Square are two examples of successful companies that have largely proved that they can fulfill this job in an excellent way.[37]

Large financial organizations have spent years in order to maximize their internal efficiency, focusing their efforts on getting their processes leaner and more cost-efficient. At the same time, they have not properly estimated the future developments of their external environment and its variability. Fintech startups have taken advantage of the advances in digital and communication technologies. Today, traditional organizations are still trying to fill the technological gap, by leveraging not only on product innovations, but also on process and organizational innovations.

"Organizational innovation means the implementation of a new organizational method in the undertaking's business practices, workplace organization, or external relations."[38]

An organization is defined by (see Fig. 3.3)

[37] https://community.xero.com/business/discussion/104481, Accessed 20 August 2016.

[38] Community Framework for State aid for research and development and innovation (2006/C 323/01).

- its components;
- its communication;
- its autonomy; and
- its rules of action compared to internal and external events.

Changing the organization does not necessarily mean innovating: as always, there must be an innovative culture leading the change. Startups are usually more flexible and able to better manage their organization in its various aspects. Startups may introduce new and innovative organizational strategies. They can action them with reasonable financial efforts, without the need of potentially disruptive cultural changes. One of the main issues when dealing with change is cultural problems. Internal resistance, either formal or tacit, could be a serious threat to an organization that is setting the stage for innovation: traditional organizations that still have old routines and consolidated cultures may face cultural barriers in their aim of innovating their organizational structure. On the other hand, the magnitude of these threats in a startup is significantly lower, sometimes almost null: agility, flexibility, openness to change, and readiness to take risks are usually intrinsic attributes of modern startups, especially in the financial services industry.

According to this classification, another form of innovation is the one referred to the business model. A business model describes the rationale of how an organization creates, captures, and delivers value (Ostwalder et al. 2010). It represents all the core aspects of a business:

- Purpose
- Infrastructure
- Trading practices
- Business process
- Target customers
- Offerings
- Strategies
- Operational processes and policies
- Organizational structures
- Sourcing

The literature has moved further, identifying the primary dimensions of a business model:

- The value architecture or creation
- The value proposition or delivery
- The value finance or economics
- The value network or the network effect

The model, developed by Al-Debei and Avison (2010), in Fig. 3.4 explains the main dimensions of a business model. In terms of innovation, any strategical and considerable change in the 4Vs, aimed to create, deliver, or capture more value, can be identified as a business model innovation. This is fundamental especially with respect to the customers and the organizations.

There are certain modifications to the model. The most important one is to put knowledge management at the center of the value components. Newell et al. (2009) define knowledge management as: "Improving the

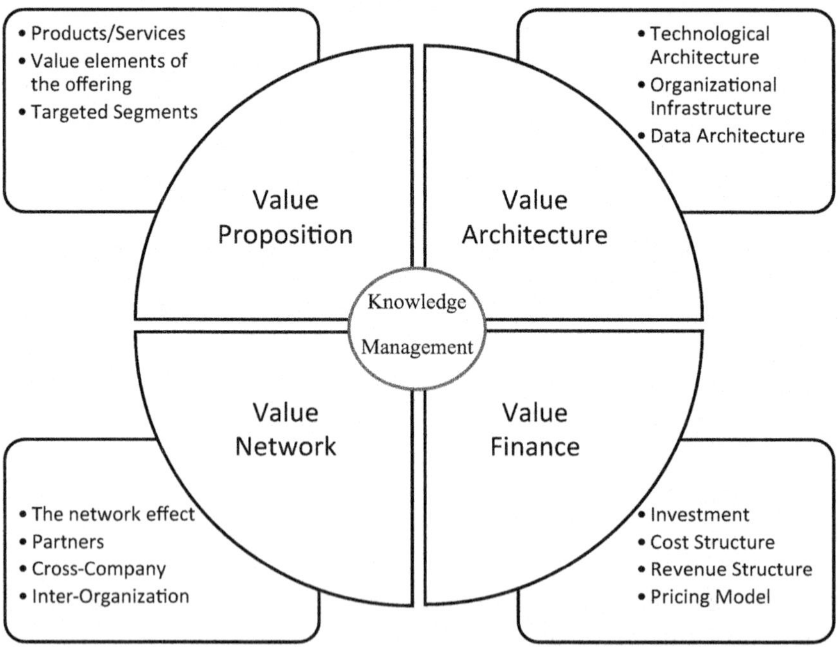

Fig. 3.4 The V4 business model framework

ways in which firms facing highly turbulent environment can mobilize their knowledge base (or leverage their knowledge 'assets') in order to ensure continuous innovation" (Morabito 2016).

Today, the focus is toward technology. This is even clearer within the financial services industry, especially when dealing with fintech initiatives. There are many examples in this direction. Bitcoin, a cryptocurrency based on the innovative blockchain technology (Skinner 2016); TransferWise, a company that allows people to transfer money internationally at considerably lower costs compared to traditional systems[39]; or Satago, which aims to completely automate the account receivable department of a business organization.[40]

Nevertheless, even new and connected business models may show some differences. According to a recent report developed by the World Economic Forum (Stein et al. 2015), one of the most intriguing markets in terms of business model innovations is the P2P lending; analyzing successful startups such as Lending Club, OnDeck, Kabbage, and Credibly, the report has shown an interesting comparison between the innovating business models of these companies from three perspectives. The business models followed by the companies operating in this business may differ in terms of three base components, that is, 3 Ps:

Peer relationships

- Balance sheet lenders
- Marketplace lenders
- Hybrid model

Financial products

- Revolving lines of credit
- Merchant cash advances
- Unsecured term loans (3–8 months)

---

[39] https://transferwise.com/gb/blog/sir-richard-branson-joins-our-mission-to-stamp-out-hidden-fees, Accessed 20 August 2016.

[40] https://www.satago.com/, Accessed 20 August 2016.

Processes

- Direct flow
- Mediated flow

A Business Model

The Business Model Approach

One of the most important aspects to consider in studying innovation is the business model of an organization (Chesbrough and Rosenbloom 2002). An organization may be either a single entity or a collection of entities working together to deliver a product or service that creates value for their target customers (Grönroos and Voima 2013). The entrepreneurs interested in launching a fintech initiative should first get an answer to some basic questions: which value are they adding to the customers? What will be their business model? How will they earn money? Answering these certainly requires a specific framework for describing the business.

The business model literature found its origins in the entrepreneurship and strategic management literature describing the phenomenon of fast-growing internet businesses, which outperform traditional companies (Moser and Gassmann 2016). Research on business models aims to answer the question on how organizations create value. Business models either have been described as a concept from a customer-centric perspective or are used to highlight aspects which are boundaries to the business aspects. Despite the fast-growing body of literature, there is still a lively debate on the theoretical foundation and the conceptualization of business models. Zott et al. (2011) argue that no theory fully describes value creation through business models, while different domains on the topic, developed independently, result in various concepts and definitions. Most of the researchers agree on value creation, value delivery, and value capturing as describing parts of a business model (Casadesus et al. 2010; Osterwalder et al. 2010). What customers value in products varies by industry. A survey has found that the top five elements influencing loyalty in consumer banking are (Almquist et al. 2016):

- Assure quality
- Provides access
- Continue tradition
- Avoids hassles
- Reduces anxiety

In the case of auto insurance, the survey found that the following elements influence loyalty (Almquist et al. 2016):

- Assure quality
- Reduces anxiety
- Reduces cost
- Provides access
- Provide variety

A Business Model for Fintech

Osterwalder and Pigneur (2010) defined their model as the business model canvas (BMC). The BMC is an effective visual framework for analyzing a business model. It explains the rationale of why, how, and through which tools an organization creates, delivers, and captures value. From a visual point of view, the BMC is a poster format chart (a canvas) that describes nine elements of a business model and enables a discussion on them by a group of people working together. The nine elements are (see also Fig. 3.5) as follows:

- Market: This includes three important aspects. The 3 Cs: the target customers, the competitors, and the compliance with the operative regulation. For whom does the fintech initiative aim to create value? Who are its target customers? Which are the rules it must respect?

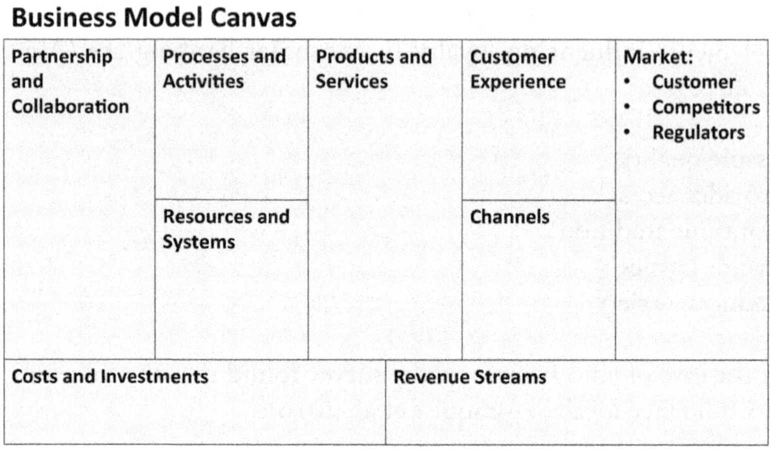

Fig. 3.5 The business model canvas (adapted by the author from Osterwalder and Pigneur 2010)

- Value propositions: Which are the products and/or services included in the organization offering? What value does the fintech initiative deliver to a customer in a given segment? Which needs are important to satisfy?
- Channels: How does the company intend to reach the target customers? What is the most convenient channel for the customer? Are the different channels integrated with an omnichannel approach (Bell et al. 2014)?
- Customer experiences: Which will be the customer experience? How can the company build, maintain, and improve it to delight the customer? Will it perfectly fit with the aims of both the organization and of the customers?
- Key resources and systems: Which resources are critical to deliver the value proposition through the channels and to maintain, enhance, and improve the customer relationships? Which organization should be set up?
- Key processes and activities: Which are the most important activities and processes to make the business successful?
- Key partnerships and collaborations: Who are the key partners and vendors? Which key resources do they provide and what key processes/activities do they operate? What is in it for them? Which relationship should be built with them?

- Revenue: What will the customers pay for? How much? Which is the pricing model?
- Costs and investments: Which are the finance (costs and investments) implied by the business model? Which are the most relevant? What is fixed and what is variable? Which are the main cost drivers and risks to consider?

The BMC comprises nine interconnected components. Each of them is critical and deserves the right attention. It is important to consider how innovation could be implemented in the different components of the business model. All these types of innovations are equally important, either if one considers innovations that cover multiple components in the canvas or if they act on a single component. It is important anyway to take into account that an innovation in one of the components normally requires adjustments also in the other components. The following sections consider the PayPal case (see Fig. 3.6) and the typical crowdfunding case (see Fig. 3.7), applying the BMC to companies that perform their businesses in the financial services industry.

The BMC of the companies operating in financial services shows some peculiarities. Following the BMC structure, it is possible to explain how a fintech company should organize its business, where to focus, and how to create a leading proactive mindset in this complex environment.

The financial technology system has such a variability that it is not possible to define a one-size-fits-all model. Furthermore, the value proposition, the market, and the structure of revenues and costs are considered to be intrinsic aspects of every organization, so they will not be taken into consideration. In the following model, the main challenges of fintech initiatives will be lumped, therefore aiming to provide general guidelines that could fit with the highly heterogeneous world of financial technology (see Fig. 3.7 for an example in the case of crowdfunding initiatives).

Every startup should address its focus toward nine important elements:

1. Market—focus on targets
2. Products and services—focus on value added
3. Channels—focus on social and omnichannel

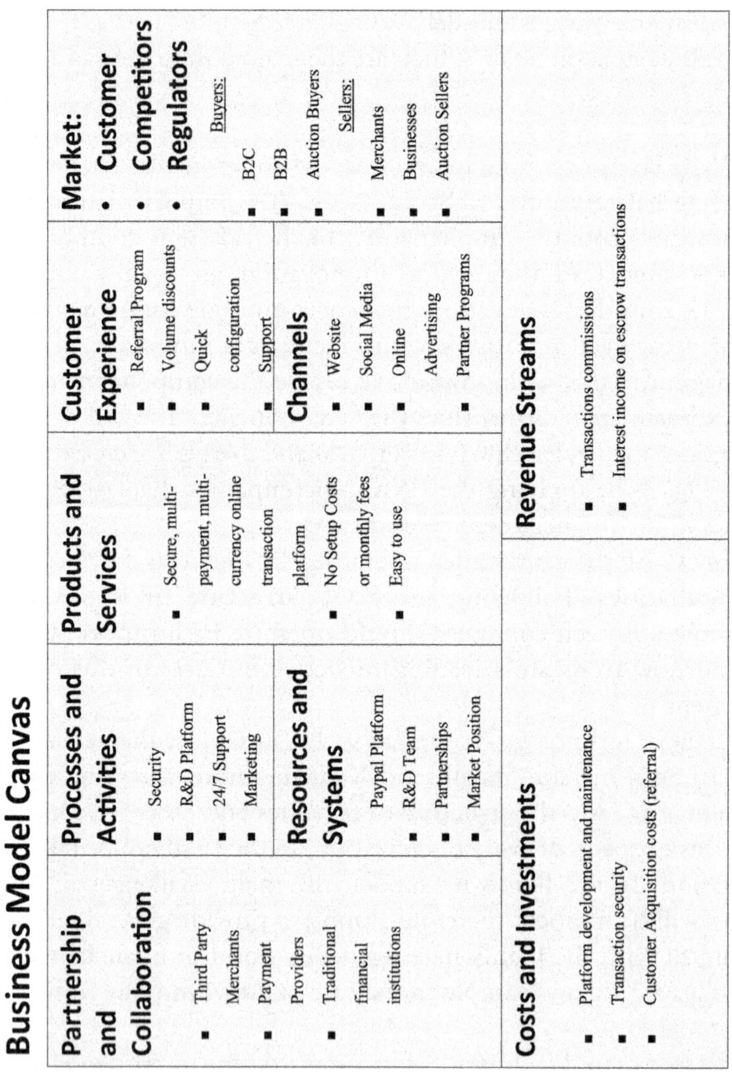

Fig. 3.6 PayPal's business model canvas (adapted by the author from multiple sites)

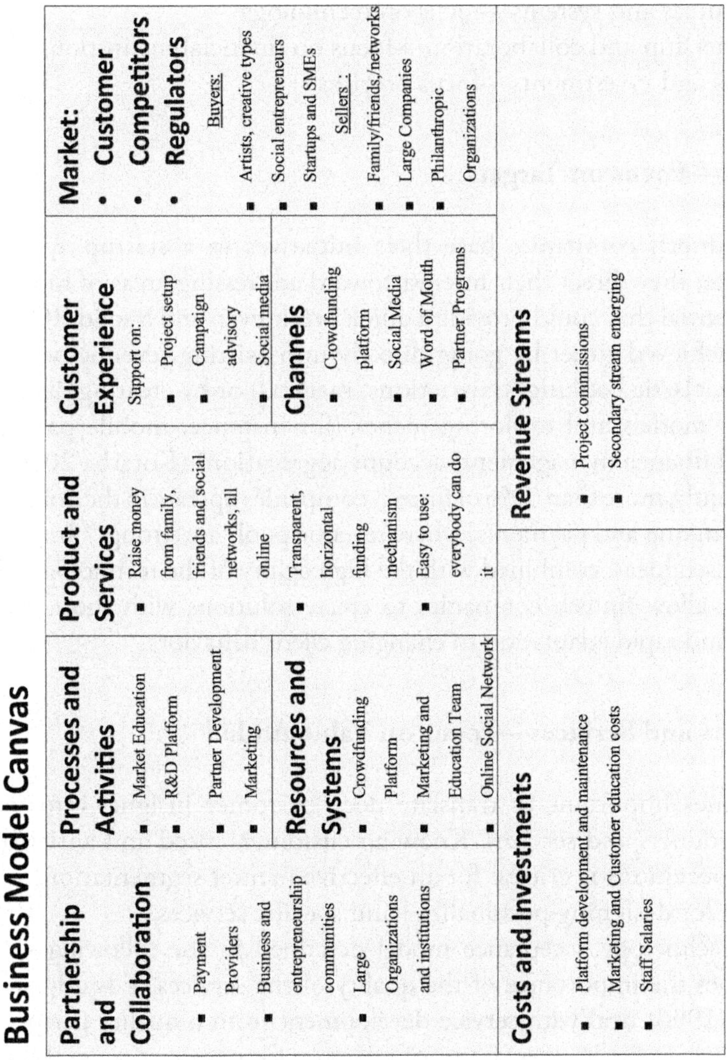

Fig. 3.7 Crowdfunding's business model canvas (adapted by the author from multiple sites)

4. Customer experience—focus on customer-centric approach
5. Revenue—focus on customer lifetime value
6. Processes and activities—focus on marketing
7. Resources and systems—focus on technology
8. Partnership and collaboration—focus on financial institutions
9. Costs and investments—focus on risks

Market—Focus on Targets

Many fintech companies base their initiatives in a startup approach. Therefore, they direct their interest toward addressing areas of high revenue potential that could provide a quick break-even and a solid ROI. This can be achieved either by going directly into existing revenue pools (for instance, classic banking, transactions, markets) or by creating disruptive business models and exploring niches (for instance, mobile payments, personal finance management, account aggregation) (Kotarba 2016).

Currently, more than 50% of fintech companies operate in the domains of classic banking and payments, where revenue pools are strong.[41] Innovative and focused ideas, combined with the high agility of the technology development, allow fintech companies to create solutions with short time to market and rapid adaptation to changing client behaviors.

Products and Services—Focus on Value Added

It becomes important to translate deep customer insights into tailor-made products and services. Knowing customers' need and anticipating their expectations is critical for an effective market segmentation, which is useful for designing personalized and specific services.

The technology acceptance model described in the following section underlines the importance of the quality of the services. Edvardsson and Olsson (1996) deal with service development from a quality perspective. Their paper presents a new frame of reference for new service development

[41] Venture Scanner (2016). Fintech Q1 Update, [online] Available at: http://insights.venturescanner.com/category/financial-technology/, Accessed 27 July 2016.

based on empirical studies in Sweden. It argues that the main task of service development is to create the right generic prerequisites for the service. This means an effective, efficient, and economical customer process. The process must be adapted to the logic of the customer's behavior and a good customer outcome; that is, the service should be associated with quality. In this process, there are three main types of aspects to consider and develop:

- the service concept;
- the service system (resource structure); and
- the service process.

This consideration underlines the importance to devote great attention in the business model to the value added that the services and products offered by the fintech initiatives could make available to the target market.

Channels—Focus on Social and Omnichannel

Fintech initiatives should use social media to introduce new products and services. They can target customers in specific regions in a cost-efficient and effective way compared to capital-intensive paper, television, and web promotions. In this way, they can innovatively change the business model of financial services. Financial institutions can experiment with different segments and then upgrade their strategies to a higher (regional, national, or international) level.

The 2014 Global Consumer Banking survey of EY provides evidence that improvements in the CRM processes are critical to maintaining and expanding the competitive position of customer-centered organizations.[42] The study points out that traditional financial institutions are subefficient in introducing important CRM changes. As a result, their market shares could fall prey to the new, non-financial market entrants, especially to the ones in the global fintech community.

[42] http://www.ey.com/Publication/vwLUAssets/EY_-_Global_Consumer_Banking_Survey_2014/$FILE/EY-Global-Consumer-Banking-Survey-2014.pdf, Accessed 27 July 2016.

Fintech initiatives should aim to improve customer channels. By combining and making transparent direct customer connections (email, call center, agent, portal, social, faxes, reports, etc.) with indirect customer connections such as social media, blogs, log files, and so on, a more holistic, 360° view of each customer can be obtained. This what is called omnichannel. It helps create a personalized and consistent communication response, enabling marketing to achieve better brand value and gain competitive advantages. At the same time, omnichannel can directly influence the bottom-line by becoming leaner, thanks to the reduction in communication costs.

Customer Experience—Focus on Customer-Centric Approach

Traditional organizations, up to now, have not created close relationships with their customers. This is both the symptom and the cause of a "disease" that has been affecting the financial services industry for a long time. In the last few years, things have radically changed, and not surprisingly. Customers are now choosing differently due to their new needs and, especially, expectations. A new group of customers, named millennials (those born between 1980 and 2000), is causing radical shifts to customer demographics (Howe and Strauss 2009).

It is important to create comprehensive customer delight surveys and feedback. Most financial services organizations perform customer surveys using a relatively small customer sample size. New solutions enable financial institutions to survey their entire customer base (and possibly prospects through social media) and process the survey results in a fast and cost-effective way. In this way, they can obtain a truer picture of what would be available from their customer service responses.

The consequence of this process of "disintermediation" implies two critical points for traditional organizations:

- losing market shares in favor of new entrants; and
- testifying that their approach needs to change in the face of such changed environment.

Table 3.2 Fintech's impact on customer centricity (PwC 2016)

Area of most impacts from fintech	Percentage of respondents (%)
Meet changing customer needs with new offerings	75
Leverage existing data and analytics	51
Enhance interactions and build trusted relationships	42
Enhance business with sophisticated operational capabilities	42

All fintech initiatives have a "customer-centric" approach, meaning that, whichever the plan they choose to pursue, customers must play a pivotal role: "The future belongs to banks that give the customer center stage in their business model" (Auerbach et al. 2012).

The path toward a customer-centric organization is full of hurdles and obstacles (Sheth et al. 2000). For traditional companies that are willing to start this journey, there will definitively be resistances that are complex, whenever internal and old routines may become unmanageable bottlenecks.

It is then useful to analyze how fintech initiatives have sped up the whole process by fostering customer centricity in traditional organization's strategies.[43] A survey done by PricewaterhouseCoopers asked the question: "In which areas do you see the most important impact to your business from Fintech?" Table 3.2 shows the result of the survey.

According to PricewaterhouseCoopers, only 53% of the financial institutions believe that they are fully customer centric, while for fintech startup respondents this share exceeds 80%.[44]

McKinsey's suggestions (2012) for designing a customer-centric organization define a clear, effective process:

- Vision and positioning: "Create an institution that customers want to bank with and employees feel proud of."
- Customer engagement model: "Design an organization that delivers exceptional customer service where customers expect it, and excites them where they do not."

[43] PwC (2016), Blurred Lines, How Fintech Is Shaping Financial Services. https://www.PwC.com/il/en/home/assets/PwC_fintech%20global_report.pdf, Accessed 31 July 2016.

[44] PwC (2016), ibid.

- Development agenda: "Define an integrated development agenda to drive short-term gains and long-term growth."
- Organization, capabilities, and insights: "Build the insights engine, organizational capabilities, and governance needed to sustain momentum."

Fintech companies should recognize and shape customer touch points in order to ensure the right customer experience and to instill the desired brand image. Satisfaction and loyalty are primary parameters of an organization's success as they increase sales and attract new customers (Keisidou et al. 2013). A structured approach is strongly suggested, where customer insight units may be part of each line of business with the aim of enabling customer centricity in all the decision-making processes. Customer centricity should not be lived by organizations as something to "show" to their customers, but rather as something to "live" during daily operations. Organizations should design their internal functions to represent customer focus with the aim of allowing themselves to implement immediate solutions for the satisfaction of their customers (Shah et al. 2006).

It is important to build and shape a company culture that supports customer centricity; in addition, anchoring customer centricity in employees' hearts and minds is critical (McKinsey 2012). McKinsey defined a test for traditional organizations to diagnose their customer centricity. Three sets of questions compose the test (McKinsey 2012):

- Vision and positioning
  - The brand and the vision are built around a specific customer "promise".
  - Brand and vision are visible for everyone and fundamentally guide behavior.
- Development agenda
  - The bank has a clear understanding of customer insights across lines of business.
  - The bank invests intelligently in superior customer experience in a systematic and economically viable manner.

- The customer experience is centered around a few key touch points of superior customer experience.
- All customer-oriented activities are rooted in economic goals, not just satisfaction.
- The bank targets "hearts and minds" to drive attitudinal loyalty, as well as wallet to drive share.
- The bank coordinates revenue initiatives across functions and leverages the full marketing and sales toolkit.

- Organization, capabilities, and insights
  - The bank has an organizational structure in place that enables customer centricity in business decisions.
  - Employees have developed the mindsets and capabilities behind the customer-centric agenda.

Organizations should take into full consideration the changed nature of their customers, putting them at the center of their plans and strategies. These statements should be adapted to the specific situation of the company, as detailed later in this book.

Revenue—Focus on Customer Lifetime Value

Leading-edge financial institutions should work to add value to the customers and the organization leveraging external data for more accurate pricing. Using real-time location and business characteristics, data can lead to more appropriate pricing on customer risk based on how and where customers use the financial services (for instance, insurance).

From the point of view of the revenue (and hence of the pricing), it is interesting to consider three important concepts: customer lifetime value (Berger and Nasr 1998), value creation and exchange (Ballantine et al. 2003; Sheth and Uslay 2007), and value co-creation (Grönroos and Voima 2013).

These concepts are metrics for customer selection and marketing resource allocation by developing a dynamic framework that enables managers to maintain or improve customer relationships proactively through marketing contacts across various channels. They also allow maximizing value added for the customers while leveraging cross-sell and upsell potential. For example, by analyzing text and speech in a near-real time environment, organizations are presented with new opportunities to convert the call center from a cost center to a service-to-sales (S2S) center by providing cross-sell and upsell capabilities.

Processes and Activities—Focus on Marketing

Financial technology startups are delivering unique products and services to their target market. Nevertheless, these organizations are actually facing a harmful threat, able to bring them to failure. In fact, their target market, most of the times, does not even know their products or services. Besides, when it does, it is not able to perceive all the benefits.

In addition to that, according to the report developed by the World Economic Forum[45] (October 2015), market shares of fintech startups are still very low. For instance, in the case of the lending market, they are still less than 1% of total bank lending on a global scale. Although growth rates are high and these figures are going to increase in the next few years, fintech companies will highly leverage on their marketing department in getting the job done and be the winners (Gritten 2011).

Fintech startups should pursue this process with simple but systematic operations. In the very first phase of their life cycles, it is critical to give the right attention to marketing and plan for it (Luu 2016). Often seen as an afterthought, it is the most useful tool in the hands of the management in order to produce returns from the marketing department. Arranging meetings for introductions may help as well, together with the production of continuous press releases that could favor the spread of the brand throughout the market. At this point of the organization's life cycle, the management should be actively involved in the systematic update of the marketing plan. It should now include sophis-

[45] World Economic Forum (2015), The Future of FinTech : A Paradigm Shift in Small Business Finance, October http://www3.weforum.org/docs/IP/2015/FS/GAC15_The_Future_of_FinTech_Paradigm_Shift_Small_Business_Finance_report_2015.pdf.

Fig. 3.8 Components of an effective marketing plan

ticated tools. Introducing recognized members in the top management team could actually be an option. Organizations should address the education of the customers with the aim of helping them in making smarter financial decisions.

Solutions can help in leveraging for an effective marketing plan (see Fig. 3.8).

1. Big Data Analytics: New software products and tools have entered the market, making Big Data (both structured and unstructured) far more accessible, even for little startups.
2. Open data: Data publicly available with no restrictions from ownership, patents and copyrights
3. The other 3 Cs: Customized Customer Content. This is about putting in action marketing campaigns leveraging on social media channels. Accenture's Banking blog is an example of how this can have a great impact on the company's lead generation.[46]

[46] http://thefinancialbrand.com/57831/5-financial-marketing-trends-tools/, Accessed 26 July 2016.

4. Relational marketing: The primary objective of a company should be the construction of loyal and long-term relationships with its customers. This task can also be accomplished by leveraging on social media channels, Big Data Analytics, and technology. The importance of customer knowledge management is particularly important both for the consumer and in the business financial market (Cui and Wu 2016).

Resources and Systems—Focus on Technology

The present years are moments of innovation and expansion for technology in the financial services industry. Fintech companies are focusing their efforts on the production and delivery of leading-edge solutions to serve their target markets. Traditional organizations have not done that in the past. Fintech initiatives should not only be maintaining this pace of innovation. They should also actively continue toward this direction in order to survive market's feasible and physiological pullbacks in the near future.

A broader and complete answer is provided in the following chapter, which is focused on the challenges of fintech initiatives in terms of innovations and advanced technologies. Important aspects to consider are as follows:

- Using data to find prescriptive and predictive information: It is important to investigate how it is possible to improve the user experience by sensing data and responding in near-real time. Prescriptive analytics can provide alerts on risky behavior in terms of transactions or behavior. Machine learning algorithms can acquire data from various sources and use them to produce predictive information. This would especially help fintech startups, since they do not have the long history of credit worthiness that traditional financial services have.[47]
- Using natural language processing (NLP) and text analytics for social media, as well as speech analytics for call center conversations: Services based on financial technologies can improve their sentiment analysis to better meet customer service improvement objectives, even if not explicitly disclosed to the company.

[47] http://www.techweekeurope.it/data-storage/business-intelligence/machine-learning-fintech-97448#t76fXTUfIjL8odz0.99, Accessed 20 August 2016.

- Enhancing search capabilities, for instance, using semantics engines: Not many financial institutions are using these solutions to discover innovative ways to search their Intranet documents in order to provide fast search capabilities in unstructured documents. These can be used by their financial departments as well as in call-center scenarios to provide real-time recommendations.
- Optimizing call center and middle offices workload: Analyzing network data from the switches (call detail records) and combining them with transactions helps in understanding who performed, what activity was performed, and how efficiently. It helps in providing guidelines for employees and intermediaries. Temporal call patterns analysis of voluminous and raw telecom and processing data can help assist in staffing optimization as well.

Partnership and Collaboration—Focus on Financial Institutions

One of the most important aspects to consider is the growing attention of the financial services sector toward fintech initiatives. Traditional financial organizations have embraced the innovation challenge in different ways; some financial institutions have diversified, becoming venture capitalists. Some others have set up innovation labs, actively participating in business incubators with the aim of narrowing their technological gap. All in all, traditional financial organizations are adopting different solutions in order to simplify their processes and foster a move toward digital transformation. Several fintech ventures have taken approaches not explored in the past. They are exploiting opportunities not yet recognized by financial giants. The future will likely be different. Many professionals (Pollari 2016)[48] have already identified a trend of a growing percentage of startups moving toward enabling and optimizing businesses, rather than disrupting them. This is an interesting step toward collaboration of fintech startups with traditional financial institutions. This process is two-way. Up to now, fintech companies have been forcing large financial

[48] http://fintechinnovators.com/about-list, 01 August 2016.

institutions to redefine their strategies. The future will see a growing influence of these large traditional financial institutions on the strategies of financial technology startups.

Costs and Investments—Focus on Risks

Costs and investments are important issues for fintech initiatives. In the case of incumbent financial institutions, costs and risks are important factors that traditional management scrutinizes in great depth since often they are not very open to fintech initiatives. In the case of startups, money is always an issue since, normally, it is not very abundant.

Costs can be managed using lean and digitized solutions (Nicoletti 2012). The risk aspects are relatively new to the world of fintech initiatives. Customer risks arise because of a greater range of product offers available via a mobile phone or another digital device. They need to be identified, assessed, and mitigated by market players and the regulator (Buckley and Malady 2015). This risk management process is necessary before customer protection problems arise for the end users, which could negatively affect trust in fintech initiatives. Customer trust is essential for the uptake and success of these fintech initiatives. This issue is a subset of the broader topic of customer risks associated with fintech initiatives or "responsible digital finance" (Zimmerman 2014). These aspects go beyond the scope of this book. Their inclusion illustrates that it is an important emerging issue for market players and in international policy development. There is currently a general awareness among financial inclusion advocates that not much is known about this broader topic. Considerable work is underway to improve all players' comprehension of how to balance the promotion of fintech initiatives while mitigating customer risks.

Closing the loop between pricing risk, transactions, and financial effects, risk officials can evaluate the loss and fraud propensity of existing customers in order to better price risk for new prospects, especially in the insurance services. This helps in minimizing risks and insuring goods largely, pricing the risk appropriately. It can help also in improving real-time risk decisions.

Conclusions

Fintech initiatives are focusing their efforts on the production and delivery of leading-edge technologies that now serve their target markets as no traditional organizations did in the past. Why was fintech born? For whom was it born? What product does it aim to provide? Where and when does it intend to perform its business? How is fintech working? The previous chapter provides answers to these questions. It also provides multiple classifications from different perspectives.

This chapter has dealt with several classifications of fintech initiatives with the aim of offering a big picture of this industry. The boundaries between classes are not always distinct and discernible. They are instead indefinite and always changing.

By using a visual framework for analyzing a business model (BMC), this chapter describes a model that aims to support those fintech initiatives aiming to achieve a competitive advantage in this fragmented galaxy. The statements provided are general guidelines and need further adaptations for being successful. Later chapters do this fitting. Improvements in the models are desirable, but in the current form, they are already an important tool for analyzing fintech initiatives.

Every startup should address its focus toward the following important elements:

1. Market—focus on targets
2. Products and services—focus on value-added
3. Channels—focus on social and omnichannel
4. Customer experience—focus on customer-centric approach
5. Revenue—focus on customer lifetime value
6. Processes and activities—focus on marketing
7. Resources and systems—focus on technology
8. Partnership and collaboration—focus on financial institutions
9. Costs and investments—focus on risks

In this way, fintech initiatives will prosper and, especially, will not die.

Innovation is the guiding principle of this business model since fintech initiatives are required to design or to implement a new business approach in order to be competitive.

Business organizations should implement innovations (marginal or drastic) in each of the described areas. The next chapter thoroughly deals with this topic, describing how fintech initiatives are delivering innovation in the financial services industry, and especially their impacts on the overall financial system.

References

Al-Debei, M. M., & Avison, D. (2010). Developing a unified framework of the business model concept. *European Journal of Information Systems, 19*, 359–376.

Almquist, E., Senior, J., & Bloch, N. (2016). The elements of value. *Harvard Business Review, 94*, 46–53.

Auerbach, P., Argimon, R. F., Roland, C., & Teschke, B. (2012). Banking on customer centricity: Transforming banks into customer-centric organizations. *McKinsey & Company Review*, 3–14

Ballantine, D., et al. (2003). Relationship marketing: Looking back, looking forward. *Marketing Theory, 3*(1), 159–166.

Bell, D. R., Gallino, S., & Moreno, A. (2014). How to win in an omnichannel world. *MIT Sloan Management Review, 56*(1), 1–45.

Belleflamme, P., Lambert, T., & Schwienbacher, A. (2010, June). Crowdfunding: An industrial organization perspective. *Prepared for the Workshop Digital Business Models: Understanding Strategies'*. Paris, France, 25–26.

Berger, P. D., & Nasr, N. I. (1998). Customer lifetime value: Marketing models and applications. *Journal of Interactive Marketing, 12*(1), 17–30.

Buckley, R. P., & Malady, L. (2015). Building consumer demand for digital financial services—The new regulatory frontier. *Journal of Financial Perspectives, 3*(3), 122–137.

Casadesus-Masanell, R., & Ricart, J. E. (2010). From strategy to business models and onto tactics. *Long Range Planning, 43*(2), 195–215.

Chesbrough, H., & Rosenbloom, R. S. (2002). The role of the business model in capturing value from innovation: Evidence from Xerox Corporation's technology spin-off companies. *Industrial and Corporate Change, 11*(3), 529–555.

Cui, A. S., & Wu, F. (2016). Utilizing customer knowledge in innovation: Antecedents and impact of customer involvement on new product performance. *Journal of the Academy of Marketing Science, 44*(4), 516–538.

Dietz, M., Moon, J., & Radnai, M. (2016, July). Fintechs can help incumbents, not just disrupt them. *McKinsey Review*. Retrieved August 24, 2016, from http://www.mckinsey.com/industries/financial-services/our-insights/fintechs-can-help-incumbents-not-just-disrupt-them

Edvardsson, B., & Olsson, J. (1996). Key concepts for new service development. *Service Industries Journal, 16*(2), 140–164.

Ernst and Young. (2014). *Landscaping UK Fintech*. UK Trade and Investment, London, UK.

Fairview Capital. (2009). *Financial technology: Fintech primer industry overview from a venture capital perspective*. Retrieved July 31, 2016, from http://www.fairviewcapital.com/pdf_downloads/fintech_Industry_Report.pdf

Fintech 100. (2015). *Leading Global Fintech innovators*. Report 2015. Retrieved August 24, 2016, from http://www.fintechinnovators.com/

Gritten, A. (2011). New insights into consumer confidence in financial services. *International Journal of Bank Marketing, 29*(2), 90–106.

Grönroos, C., & Voima, P. (2013). Critical service logic: Making sence of value creation and co-creation. *Journal of the Academy of Marketing Science, 41*, 133–150.

H2 Ventures, KPMG and Matchi. (2016). Fintech 100. *Leading Global Fintech innovators, Report 2015*. Retrieved July 31, 2016, from https://www.kpmg.com/FR/fr/IssuesAndInsights/ArticlesPublications/Documents/Etude-Fintech100-2015.pdf

Howe, N., & Strauss, W. (2009). *Millennials rising: The next great generation*. New York, NY: Vintage.

Keisidou, E., Lazaros, S., Maditinos, D. L., & Thalassinos, E. I. (2013). Customer satisfaction, loyalty and financial performance: A holistic approach of the Greek banking sector. *International Journal of Bank Marketing, 31*(4), 259–288.

Kipling, R. (2013). *Just so stories*. CreateSpace Independent Publishing Platform.

Koen, P. A., Bertels, H. M. J., & Elsum, I. R. (2011). The three faces of business model innovation: Challenges for established firms. *Research-Technology Management, 54*(3), 52–59.

Kotarba, M. (2016). New factors inducing changes in the retail banking customer relationship management (CRM) and their exploration by the fintech industry. *Foundations of Management, 8*(1), 69–78.

Luu, T. (2016). *The ultimate compendium of internet marketing tools & resources*. Luxembourg: Amazon Media EU, s.a.r.l.

McKinsey & Company. (2012). Banking on customer centricity: Transforming banks into customer-centric organizations. Retrieved February 21, 2017, from http://www.mckinsey.com/~/media/mckinsey/dotcom/client_service/Financial%20Services/Latest%20thinking/Consumer%20and%20small%20business%20banking/Banking_on_customer_centricity_Transforming_banks_into_customer-centric_organizations.ashx

Morabito, V. (2016). *The future of digital business innovation: Trends and practices*. Heidelberg, Germany: Springer Verlag.

Moser, D., & Gassmann, O. (2016). Innovating platform business models. *Proceedings of ISPIM—International Society for Professional Innovation Management* (pp. 1–14). Porto, Portugal.

Newell, S., Robertson, M., Scarbrough, H., & Swan, J. (2009). *Managing knowledge work and innovation*. London, UK: Palgrave Macmillan.

Nicoletti, B. (2012). *Cloud computing in financial services*. London, UK: Palgrave Macmillan.

Nicoletti, B. (2014). *Mobile banking*. London, UK: Palgrave Macmillan.

Osterwalder, A., Pigneur, Y., Smith, A., & 470 practitioners from 45 countries. (2010). *Business model generation*. Self-published.

Pollari, I. (2016). The rise of fintech. *JASSA* (3), 15.

PwC. (2016). Blurred lines. How Fintech is shaping financial services. Retrieved February 22, 2017, from https://www.pwc.com/il/en/home/assets/pwc_fintech%20global_report.pdf

Schumpeter, J. (2013, January 5). Lending club: Peer review. *The Economist*.

Shah, D., Rust, R. T., Parasuraman, A., Staelin, R., & Day, G. S. (2006). The path to customer centricity. *Journal of Service Research, 9*, 113.

Sheth, J. N., Sisodia, R. S., & Sharma, A. (2000). The antecedents and consequences of customer-centric marketing. *Academy of Marketing Science Journal, 28*(1), 55–66.

Sheth, J. N., & Uslay, C. (2007). Implications of the revised definition of marketing: From exchange to value creation. *Journal of Public Policy and Marketing, 26*(2), 302–307.

Skinner, C. (2016). *How Fintech firms are using bitcoin blockchain and mobile technologies to create the Internet of value*. Singapore: Marshall Cavendish International (Asia) Pte Ltd.

Square Capital. (2015). We've now extended $225 M in business financing. Retrieved August 20, 2016, from https://squareup.com/townsquare/weve-now-extended-225m-in-business-financing/

Stein, P., Ventura, A., & Tufano, P. (2015, October). The future of FinTech: A paradigm shift in small business finance. *World Economic Forum*, 1–35.

Teece, D. J. (2010). Business models, business strategy and innovation. *Long Range Planning, 43*(2–3), 172–194.

Venture Scanner. (2016). Fintech Q1 update. Retrieved July 27, 2016, from http://insights.venturescanner.com/category/financial-technology/

World Economic Forum. (2015). *The Future of Fintech : A paradigm shift in small business finance*. Geneva, Switzerland: World Economic Forum Publications.

Zimmerman, J. (2014, 21 July). The emergence of responsible digital finance. *Centre for Financial Inclusion*. Retrieved August 24, 2016, from https://cfi-blog.org/2014/07/21/the-emergence-of-responsible-digital-finance/

Zott, C., Amit, R., & Massa, L. (2011). The business model: Recent developments and future research. *Journal of Management, 37*(4), 1019–1042.

4

Fintech Innovation

Introduction

One of the critical aspects in fintech initiatives is their intrinsic innovative attitude. This is a global phenomenon aiming to provide innovations in the financial services industry. Fintech initiatives have been leveraging on innovation, especially by means of new technologies, often delivered through online and mobile channels, in order to act upon the industry by disintermediating traditional financial institutions.

Fintech initiatives can deliver innovation to the market in different ways:

- Product innovations
- Process innovations
- Organizational innovations
- Business model innovations

This categorization is at the base of this chapter and leads to further insights and considerations. The chapter provides real-life examples for

B. Nicoletti, *The Future of FinTech*,
DOI 10.1007/978-3-319-51415-4_4

each one of these categories with the aim of connecting theory with practice. It is necessary to underline that fintech initiatives are extremely dynamic. Examples are useful, but they may disappear over times. This is the reason why this book underlines models rather than relying only on examples.

This chapter analyzes some important innovations in connection with the previous classification (see Table 4.1).

Mobility, Big Data Analytics, robots, and tech organizations can be considered the reflection of this categorization in some fintech initiatives. Analyzing real cases helps to evaluate the current shift that is disrupting the financial services industry.

Innovation and Fintech

The model developed in the previous chapter is consistent with the report produced by EY. The customer-centric approach, the focus on technologies and on digital channels, and the enlargement and empowerment of the customer base are primary elements to consider in fintech initiatives (see Table 4.2).

Digital Transformation and Fintech

One important question is when it makes sense for a traditional organization to embrace the fintech wave.

Some believe that a digital transformation is simply a matter of using digital technologies to sell and service clients more effectively, more efficiently, and in a more customized way.

Table 4.1 Innovation classification

Category	Example of innovation
Product innovation	Mobility
Process innovation	Big Data Analytics, etc.
Organizational innovation	Robots
Business model innovation	Tech organizations

Table 4.2 Innovation in financial services (adapted from Lopez et al. 2015)

Traditional model	Digital innovations	Why are they innovative?
The main objectives of technology are employee productivity, compliance, and integration of disparate and legacy ICT systems.	Well-designed platforms, focused on simplicity, speed, and intuitive workflows through digital and mobile channels	Technology aims to improve the customer experience with financial advices for the investors.
Traditional marketing and advertising through brochures, company websites, and direct mail campaigns	Compelling editorial content and financial education distributed openly online with a focus on human connection; provision of constant feedback on the customer's financial health	Focusing on the human connection and financial education in plain language through digital/mobile channels improves investor awareness. It also brings greater confidence, trust, and engagement.
Fees on assets under management typically above 100 basis points, difficult to understand, and with low visibility for investors	Average fees between 25 and 50 basis points; provision of free tools to analyze fees across accounts while offering cost-savings options	Leveraging low-cost exchange-traded funds (ETFs) and share/bond indexing enables portfolio diversification at lower prices with a transparent fee structure.

There are also other interpretations of what digital transformation is:

- A new application of digital initiatives, such as marketing
- A matter of using technology to drive business process innovation
- Nothing less than to be the Uber of taxi or the Airbnb of hoteling, and more

The real problem is not so much a definition of what digital transformation is, but what should be the strategy in face of this challenge/opportunity and how do we align an organization behind the digital transformation vision? A definition affects strategy and the level of its conversation, so it matters. What executives often do not know is how to bring about the changes that will help their organizations to be profitable, sustainable, and competitive in an era of disruptive change.

The reality is that most companies are reluctant to disrupt their own industries. Their concern is often because they fear cannibalizing their customer base or eroding their own margins. Hence, many executives prefer to make minor changes to their business with digital technologies rather than to innovate their business models in a fundamental manner. Many scholars such as Clayton Christensen (2013) suggest that a new business, outside of the current business, is often the best way to have the better of two worlds. It means an organization can become more customer-centric by using data and technology well in its current business, while experimenting with more disruptive solutions enabled by technology.

The recommendation is that executives should start by discussing their business' 4 Cs—context, customers, challenges and costs, and competitors—so that they can have a clear view of how digital transformation, technologies, and customer behavior can affect their organizations in the years to come. This exercise is about clarifying language so the organizations can build a digital strategy based on a shared understanding of their challenges and desired outcomes.

However, according to the study done by Forrester Research, the positive results of these investments are not clear: 73% of executives believe that a company has a digital strategy, but only 21% believe that it is the right strategy and only 15% believe that they have the skills and capabilities to execute it.[1]

It is important to analyze the digital transformation in order to assure that it is more successful. In this respect, it might be interesting to refer to the sentence of Rudyard Kipling mentioned in Chap. 3 of this book[2]: five Ws, and one H. It is important to answer these questions, each starting with an interrogative word, for considering complete the analysis of a problem. In the case of digital transformation, this would mean to answer the following questions:

- Why digital transforms the organization?
- For whom to do the transformation?

[1] Forrester Research 2015. The State Of Digital Business 2014, [online] Available at: http://blogs.forrester.com/f/b/users/NFENWICK /Infographic_1v4.pdf, Accessed 27 July 2016.

[2] Kipling R. (2013), Just So Stories, CreateSpace Independent Publishing Platform.

- What is the product it should aim to provide?
- Where can it take place?
- When can it take place?
- How to implement a digital transformation?

The broad questions executives should be asking are then:

- Why: The reason to do a digital transformation is to improve the business from an effectiveness, efficiency, and economic point of view. The real nature of the digital transformation of an established industry is not always obvious. Think, for example, about Uber, which may have a drastic impact beyond the taxi industry in the years to come. By making personal transport an affordable service commodity, it could eat away at the edges of the car and auto insurance industries.
- What are the best companies across the spectrum of digital enablement? What can executives learn from them about the future of the industry and the business? Organizations must understand how customers behave rather than simply looking at direct competitors. Remaining relevant is not simply a matter of creating an app or smartening up their website. It is essential to find ways to use customer data to create more meaningful and relevant customer experiences at every contact, physical or virtual.
- Who: Digital transformation requires a change in how institutions understand and engage with customers with the aid of digital tools and channels. This is an imperative and no longer up for debate. Unless this is done, nothing else is possible. This approach has the advantage of being realistic and manageable to implement.
- Where should the organization change to defend and extend market share, grow profits, and ensure relevance as digital technology evolves in the years to come?
- When should the organization invest in financial technologies? The simple answer "always" is in contrast with the realities of the possibilities of any financial institutions. By looking closely at competitors and the technology landscape, executives need to intercept low signals on how emerging technologies and disruptive rivals could attack their market shares. They need to create, deploy, and manage the strategies necessary to protect their market share and possibly identify ways to

expand into new service/market domains using the digital transformation.
- How exactly is digital technology changing the way the organization's customers behave and the way that existing, emerging, and potential competitors do business?

The next step is how to implement the new strategy. The answer is not the same for every business. Some businesses will have visionary leadership, agile processes, innovative cultures, open workforces with digital skills, and modern technology platforms, so they are able to embrace digital transformation more wholeheartedly.

In dealing with this digital innovation, it is important to refer to a model of innovation (Nicoletti 2016). Organizations should approach digital innovation in a holistic way. To approach this challenge, it is possible to refer to the combination of the Chandler model of connecting strategy and structure (1962) and the Leavitt Diamond model (1965), by considering the four connected variables:

- Structure (organization)
- Processes
- Technology
- Persons

An example of this approach applied to a digital strategy is shown in Fig. 4.1.

Conservative leadership, legacy technology, regulation, siloed processes, and non-receptive workforces may affect many organizations. Organizations will need to look at their assets—data, customers, resources, and channels—and find ways to put them to work in a digital world. In some cases, they might need to launch new products, or accept new business models or innovation groups to fast-track their digital programs.

On the other side, for the digital transformation, it is important to look at the 3 Ps (Nicoletti 2014a):

- Products: The definition of services to be offered to the customers of the organization is really essentially.

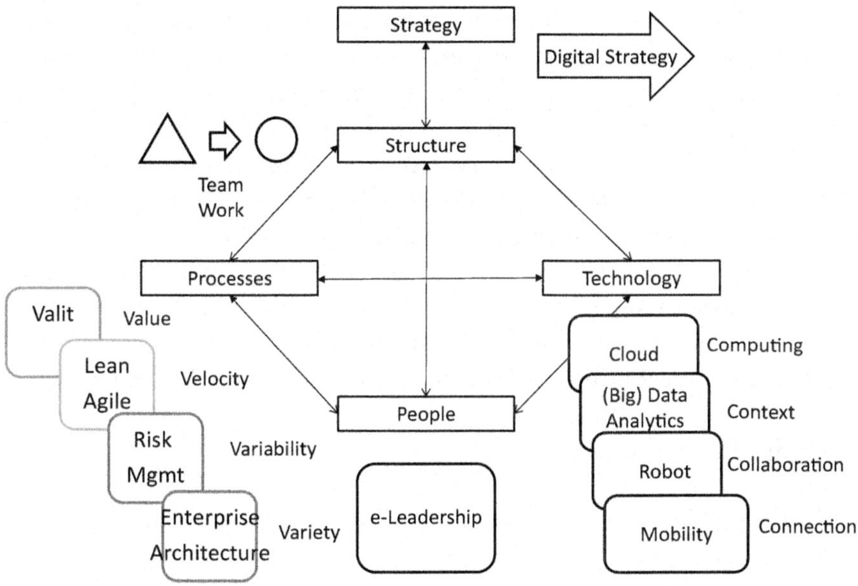

Fig. 4.1 A model for an integrated innovation strategy (Nicoletti 2016)

- Processes: The introduction of new products needs to consider also the changes in the processes. The two goes together in an innovation.
- People: Finally yet importantly, people must deploy and deliver the innovation. Executives should devote to them a very strong consideration and help individuate and foster the talents.

So ultimately, underpinning the organization's ability to perform a digital transformation lies in its ability to define a vision, define a plan, organize, and make it real.

Types of Innovation

"Companies must accept the inevitability of change by valuing innovation above past success" (Utterback 1994). In order to maintain a competitive advantage and to countervail the influences of a non-friendly environment, companies should struggle in continuously innovating. As Michael E. Porter states in *The Competitive Advantage of Nations* (1990),

"Companies achieve competitive advantage through acts of innovation." and "They approach innovation in its broadest sense, including both new technologies and new ways of doing things". These statements focus on the centricity of innovations in every industry, both as disruptive innovations, which are able to change radically an industry thanks to their impact, and as evolutionary or marginal innovations, renovating products or processes without completely disrupting them.

The financial services industry is on the brink of major innovation. This is important since there is strong evidence that the development in this sector contributes to the economic growth.

From a practical point of view, the innovation can be in the following:

- Product (or services)
- Process
- Organization
- Business models

Products

There are many opportunities for financial institutions in product innovation. Customers have a strong interest in seeing these institutions develop innovative services that apply new capabilities and deploy them close to the source of their needs. Financial institutions need to add value to their customers by addressing these customer expectations and operate much more effectively, efficiently, and, especially, economically. This standing is not easy for incumbent companies. They need to pick up these challenges.

For example, there are a significant number of applications in insurance for connected sensors and devices included in the IoT (or IoE, as Cisco calls it[3]). IoT is a scenario in which objects, animals, or people have unique identifiers. There is the ability to transfer data over a network without requiring human-to-person or human-to-computer interaction. With IoT, financial institutions are able to collect new datasets and

[3] http://www.cisco.com/c/m/it_it/tomorrow-starts-here/ioe.html, Accessed 27 July 2016.

assess risk in completely different ways with respect to today. This has the potential to radically reshape product propositions and reduce the size of global risk pools. With IoT, property and casualty insurance is likely to see the biggest long-run impact from technology disruptions as it moves from actuarial risk assessment using statistical techniques to structural risk modeling based on real-time observations, such as the use of vehicles and potentially their speed. Similar changes are likely over time in health insurance and life protection. Financial institutions, by using these opportunities, can become the leaders in the markets. Those that do not could slowly decline, and possibly disappear, from the market.

Processes

Financial institutions need to rethink completely their customer engagement processes. Customers' overall digital experience with financial services lags that of other industries (McKinsey 2016). This is true when it comes to the "moments of truth", such as getting a credit line (Carlzon and Peters 1987). As customers continue to integrate digital experiences into their lives, they expect these experiences, as well as their relationship with financial institutions, to become more direct, simple, seamless, and effective.

Organizations

Better processes require better organizations. This will require, for instance, very effective contact centers in order to assure the management of the quality and non-quality of the services provided (Zeithaml et al. 1996). There are other innovative ways to create contacts and service customers.

Financial institutions started mainly through physical channels, such as branches and agencies. Later, many financial institutions started to set up contact centers to market and service customers and, in some cases, to sell financial products and services. More and more, financial institutions sell their products directly through contact centers or websites or mobile apps. Financial institutions or some intermediaries manage them directly. For instance, in the case of insurance companies, there are the so-called comparators: a sort of "virtual brokers", a different type of brokers (Nicoletti 2016). They are third parties that use a web application that draws together syndicated contents from various insurance companies' online sources and displays them in a single location for the user's convenience. In less than a decade, insurance comparators have become the dominant distribution channel for auto insurance in several important markets. Customers in the United Kingdom buy more than 60% of auto insurance policies online, but not directly from insurance companies' websites. Apart from the comparators, another important channel, especially for life insurance products, is the banks, through the so-called Bancassurance. Bancassurance is now moving to sell property and casualty insurance products.

From the point of view of financial institutions, with more virtual channels, such as the Web or the mobile, it is essential to have a way to "know your customer" (KYC). KYC is important from several points of view: not only risk management, but also marketing and finance. More and more, it is possible to use Big Data Analytics to support KYC. This is the process of examining relatively large datasets containing a variety of data types—for instance, data external to companies—to uncover hidden patterns, unknown correlations, market trends, customer preferences, risky behaviors, and other information. In this way, it is possible to provide very personalized financial services offered.

The idea is to consider, in the Big Data Analytics, also structured and unstructured content available in social networks. This means an onsite or an online service that facilitates communication among a community of people with a common interest, where the people use the website or other technologies to communicate with each other and share information, resources, and so on. Social networks can also be an extremely important channel for promotion and advertising of the financial services offered.

Due to the distributed nature of almost all financial services, the best platform to distribute them is the so-called cloud computing. As per the definition of the National Institute of Standards and Technology (NIST), cloud computing is a model for enabling ubiquitous, convenient, on-demand network access to a shared pool of configurable computing resources (for instance, networks, servers, storage, applications, and services) that can be rapidly provisioned and released with minimal management effort or service provider interaction.[4]

Business Models

More and more, financial institutions need to change their business models and consider possible ecosystems suitable for today's markets. In these models, multiple players collaborate. Financial service providers will need to agree on or extend, for instance, partnerships with technology providers that can supply and service connected devices or with other financial institutions, which can support other channels. They will also need to set up broader partnerships to secure direct access to customers and valuable information.

The rising importance of ecosystems entails the risk that new players will enter the financial services markets at different points of the value chain. New players could also take control of these ecosystems—potentially leveraging far more detailed customer insights than the ones available to financial institutions. The long-term result could be lower returns for traditional financial institutions if they lose control of the relationships with the customer. As mentioned before, Big Data Analytics can help in this respect.

To defend their markets, financial institutions must aggressively build new business models that focus on meeting consumers' expectations for digital experiences. They should apply the capabilities of new technologies to improve the ways they assess risk and operate their businesses. The biggest winners will be financial institutions, be them traditional or startups, with the foresight to identify new game-changing innovation that may not be ready for immediate utilization (for instance, in marketing) but could have a significant medium-/long-term impact on the industry. Virtual robots provide a clear example in this direction.

[4] http://faculty.winthrop.edu/domanm/csci411/Handouts/NIST.pdf, Accessed 27 July 2016.

Examples of Innovation

The following sections present the relevant innovations exploited by fintech initiatives.

Product Innovation

Mobility is at in the center of several financial institutions' business plans. It is interesting to analyze what mobility is and why its adoption has grown up at such an unpredictable pace.

According to the academic model presented by Tiwari and Buse (2007, pp. 73–74), mobile financial services "refer to the provision and availability of banking- and financial services with the help of mobile telecommunication devices. The scope of offered services may include facilities to conduct bank and stock market transactions, to administer accounts, and to access customized information."

In simpler words, mobile financial services are services delivered by a financial institution which allows its end-users to perform financial transactions by means of two specific components (Nicoletti 2014a):

- a mobile device, such as a tablet or a smartphone; and
- a software designed for being executed on mobile devices, usually with an "App".

Handling transactions may be expensive for a financial institution: the need of physically visiting a branch is reduced by allowing customers to perform a set of financial transactions directly through their online or mobile devices. Speed of access is an important element of value for the customers too. Even though companies are moving toward a full digitalization of their internal processes, it is difficult to imagine the world where phones act as ATMs; indeed, banks and some of their branches are still a relevant reference, especially for complex financial transactions, such as mortgages or large investments.

Figure 4.2 shows the categories of services that mobile banking can provide to its users, from a broader perspective.

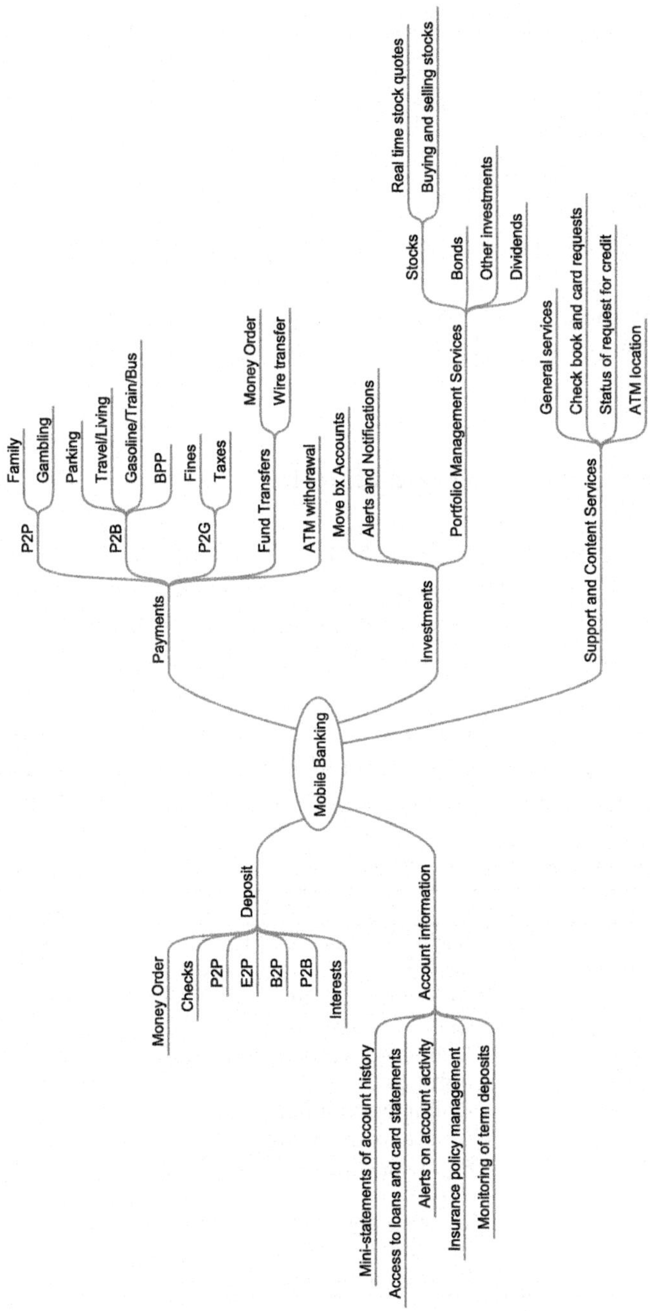

Fig. 4.2 Services in mobile banking

The Classification based on product innovation includes five areas:

- Account information
- Payments
- Deposits
- Investments
- Support and content services

Currently, most of the financial services provided are transactional: making payments and transferring money are the main scopes for the transactions.

Mobile Financial Services and Fintech

According to a survey conducted by EY ("EY Fintech Adoption Index" 2016), most of the digitally active population makes use of fintech services to make payments and transfer money. These are the typical services provided by mobile banking apps. Table 4.3 shows the results of the EY survey.

As stated in the model presented in Chap. 3, one of the main challenges for traditional financial institutions and fintech startups is to maintain a customer-centric approach to their business. The approach followed by

Table 4.3 Most used Fintech services (Ernst & Young 2016)

Transaction	Event	Percentage (%)
Money transfers/ Payments	• Use of non-banks to transfer money • Online foreign exchange • Overseas remittances	17.6
Savings/Investment	• Online stockbroking/spread bettings • Online budgeting/planning • Online investments • Equity and rewards crowdfunding • P2P	16.7
Insurance	• Car insurance using telematics • Healthcare premium aggregators	7.7
Borrowing	• Borrowing via P2P websites	5.6

fintech startups manages to develop richer interactions with their users, in a goal-oriented and proactive environment able to turn mobile devices into virtual advisors. A clear, big picture of the business may support the whole process. Mobile financial services apps may combine with other innovations, generally categorized as non-product innovations: for instance, a combination of Big Data Analytics technologies with robo-advisors could be a line of action. These technologies, by analyzing and processing user and market information, help in delivering high-tailored products and "advice" to the end-users of the product. For instance, they could advise elderly people with dependent family members to keep a low percentage of their portfolios into equities, for example.

The previous chapter analyzed some of the product innovations delivered to the market in recent years. Each of them has its own peculiarity that actually differentiates its business from the rest of the market. It is interesting to consider the framework developed in Chap. 3 to suggest fintech organizations how to manage their mobile financial services in the best suitable way.

Applying the Model to the Mobile Financial Services Providers

The previous chapter built a framework suitable for all startups that are performing their business in the financial services industry. In order to provide general guidelines for this highly heterogeneous universe of fintech initiatives, the main challenges address the following critical issues (see Fig. 4.3):

1. Market—focus on targets
2. Products and services—focus on value added
3. Channels—focus on social and omnichannel
4. Customer experience—focus on customer-centric approach
5. Revenue—focus on customer lifetime value
6. Processes and activities—focus on marketing
7. Resources and systems—focus on technology
8. Partnership and collaboration—focus on financial institutions
9. Costs and investments—focus on risks

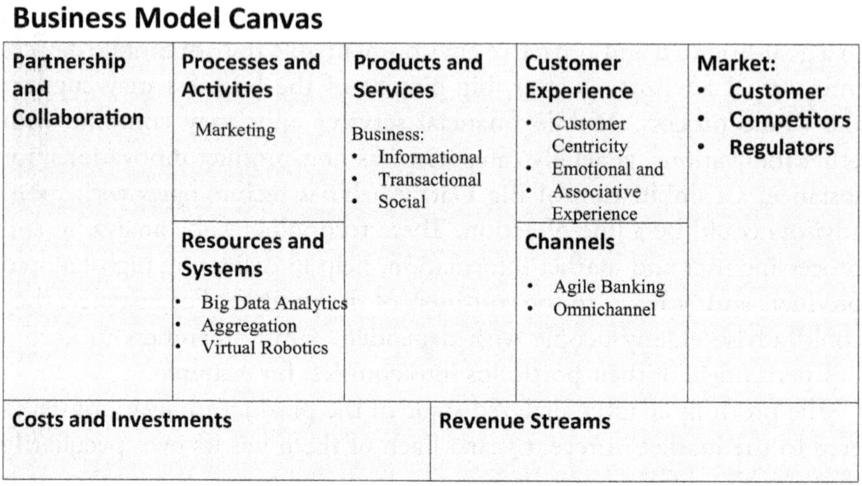

Fig. 4.3 Fintech business model canvas

The following pages detail the model introduced in this book to the mobile financial services area (see Fig. 4.3). The model identifies what can support traditional organizations and startups to set up a convenient and forward-looking business (Fig. 4.4).

Unlike the original model, built for fintech startups and new entrants, this framework is suitable for every organization that is delivering a mobile financial service to its customers. The organization's focus should be on five elements:

- The centricity of customers in all aspects of the value proposition
- The enlargement of the business, from informational to transactional
- The creation of synergies between the product and other solutions, as Big Data Analytics and virtual robotics
- The importance of being agile and forward-looking
- The building of a simple but secure solution

Several fintech startups have already set the stage for being in line with future trends. A relevant percentage of them are moving in the right direction toward the ways suggested by the model.

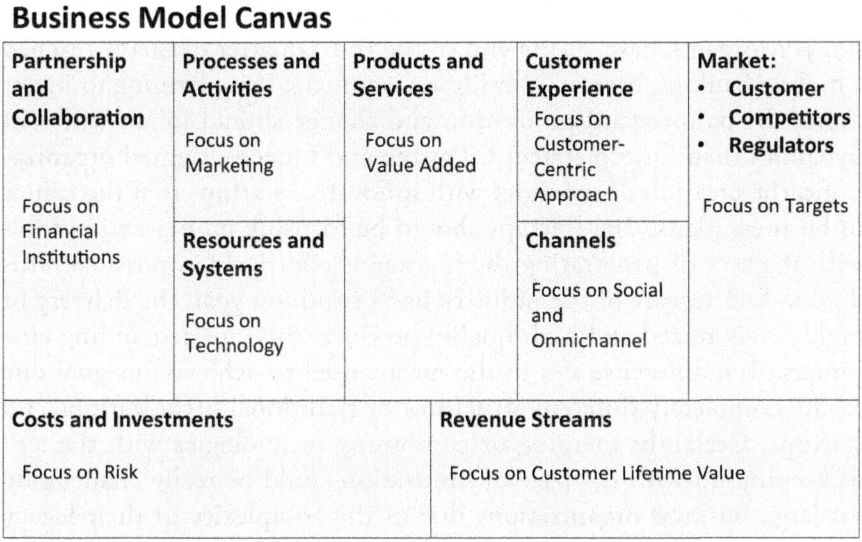

Fig. 4.4 Mobility focus in the business model canvas

According to what the consultancy company EY suggests in its report "EY Fintech Adoption Index" (2016), mobile financial service apps are mostly conceived by customers as payment "facilitators". They help in avoiding the need of visiting a branch or an agency in order to perform some basic financial transactions. Certainly, this factor has played a primary role in the past, so that, alone, it could be able to justify such a growing rate of adoption of mobility apps by "digitally active users" (Gulamhuseinwala et al. 2015).

If financial institutions do not understand the importance of change and innovation, most likely they will be missing growing and potentially market-changing opportunities. It is important that financial institutions enlarge their mobile offering in order to seize these opportunities, especially when referring to the ongoing shift in mobile financial services apps from "payment facilitators" to "digital advisors". The accomplishment of this task is not an easy job due to a large amount of information needed and its accuracy. This is the reason why Big Data Analytics solutions are of central importance in this process.

Large financial institutions are showing a great interest in this sector. JPMorgan Chase, at the end of the third quarter of 2015, reached a mobile banking base of 22 million customers. It is planning to invest more.[5] Its path toward innovation and change should follow different dynamics than fintech startups. For big and fintech-oriented organizations, the creation of synergies with innovative startups is at the center of business plans. The startups should be focusing on marketing tools with the aim of penetrating the market as effectively as possible. This double-fold feature of the industry has a common goal: the delivery of highly customized and high-quality products to more demanding customers. The difference lies in the means used to achieve this goal due to the completely different structures of traditional organizations and startups. Certainly, merging or combining technologies with the aim of keeping up with the pace of innovation could be really challenging for large business organizations due to the complexity of their legacy ICT infrastructures. For new entrants or small organizations, more flexible by nature, the whole process is less costly and simpler to play out. Sometimes, those business ventures do not even own an internal information technology (IT) infrastructure. They can move to cloud computing without needing complex "hybrid" (cloud-onsite) models. On the other side, the cloud allows them to eliminate any geographical limitation and, especially, to get the scalability and the pay-per-use that they need (Nicoletti 2012).

Aggregations are the next step that every organization should consider in its business plans, where Big Data Analytics solutions are one of its main tools.

It is possible to look at customer centricity from different perspectives such as, for example, the ones provided by other companies, not even working in the financial services industry. Google and other successful tech giants have indeed taken on their experiences in creative ways by diversifying their business and directing it toward present and future "customer needs". This is exactly the way that Google and Apple managed to reach unforeseeable markets, such as the financial services industry itself

[5] http://www.cnbc.com/2016/01/14/jpmorgan-chase-reports-q4-earnings.html, Accessed 27 July 2016.

(Apple Pay, Google Wallet), earning very large profit margins. This can apply also to the model presented in this book. Financial institutions and fintech organizations could provide access to the purchase of other products and services. In addition, they could facilitate or even build platforms that will be able to link their customers on common bases, as P2P networks or communities.

Chapter 10, on the future of fintech, covers more on this subject.

Process Innovation

Big Data Analytics

Big Data Analytics is the use of a large collection of data gathered and collected from inside and outside the company. Making use of such datasets is generally a very complex thing to do and using traditional processing applications may not be enough. This gap in the traditional processing applications has actually stimulated the burgeoning and growth of multiple companies, interested in capitalizing on Big Data Analytics.

There are several definitions of Big Data Analytics. This can create complexity, given the presence of complex linkages and hierarchies among all data (Troester 2012). Academic literature does not agree on one unique definition of Big Data Analytics. Three different perspectives (Hu et al. 2014) are possible:

- According to the attributive definition, "Big Data technologies describe a new generation of technologies and architectures, designed to economically extract value from very large volumes of a wide variety of data, by enabling high-velocity capture, discovery, and/or analysis" (Carter 2011).
- Based on the comparative definition, instead, "Big Data are datasets whose size is beyond the ability of typical database software tools to capture, store, manage, and analyze" (Manyika et al. 2011).
- The architectural definition cites Big Data as projects "where the data volume, acquisition velocity, or data representation limits the ability to perform effective analysis using traditional relational approaches or

requires the use of significant horizontal scaling for efficient processing." (NIST)[6]

Big Data Analytics provides opportunities in existing environments. It also creates new opportunities for financial institutions' stakeholders. These opportunities were not possible by dealing with structured content in traditional ways. Big Data Analytics has three characteristics—the so-called 3 Vs:

- Volume: The quantity of data should be relatively large. The word "relative" refers to the organization: a small organization might consider as Big Data Analytics a relatively lower volume of data with respect to large organizations. Big Data Analytics refers to the large—and exponentially growing—amount of data flooding in and out of every financial services company and that have been internally generated. Examples of these can be found in a variety of sources, including:
  - the structured granular call detail records (CDR) in a call center;
  - the detailed sensor data from telematics devices, such as personal computers (PCs)s, mobile, ATM, Point of Sale (POS), and so on;
  - external information, including open data, marketing research, and other behavioral data;
  - unstructured data from social media, reports of different types, and so on.
- Velocity: Financial institutions must be able to process, access, analyze, and report huge volumes of information as quickly as possible in order to make timely decisions, especially in the operational environment. Financial institutions also need to (Bhargava 2014)
  - reduce latency to optimize transparency, cross-selling, and upselling in the different channels;
  - provide quick enterprise Intranet documents search to study the impact of different events and decisions;

[6] http://csrc.nist.gov/groups/SMA/forum/documents/june2012presentations/fcsm_june2012_cooper_mell.pdf, Accessed 06 August 2016.

- decrease the business delivery time for reports in a data warehousing environment. There is the need of resources and solutions for fast processing of the data, in such a way that they cannot "age" too much:
- clickstreams and ad impressions capture user behavior at millions of events per second;
- machine-to-machine processes exchange data between billions of devices; and
- infrastructure and sensors generate massive log data in real time.

* Variety: The majority of organization's data (estimated on average around 85%) is unstructured. This means that further elaborations are necessary in order to analyze data that do not flow into the organization in a constant manner; peak loads may occur with daily, seasonal, or event-triggered frequencies. Furthermore, different sources may require different architectures and technologies for the analysis (audio, text, video, and so on). Data can come from disparate sources beyond the usually structured environment of data processing. It would include mobile, online, agent-generated, social media, text, audio, video, log files, and more. Big Data Analytics is not just numbers, data, and strings. Big Data Analytics is also documents, geospatial data, three-dimensional data, audio, photos and videos, and unstructured text, including log files and social media. The processing of such variety of information is not easy. Traditional database systems address smaller volumes of structured data, fewer updates with a predictable, consistent data structure. In general, it is possible to classify Big Data Analytics as:

  - Structured: Most traditional data sources are structured.
  - Semi-structured: Many sources of Big Data Analytics are semi-structured.
  - Unstructured set of data: such as video data and audio data.

The analysis of unstructured data types is a challenge. Unstructured data differ from structured data in that their format, which varies widely. They cannot be stored in traditional relational databases without significant effort at data transformation. Sources of unstructured data, such as email, word documents, pdfs, geospatial data, and so on are becoming a relevant source of Big Data Analytics, and also for financial institutions.

There are three other Vs that are important to consider:

- There should be a concern about the "veracity" of data. It refers to the messiness or trustworthiness of the data. With many forms of Big Data, quality and accuracy are less controllable. The quality, dependability, reliability, and consistency of data are critical issues for financial institutions looking to extract from data meaningful information to support their decision-making processes. The consequences are different. The impact of veracity on Big Data Analytics is much wider than on small data. In some cases, such as in voice-to-text conversions or social network conversations, data quality can result in meaningful information. This is true especially if financial institutions are trying to analyze macro-level phenomena, such as in sentiment analysis.
- "Vulnerability" is also important. Due to the variety of Big Data Analytics, ensuring data privacy for unstructured data might be a challenge.
- Last but most important, "value" refers to the ability to turn the data into value. Value for the customer is the most important of the Big Data Analytics' characteristics. If the customer finds value in the relationship with a financial services company, the value should accrue also to the company. Big Data Analytics use should add value for the customers and the organization. Financial institutions that adopt customer-centric approaches can get valuable insights from data analysis. It is important that financial institutions make a case for any attempt to collect and leverage data. It is easy to fall a victim to the latest fashion and launch Big Data Analytics initiatives without a clear understanding of its business value. In order for financial institutions to derive true value from Big Data Analytics, they must enable innovations in products, processes, organizations, and business models.

Scholars and practitioners have identified the main challenges of Big Data Analytics governance in (Cavanillas et al. 2016):

- Analysis
- Capture

- Data curation and quality
- Querying
- Data security and privacy
- Search
- Sharing
- Storage
- Transfer
- Visualization

This chapter focuses on the extraction of value from data: large amounts of structured and unstructured data contain a variety of useful information that managers can use in pursuing their objectives in a more efficient, effective, and economical way.

In the survey "Big Data in Big Companies" (2013), Tom Davenport interviewed managers from more than 50 businesses in an effort to understand the ways through which companies create value. According to Davenport, Big Data Analytics allow significant cost reductions not by simply bringing cost advantages. It also helps in identifying new paths and ways for doing business. Implementing Big Data Analytics implies better decision-making processes, with reference to both time and quality; decision-makers have the opportunity to analyze new sources of data in a faster way. That could end up in the discovery of completely "uncharted oceans", as new markets, products, or services. Big Data Analytics can help also in cross-selling and risk management (see Fig. 4.5).

Definition of Big Data Analytics

Big Data Analytics is one of the next Big Thing in organizations. Big Data Analytics came into the scene in the beginning of the twenty-first century. The first organizations to embrace it were online and startup companies. Companies such as Google, eBay, LinkedIn, and Facebook relied on Big Data Analytics from the beginning. Google succeeded in the business of helping persons in searching through millions of websites and zettabytes of data in order to provide near-instantaneous results with pinpoint accuracy (Cutroni 2010). Various Big Data Analytics methods and solutions help in obtaining this result. In the past decade, a variety

Fig. 4.5 The objectives of Big Data Analytics

of industries in the finance, manufacturing, retail, and technology sectors have been using Big Data Analytics to improve their processes or to better understand and deliver services to their customers.

Big Data Analytics generates value from the storage and processing of very large quantities of digital information. Traditional computing techniques are not efficient in this case. Big Data Analytics is similar to "small data" but relatively bigger in volume. Having more data requires different approaches:

- Techniques, solutions, and architecture
- Solutions for new problems or for old problems in a better way

The reasons for the interest in Big Data Analytics are as follows:

- The growth in the quantity of processable data
- The increase in data storage capacities
- The increase in data processing power
- The availability of data (different data types)

The use of Big Data Analytics makes sense for the large amount of processable data more and more available:

- Wal-Mart handles more than 1 million customer transactions every hour.
- Facebook handles 40 billion photos stored by its user base from its user base.
- Decoding a person's genome originally took 10 years to process; now it can be achieved in less than one week.

Every day, over 2.5 quintillion bytes of data is generated globally. Around 90% of the existing processable data in the world today has been created in the last two years alone (Zhang et al. 2012). A definition of processable is: "Able to be processed; suitable for processing" (by other computer applications) (Hey et al. 2009).

Big Data Analytics are normally

(1) automatically generated by a machine (for instance, sensors embedded in a vehicle);
(2) typically extracted from an entirely new source of data (for instance, use of the IoT);
(3) data not designed to be computer-friendly (for instance, text streams); and
(4) Focused on important data.

On the other side, if you cannot handle the data it does not make sense to store them.

Big Data Analytics are the results of processes such as:

- Transactions
- Data from sensors
- Social networks, etc.

The data to use are as follows:

- The data produced by the same company
- The data produced by users, customers, and vendors

- The open data such as social media, on the markets (the 3Cs: customers, competitors, and compliance).

Characteristics of Big Data Analytics

Big Data Analytics are the solutions, processes, and procedures that allow an organization to create, manipulate, store, and manage a relatively large amount of data to get information. This book uses the term Big Data Analytics since a large amount of data (Big Data) in itself cannot really be useful. It is the combination of a large amount of data (Big Data) and the capability to analyze them (analytics) that can bring large benefits.

Big Data Analytics means:

- storing a large amount of data;
- examining (or mining) them;
- getting appropriate information; and
- identifying hidden patterns, unknown correlations, and similar things in support of decision-making.

Around 15–20% of available data is in structured form, while the remaining information is available in an unstructured format (Feldman and Sanger 2007). While managing the overwhelming data flow can be challenging, financial institutions that can capture, store, search, aggregate, and possibly analyze the data can obtain real benefits such as increased productivity, improved competitive advantage, and enhanced customer experience. This value, however, does not necessarily come from simply managing Big Data Analytics. It comes from harnessing the actionable insights from them. Financial institutions that can obtain objective-driven business value by applying science to effectively mine data for customer insights, support, and offer new products/services will have clear competitive advantages and stay ahead of the curve in this information age.

Big Data Analytics develops from analytical technologies that have existed for years. Now organizations can use them faster, on a greater scale, and they are more accessible. Analytics is the discovery and communication of meaningful patterns in data. It is especially valuable in areas rich in recorded information. Analytics relies on the simultaneous application of statistics, computer programming, and operations research to quantify performance. Data visualization is particularly important in getting value from harvesting the data.

These challenges are the current inspiration for much of the innovation in modern analytics information systems. They give birth to relatively new automatic analysis concepts such as complex event processing, full-text search and analysis, and even new ideas in presenting the information to support successful decisions.

Big Data Analytics operations can be processed on site. As organizations migrate to the cloud, so will their corporate data. Cloud-based architectures will become more important as individual entities (both devices and resources) generate continuous data streams. With cloud computing, organizations can collect, store, process, analyze, use, and report them.

The volume, speed, and power of technology have transformed the economic environment into a sophisticated data economy. It allows for the execution of complex global transactions at the push of a button. From high-frequency trading to e-commerce to mobile telephony, computers all over the world are generating huge amounts of data. Like individuals, institutions might be facing an information overload that is limiting the promise and opportunity of technology. All of these data provide a large amount of information from more sources than ever before—from social media to e-commerce transaction records to cell phone and global positioning system (GPS) signals to an increasing number of sensors.

Because the majority of data is unstructured and requires unique expertise to understand, organize, and analyze, most of the information sits idly. The good news is that there is a growing set of Big Data Analytics solutions. They can help organizations use and monetize this valuable commodity by finding important insights into their activity. They can help in analyzing their customers' transaction flows. In this way, organizations can support their customer in a more effective, efficient, economical, and ethical way with their offerings.

Research has found that Big Data Analytics holds the capability to generate profits by improving the margins around transaction flows.[7] The

[7] Banking on Big Data, *Banking Technology*. 3 December (2014).

organization and analysis of the data can highlight flows and offer unique insights into trends, destinations, values, volumes, and fees, which can ultimately drive opportunities for organizations (Albright et al. 2010).

In today's ever-changing economic environment, all sectors need to rethink traditional value propositions. Big Data Analytics is emerging as a cutting-edge option. It is an innovative way to access and visualize key information to be more effective, efficient, economical, and indeed ethical. By unlocking the data available in the organization, persons are able to better understand opportunities for growth and cost savings and, therefore, to be better prepared for success on all fronts.

Big Data Analytics' superior value is twofold in that it not only provides key information on the business and the market. It also offers a look at the internal processes. This can support their improvement, taking into account the changing economic landscape. This visibility will give organizations the option to fill gaps, improve efficiencies, and ultimately make better decisions. It will also help to create customer-centric strategies and improve the overall customer experience.

As technology continues to push for faster, more interconnected organizations, Big Data Analytics will become an increasingly valuable tool. Through this untapped information, organizations will be able to understand their businesses and customers in new and insightful ways. For many organizations, using Big Data Analytics to identify trends is a very new approach. Only now, some financial institutions are beginning to understand the importance of information as an asset and what this information can offer, and are continuing to gain new insights. Organizations are talking more and more about "data monetization" (Woerner and Wixom 2015). Diving into Big Data Analytics may seem like diving into unchartered waters for some. Big Data Analytics is the future also for financial institutions. There is only the need to take advantage of it in order to remain relevant and use the increasing amount of data available.

It is important to follow a correct process in storing Big Data Analytics:

- Selecting data sources for analysis
- Defining data models: key value, graphics, document
- Analyzing the characteristics of the data
- Improving the data quality, for instance, eliminating redundant or duplicated data

- Overviewing data storing, storage, and retrieval

There are several actions important in storing large sets of data:

- Choosing the correct data stores based on the characteristics of the data
- Moving code to data
- Implementing polyglot data store solutions
- Aligning business goals to the appropriate data store
- Integrating disparate data stores
- Mapping data to the programming framework
- Connecting and extracting data from storage
- Transforming data for processing
- Monitoring the progress of job flows
- Using advanced tools, such as D3.js (data-driven documents) (Zhu 2013)

There are a certain number of questions that need to be answered when dealing with Big Data Analytics:

- Which types of solutions to be used in Big Data Analytics?
- Where data are stored: centralized or distributed or cloud storage?
- Where processing is done: mainframe, distributed servers/cloud?
- How data are stored and indexed: high-performance schema-free databases?
- What operations are performed on data: sequential, analytic, or semantic processing?
- What are the risks?
- Are the right talents available capable of choosing the right data to solve the right problem?

Analytics 3.0

In an article in the *Harvard Business Review*, Tom Davenport presented a model of the development of analytics (2013):

- Analytics 1.0 is the business intelligence before the Big Data Analytics. It was mainly devoted to analyzing small internal problems since the amount of data available was small.
- Analytics 2.0 was a step forward thanks to the rise of Big Data Analytics. It can be used also for predictive analytics besides historical analysis.
- A new wave is Analytics 3.0. It is a new resolve to apply powerful data-gathering and analysis methods to a company's operations and to its offerings—to embed data smartness into the products and services customers buy.

A quotation from Tom Davenport is interesting (2013):

"The most important trait of the Analytics 3.0 is that not only online companies but virtually any type of companies in any industry, can participate on in the given economy."

Table 4.4 reports a synthesis according to Davenport of the characteristics of each generation of analytics.

With Analytics 3.0, a new architecture was born. The use of technologies existing in many large organizations is not abandoned. It is possible the use of solutions of analysis of Big Data Analytics (such as Hadoop) in the cloud and open source.

An example of the use of Analytics 3.0 in financial services is mass private financial services: a low-cost, customer-centric version of financial services:

- low costs since it can use the lower costs of processing a large amount of data made possible with the Big Data Analytics solutions;
- personalized to each customer, thanks to a powerful Big Data Analytics.

This would require

- recording the behavior of the customers: through his/her accesses, transactions, and, if available, social networks, with their consent;
- processing of all these data versus a "model" which might provide useful information for marketing, investment, or risk-averse actions;

Table 4.4 Characteristics of the three generations of analytics (adapted from T. Davenport 2013)

Era	1.0 Traditional analytics	2.0 Big data	3. 0 Data economy
Timeframe	Mid-1970s to 2000	Early 2001 to 2020	2021 and in the future
Culture	Competition not on analytics	New focus on data-based products and services	Agile method where all decisions are driven (or at least influenced) by data
Type of analytics	95% reporting, descriptive	85% reporting, descriptive	90%+ predictive, prescriptive, automated reporting
	5% predictive, prescriptive	15% predictive, prescriptive (visual)	
Cycle time	Months	An insight a week	Millions of insights per second
Data	Internal, structured	Very large, unstructured, multisource	Seamless combination of internal and external data; analytics embedded in operational and decision processes
		Explosion of sensor data	Tools available at the point of decision
Technology	Rudimentary business intelligence (BI), reporting tools; dashboards; data stored in enterprise data warehouses or marts	New technologies: Hadoop, commodity servers, in-memory, open source. Master data management	New data architectures, beyond the data warehouse; new application architectures
		Standards appear for data quality	Specific apps, mobile; data dictionaries; full data governance

(*continued*)

Table 4.4 (continued)

Era	1.0 Traditional analytics	2.0 Big data	3. 0 Data economy
Organization	Analytical people segregated from business and ICT	Some chief data officers appear in some advanced companies; data scientists are on the rise	Centralized teams, specialized functions among team members; dedicated funding
	Back-room statisticians	Talent shortage; educational programs starting	Chief analytics officers; training and educational programs

- suggesting or taking actions with the customers, which would add value to him/her; and
- reporting and getting the feedback of the customer to improve the services.

Such a potential sequence suits especially the case of services based on financial technologies. Mobility would add also information on the location of the customer. If the customer is in a mall, it would be possible to provide her/him with some proximity information of the nearest agency.

From a privacy point of view, it would be necessary to have the acceptance of the customer of such tracking of his/her activity. In some cases, for instance, if the customer has some funds available, he/she would really appreciate suggestions on how to invest the funds available through the financial services. The acceptance of the suggestion sent by the financial services company to the mobile might even not require pushing a key on the smartphone, but simply a "double shake" of the mobile.

A similar type of functions would be particularly useful in the case of mobile corporate/institutional financial services. The financial services company should send (on request) such messages to the corporate treasury to alert about the need to take an action, such as renew a policy or assign to a different value of the line of credit. That would help the treasury in properly covering corporate risks. Small- and medium-sized companies would appreciate such services. In such companies, often, the managers do not have the time or the skills to follow liquidity or do not have the necessary skills to optimize the financial services management.

Value Creation from Big Data Analytics

According to McKinsey, Big Data Analytics can create value for the customers and the organizations in five ways (Manyika et al. 2011):

- Can increase transparency, making data more easily accessible to relevant stakeholders;
- Create and store more transactional data in digital form. In this way, organizations can collect accurate, detailed performance data in real time or near real time. This would enable proof of concept (POC) to identify needs, improve performance, but especially be able to offer new products and services adding value to the customer;
- Can provide organizations the tools to improve customer segmentation and then better develop and tailor products, services, processes, and promotions to each specific segment (in the limit, to each specific customer, in a one-to-one relationship);
- Include advanced analytics to provide actionable customer insights that minimize risks and improve decision-making;
- Be useful for organizations looking to create new business models and improve products/services, processes, organizations, and business models.

Harnessing and Harvesting Big Data Analytics for Digital Financial Services

Big Data Analytics platforms do not replace existing traditional data management and analytics platforms. They simply complement, extend, and improve upon existing environments and capabilities. Big Data Analytics consists of two processes: harnessing, which involves the collection, extraction, transformation, loading, administration, and management of Big Data Analytics; and harvesting, which involves the skills and solutions required to apply science to the data in order to derive actionable and meaningful insights from this to drive actions.

The harvesting and harnessing processes are complementary. They are two sides of a Big Data Analytics initiative (Hussain and Prieto 2016).

Harnessing Big Data Analytics

At the most basic level, the harnessing process consists of

- the collection of data;
- the extraction, transformation, and loading of data;
- the management of data; and
- the setting up of an ecosystem that can not only create Big Data Analytics but sustain it as well.

In the past, the data harnessing process was much easier than it is today. The benefits of using these data were more limited. Today, the complexity arises from

- a combination of additional sources of data, such as social media;
- the complex technology that exists today to give financial institutions access to those data as well as the ability to analyze them;
- the diversity of data. Gartner estimates that between 80% and 90% of all data produced today are unstructured.[8] Today, financial institutions can tap into a treasure trove of unstructured data of all varieties: text, audio, video, adjustor notes, click streams, and log files, for instance, and combine them with other structured types, such as currency exchanges, stock exchange performances, demographics and geographic data, and so on.

Harvesting Big Data Analytics

It is possible to classify Big Data Analytics harvesting in two ways. Big Data Analytics uses descriptive and predictive models to gain valuable knowledge from data. It uses this insight to recommend actions or to

[8] Lohit, N, (2013), Big data, Bigger Facts, July 5. http://blogs.sap.com/innovation/big-data/big-data-bigger-facts-098520, accessed 04 October 2013.

guide decision-making and communication. It is not possible to use data in their raw form. It is necessary to process them to generate information. Information is useful to generate knowledge. Based on the knowledge, it is possible to take better decisions. This is called operational analytics when decisions support operational tasks (Nicoletti 2014b).

The harvesting process utilizes technology and algorithms that enable financial institutions to

- analyze data;
- deliver actionable insights;
- support process intelligence; and
- get real value from Big Data Analytics.

One more emerging challenge is dynamic regulatory needs. For example, in the financial services industry, Basel III or Solvency II or capital adequacy needs are likely to force even smaller financial institutions to adopt internal risk models. In such cases, cloud computing and open-source solutions can help smaller financial institutions adopt risk analytics and support agency-level monitoring by applying predictive analytics.

Organizations may commonly apply analytics to financial institutions' data to describe, predict, and improve business performance. Specifically, areas within analytics include:

- enterprise decision management;
- marketing optimization and marketing mix analytics;
- web analytics;
- sales force sizing and optimization;
- price and promotion modeling;
- predictive science;
- risk analysis; and
- fraud analytics.

Skill sets such as statistics, data mining, econometrics, business analytics, visualization techniques, and more are in high demand as they provide a solid foundation for deriving useful insights from the data. Academic institutions have started filling the supply-demand gap by offering various schools programs to prepare for the next-generational skills needed to mine actionable insights, producing the so-called data scientists (Nicoletti 2016).

Celent surveyed many financial institutions (Monks and Michellod 2014). The survey showed that in Europe company structure or culture constraints (90%), lack of skills (70%), and channel conflicts (67%) are the top three challenges to executing a company's digital strategy. Although company structure/culture is also the top global challenge (albeit at a lower 68%), lack of skills (50%) and channel conflict (46%) are viewed as less of a challenge globally. European non-life insurance companies feel particularly challenged by the scarcity of skills/expertise and channel conflicts: 79% and 74% cite these challenges, compared to only 66% of life insurance companies. European financial institutions need analytics and technology capabilities, suggesting that the recruitment battle will be intense for people with these skill sets.

While the ability to successfully harness and harvest data is critical to a Big Data Analytics strategy, the harvesting process is where financial institutions can derive the true value from their data, with the help of analytics and process management. Defining use cases and hypotheses becomes critical when following a focused "top-down" approach to creating actionable insights.

Although this is a focused approach, many times, financial institutions need to do some initial work in order to perform data exploratory analysis in order to come up with the use cases that can exploit Big Data Analytics. This initial bottom-up approach is a prerequisite for determining and prioritizing use cases to support POCs for Big Data Analytics.

To derive real value, it is necessary that actionable insights can make a positive difference in achieving the strategic objectives and especially adding value to the customers and eliminating waste in internal processes.

Big Data Applications in Fintech

A research developed by the consultancy company PricewaterhouseCoopers has predicted an interesting future thanks to the growing importance of data into all businesses[9]:

---

[9] PwC (2015), Business Booster Data Analytics, PwC Report, August.

- Companies that consistently use analytics to inform decision-making will beat their competitors.
- About 50% of today's service jobs will be taken over by computers.
- Providing trustworthy data is a necessity and will become increasingly important in dealing with regulators or third parties.
- Data ecosystems will rapidly grow in importance.
- While Big Data posits "the more the better", effective management is based on reliability of controls and sound analysis.
- Data governance, quality, and security are particularly important.

The financial services industry should then address its focus on data in order to keep abreast of times. The majority of fintech startups have already identified the analytic, data-driven approach as the best in class. It is possible to consider multiple applications of Big Data not only as a first step but also as a mere evidence of their forward-looking attitude.

Fintech should not only take into proper consideration data but also analytics: "it'll become like using weather forecasts—those who don't use them will get wet."[10]

In order to better position their brands and be more attractive, fintech initiatives should deepen their understanding of the environment and especially of their customers. It is important, for instance, to understand how their customers behave online or how they generally behave when they are not dealing with a specific fintech company. Multi-source data and tools that are able to gather, collect, and process them will then become essential for every company willing to be competitive in the market.

ZhongAn

"ZhongAn Insurance was the first to get an auto insurance license from the Insurance Regulatory Commission and has the business scope to expand into compulsory traffic accident liability insurance, motor vehicle business insurance, and insurance information services."—Chen Jing, CEO of ZhongAn

(*continued*)

[10] PwC (2015), ibid.

ZhongAn (continued)

ZonghAn is a Chinese online property insurance company that leverages on Big Data Analytics in order to "to assist with product design, automatic underwriting, auto claims, precision marketing, and risk management".[11]

It is a joint venture between Alibaba Group Holding, Tencent Holding, and Ping An Insurance. This company provides a large base of insurance services to the rich Chinese market, while leveraging on Big Data technologies in order to deliver a value proposition considered by the research developed by H2 Ventures, KPMG, and Matchi, the one with the highest potential within fintech's boundaries.[12]

Kreditech

"In three years, Alexander and I have built Kreditech into an industry leader tackling a serious mission in a very innovative way—and it works."—Sebastian Diemer, Co-founder of Kreditech[13]

Kreditech (Kreditech Holding SSL GmbH) is a German company providing a wide range of tailored financial services by using proprietary algorithms and technologies. In particular, this company makes use of Big Data Analytics technologies to gather and process financial data from its customers and elaborates the resulting datasets for providing completely innovative, highly tailored services to the market. Kreditech uses an innovative self-learning algorithm able to analyze large datasets (see Figs. 4.6 and 4.8).

The application does not compute the individual's credit score based on traditional data. Information: online behavior becomes key in order to understand the creditworthiness of the individuals. Only in recent times, this has become possible, thanks to the diffusion of Big Data Analytics technologies.

[11] Fintech 100 (2015), Leading Global Fintech Innovators, Reports, http://fintechinnovators.com/uploads/H2-Fintech-Innovators-2015.pdf, Accessed 07 August 2016.

[12] Fintech 100 (2015), Leading Global Fintech Innovators, Reports, http://fintechinnovators.com/uploads/H2-Fintech-Innovators-2015.pdf, Accessed 07 August 2016.

[13] http://fintechinnovators.com/company/470, Accessed 13 August 2016.

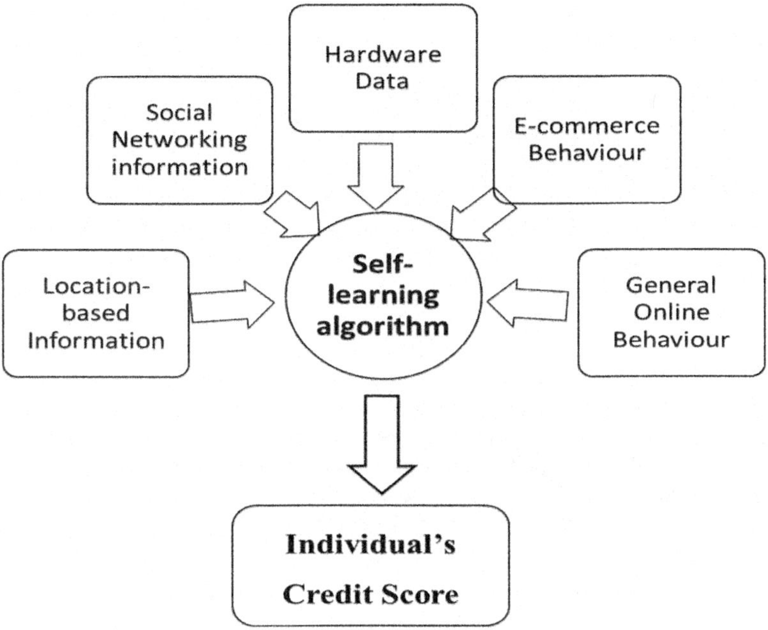

Fig. 4.6 Kreditech's self-learning algorithm

Progressive

"Over the last five years, we've had countless discussions about the need for an internal 'lab' to test and learn. Innovation requires some degree of speed, so BIG allows us to fail fast, innovate faster, and get best-in-class products to market in such a highly-regulated environment like the insurance industry."—Ray Voelker, Chief Information Officer (CIO) of Progressive Insurance[14]

Progressive USA has sold more than one million snapshot policies. The premium depends on monitoring the driving behaviors. The data collected help tailor the pricing.[15] Harvesting digital data has big potential in a world

(continued)

[14] http://www.the-digital-insurer.com/dia/progressives-business-innovation-garage/, Accessed 26 August 2016.

[15] https://hbr.org/2014/03/insurance-companies-untapped-digital-opportunity/, Accessed 28 May 2015.

Progressive (continued)

where people leave vast amounts of information behind from the websites they visit, the words they search, and the social media posts they make. Several companies are already mining data on social media to provide their (physical or virtual) agents with real-time information about their policy-holders' life events (moves, job changes, vehicle and real-estate investments, new babies) for sales, and similarly using digital data to curb fraudulent claims.

Avant

"Avant is serving the unmet demand on a global scale and providing millions of consumers with access to responsible credit in a clear and timely manner. We are proud of Avant's tremendous growth, over the last three years and continue to believe in the power of technology to innovate and, improve the customer experience."—Al Goldstein, CEO of Avant

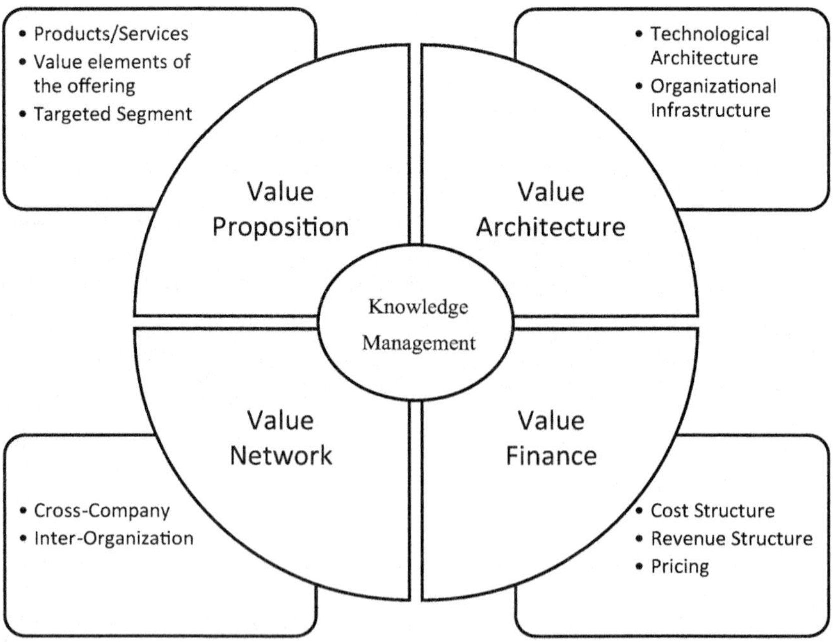

Fig. 4.7 The V4 business model framework

Avant (continued)

Avant is an Illinois-based company actually operating in the fintech industry. Kreditech makes use of Big Data Analytics to evaluate the creditworthiness of its customers. Avant focuses its efforts on the development of a proprietary software, able to mitigate efficiently default risk and fraud. In particular, the software applies self-learning algorithms and protocols to determine a tailored rate, length, and amount of a loan, while significantly simplifying the borrowing process.

Lufax.com

"Lufax is one of the largest peer-to-peer lenders in China. It connects individual investors with borrowers for loans of around $10,000."—*Wall Street Journal*[16]

(continued)

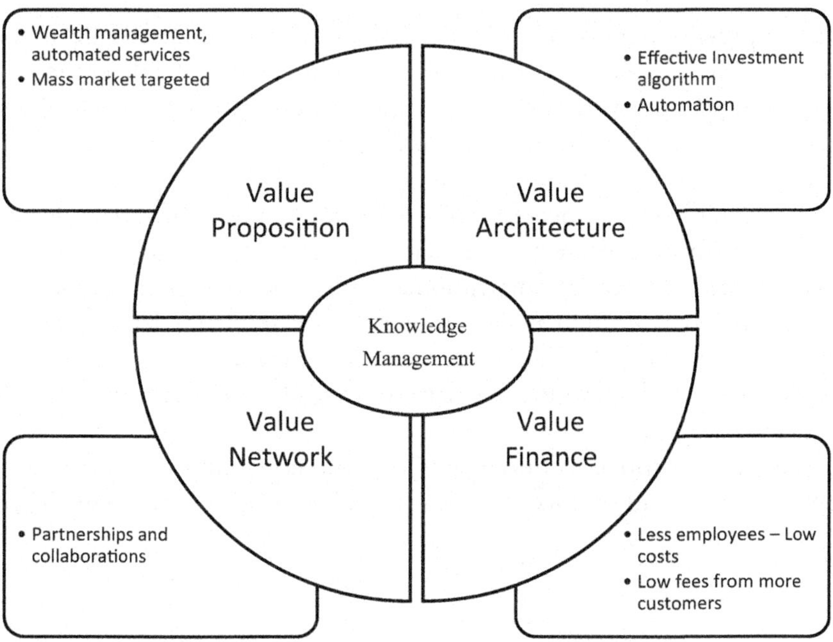

Fig. 4.8 The V4 business model framework for Betterment

[16] http://www.fintechinnovators.com/company/485, Accessed 10 August 2016.

Lufax.com (continued)

Lufax (Shanghai Lujiazui International Financial Asset Exchange Co., Ltd) is a P2P lender operating in China.[17] Founded in 2011 and headquartered in Lujiazui, Shanghai, Lufax provides a marketplace for trading and originating financial assets: $2.5 billion collectively since the launch of Lufax. Taking advantage of leading-edge Big Data technologies, the company has managed to become the world's most valuable financial technology startup,[18] also thanks to a recent fundraising campaign that increased its value up to $18.5 billion.

Lufax operates also from around 100 shops located in over 80 cities. It is owned by Ping An Insurance, a unicorn in its own right.

Internet of Things

Internet of (Everything) Things

One impressive development in technology is the IoT. Cisco calls it also the IoE.[19] IoT is the interconnection of uniquely identifiable embedded computing devices within the existing internet infrastructure. IoT allows using the internet to connect not only persons but also objects of any type.

In order to be "connected" to a network, sensors and other devices need a networking device: some examples are switches, hubs, gateways, and routers. For instance, smartphones, tablets, or printers can connect to a home network through a Wi-Fi router. To transfer data, devices need an identification through network and internet protocols: IPV4 and IPV6 are used to address computers, where IP stands for Internet protocol (Fall and Stevens 2011).

The real disruptive technology will be the possibility to connect processes, devices, and sensors. Businesses and people act on processes. These

[17] http://www.bobsguide.com/guide/news/2016/Aug/8/5-chinese-fintech-unicorns-to-watch/, Accessed 10 August 2016.

[18] http://www.gruenderszene.de/allgemein/deutsche-banken-fintech-unicorn, Accessed 20 August 2016.

[19] http://www.cisco.com/c/m/it_it/tomorrow-starts-here/ioe.html, Accessed 27 July 2016.

are essentially a series of activities that help to reach a target. In the case of businesses, the target could be a sale. In the case of people, it could be a more convenient insurance, which takes into account the use of the insured object. Most of these processes today are unconnected between themselves. People will need to move from one activity to the following one, at best supported by an automatic workflow. Most of the times, people are moving without any help at all.

IoT will change substantially this situation. Thanks to various types of sensors, embedded more and more in objects, IoT will be able to sense where an object or a person is, what it/he/she is doing, and which object or person is it/he/she in contact with. IoT, together with predictive computing, is able to forecast what one person is planning to do next and then help to accomplish it (Gubbi et al. 2013). Somebody might be afraid of this big brother. This is certainly true for some activities, but for other ones, it will be a great support. Think of the case of black boxes mounted on vehicles. IoT will provide a huge amount of data and make possible innovations.

Typically, IoT offers advanced connectivity of devices, systems, and services. It covers a variety of protocols, domains, and applications. The interconnection of these embedded devices (including smart objects) allows automation in nearly all fields. In insurance, IoT can refer to a wide variety of devices, such as health monitoring implants, biochip transponders on farm animals, vehicles with built-in sensors, or field operation devices that assist in remote monitoring plenty of apparatus and situations.

According to Gartner, there will be nearly 26 billion devices on the IoT by 2020 (Rivera and van der Meulen 2013). ABI Research (2013) estimates that IoT will connect wirelessly around 30 billion devices by 2020. In a survey done by Pew Research Internet Project, a large majority of the technology experts and engaged internet users who responded—83%—agreed with the notion that the IoT/Cloud of Things and embedded and wearable computing will have widespread and beneficial effects by 2025 (Anderson and Rainie 2014).

IoT will allow near-real-time remote monitoring of a specific situation and make possible a much more flexible pricing of financial services, such as insurance products. For instance, it would be possible to collect more information on the customers' behaviors. Some insurance companies are already doing this, using telematics data from vehicles to price their auto and transport policies (Desyllas and Sako 2013).

The challenge is how to use IoE. It goes back to the capabilities of each organization. It will push the job of ICT from being information and communications technology to a different ICT: innovation, collaboration, and transformation. This is really a challenge for some ICT managers. They require moving from being Chief Information Officers to Chief Innovation Officers. If they will be able to accept, the challenge will depend very much on the person.

Internet of Things and Fintech

It is interesting to analyze the general use of IoT in fintech. IoT finds its best applications in the insurance industry. Chapter 8 analyzes this aspect. Being in the early phases of its life cycle, this technology does not require complex and expensive resources to operate. It can operate with devices having limited computational power.[20]

IoT is a potential game-changing factor and a highly disruptive element in the financial services industry, similar to what have been smartphones and tablets (Deloitte 2015).[21]

It is important to emphasize the relevance of IoT for every business that leverages on data to deliver its products or services, especially for personalizing the product and the pricing for specific customers. Customers will have the opportunity to make smarter financial decisions in just a few seconds through their smartphones or wearable devices. Financial interactions, delivered through mobile devices, will be entirely contactless, whereas traditional financial services, made of cards, papers, and forms are becoming obsolete. While, still today, most of the financial information needed by people for their decisions need to be accessed in some steps, in the era of IoT, they will most likely be retrieved in real time.

---

[20] http://www.gartner.com/newsroom/id/3165317, Accessed 20 August 2016.

[21] Deloitte, Financial Services in the age of the Internet of Things, 2015. https://www2.deloitte.com/content/dam/Deloitte/cn/Documents/about-deloitte/aff2015/deloitte-cn-aff-postcon-leaflet-en-150227.pdf, Accessed 20 August 2016.

Perhaps one of the biggest potential benefits would be in claims management: in insurance, by using IoT, it could be possible for insurance companies to use such sensors to record and possibly anticipate and prevent damage. This might save costs in the end not just for reinsurers and investors, but also for individuals and communities.

This path has a certain number of challenges. There are privacy, security, and regulation issues. Even if customers would benefit from all those innovations, most of them will not be comfortable knowing that each detail of their activities is accessible. Most likely, focus will be on the ability of financial services providers to establish trust-based relationships with them and provide new services.

It is key to combine IoT with other technologies able to gather, collect, and process a large amount of unstructured and multi-source datasets. Eventually, the ability of fintech initiatives to build a solid infrastructure capable of embracing such innovations is critical in defining the success or the failure of their business models.

Visa

"We work every day to make payments faster and easier for merchants and consumers across the world. As the number of connected vehicles on the road increases, so does our ability to bring this secure frictionless option of online commerce to consumers everywhere."—Jim McCarthy, Executive Vice President, Innovation & Strategic Partnerships, Visa Inc.[22]

Visa, collaborating with Pizza Hut and Accenture, is working on a POC-connected car to test mobile and online purchases on the go.[23] The connected car could use Visa Checkout, Visa's online payment service, cellular connectivity, Bluetooth low energy (BLE), as well as beacon technology deployed at Pizza Hut restaurants to alert the staff when the customer has arrived and is ready to pick up the order.

---

[22] https://www.accenture.com/au-en/success-visa-connected-commerce-car, Accessed 26 August 2016.

[23] https://letstalkpayments.com/how-to-integrate-payments-in-iot-devices/, Accessed 20 August 2016.

Blockchain Technology

Blockchain was born in connection with Bitcoin, a virtual currency.[24] It is essentially a database for recording transactions in a secure way.[25] Blockchain is a distributed database, able to generate a public ledger of all the transactions, not entirely stored at a single physical location, but rather dispersed over a network of interconnected computers.[26]

Blockchain is a decentralized solution. For instance, all participants of a P2P network have a copy of the full set of records. Consequently, there is no central authority. Each participant of the network can manipulate the ledger without causing security issues by means of cryptography and digital signatures. Through these digital tools, a real-life identity (not visible) ties with a cryptographic identity. This is useful to verify and validate transactions. Blockchain and related disruptive technologies have drawn close attention in the financial industry. Blockchain is relatively secure, transparent, and unmodifiable.

Blockchain has much greater potential than digital currency alone, even if the concept was born in connection with Bitcoin (Ngai et al. 2016). It enables point-to-point transactions without a clearing intermediary. In this way, it reduces substantially transaction time, quality, and costs. When combined with smart contracts, blockchain makes it possible to issue automatically digital securities and trade financial derivatives. For instance, the insurance sector will also provide new opportunities for the application of blockchain.

In a distributed ledger, there are two types of records[27]:

- Transactions
- Blocks

[24] There is a debate if what is Bitcoin from a taxation point of view. EU considers it a currency, SEC a security and the USA IRS a commodity (hence subject to tax). See also http://blogs.wsj.com/digits/2015/10/22/eu-rules-bitcoin-is-a-currency-not-a-commodity-virtually/, Accessed 04 August 2016.

[25] https://www2.deloitte.com/content/dam/Deloitte/uk/Documents/Innovation/deloitte-uk-what-is-blockchain-2016.pdf, Accessed 27 July 2016.

[26] Public domain material, General Services Administration (http://www.its.bldrdoc.gov/fs-1037/fs-1037c.htm).

[27] https://www.icbpi.it/block-chain-come-la-tecnologia-al-cuore-di-bitcoin-puo-cambiare-la-banca-e-non-solo/, Accessed 13 August 2016.

Transactions are at the core of the entire process. In the case of the blockchain used for the virtual currency Bitcoin, a transaction is the transfer of a Bitcoin value between users. Blocks contain the correct amount and order of valid transactions—indelibly added to the database. A generated transaction is not immediately added to the blockchain. It needs to be validated, giving rise to the so-called consensus approach. Blockchain technology makes use of its network to reach consensus: when the majority of participants agree on the validity of a block of pending transactions, then it is added to the blockchain.

Consensus protocols are essential in order to protect the public ledger from unauthorized changes. The consensus is also the object of differentiation between those companies that are leveraging on blockchain technologies in their business.

Bitcoin, for instance, relies on proof-of-work mining to secure consensus. A network of miners competes for rewards by validating blocks. According to some researchers,[28] this mining, or proof-of-work, comes with a substantial cost. At today's Bitcoin prices and reward schedule, miners receive about $1 million a day to secure the blockchain. Electricity for the data center is a significant portion of that money. Proof-of-work-based consensus protocols are also slow, requiring up to an hour to confirm, in a secure way, a payment to prevent double spending.

Due to this time and cost issues, other protocols have been proposed. Tendermint, ARBC (Asynchronous Randomized Business Consensus), BAR (Byzantine, Altruistic, Rational), SCP (Secure Copy Protocol), and so on.[29] From a theoretical perspective, the ideal protocol is an incentive-compatible Nash equilibrium such that deviating from the protocol does not result in a net gain (Kroll et al. 2013). Specialized publications can provide more technical and functional details.[30]

---

[28] Kwon, J. (2014), TenderMint: Consensus without Mining, http://tendermint.com/docs/tendermint.pdf, Accessed 31 July 2016.

[29] http://www.slideshare.net/lablogga/blockchain-consensus-protocols, Accessed 31 July 2016.

[30] https://cointelegraph.com/news/five-books-on-blockchain-and-bitcoin-you-may-need-right-now, Accessed 27 July 2016.

Nowadays, protocols are far from being ideal. They show multiple complicating factors. This is the reason why different scholars and practitioners are still directing their efforts in improving this interesting and high-potential area.

Blockchain technology has interesting potential in several fields and especially in the financial services industry.

Blockchain offers trust and provenance. These are critical aspects of the financial services industry. Still, like all technologies, it can be subject to fraud. US regulators expressed concerns that "bitcoin-like" systems were vulnerable to fraud through user collusion. In 2016, there was a big incident in Hong Kong, resulting in the stealing of $65 million.[31] This incident has shown that theft through hacking is also a risk. The more so, since there are multiple institutions operating different levels of security and providing multiple entry points. Even Bitfinex's multisignatory system, in which transaction permission was required from two of three users, proved insufficiency robust.[32] Bitfinex heist or no, trust-based blockchain security needs to improve to be fully trusted.

Different Types of Blockchain

Concerning access protocols, distributed ledgers can either be[33]

- Public: Any user who wishes to do so can access the ledger and submit transactions for inclusion. This is the blockchain technology used in Bitcoin. Many consider this the truly democratized form of the ledger and the ideal system.
- Private: Only a select few participants can view as well as submit transactions. Although the market can have many participants, only certain individuals or institutions will have access to the ledger and the devel-

---

[31] http://www.bloomberg.com/news/articles/2016-08-03/bitcoin-plunges-after-hackers-breach-h-k-exchange-steal-coins, Accessed 08 August 2016.

[32] *Financial Times*, 6 August (2016).

[33] https://www.gov.uk/government/uploads/system/uploads/attachment_data/file/492972/gs-16-1-distributed-ledger-technology.pdf, Accessed 20 August 2016.

opment of the blockchain. This approach resembles financial exchanges or modern banking due to the centralized characteristic of the process. Only a few institutions (brokers) verify these transactions, but anyone can participate in the dealing of assets. This process sacrifices potentially lower transaction costs on a public blockchain for increased reliability and security. The overseer must invite and approve the individuals or institutions that would like to participate in the verification network. In a private blockchain, the resources required for a consensus can be reduced, overcoming a big issue in the use of blockchain for virtual currencies.

In addition to public and private ledgers, blockchain falls under two similar but independent categories[34]:

- Permissionless means that anyone can contribute to the blockchain. As mentioned above, once verified, the transaction is added to the blockchain. In a permissionless ledger, anyone can choose to participate in this verification network and obtain potential rewards of participation. The verification or mining process can be very complex. The possibility of an organization or individual successfully threatening the system always exists since sufficient concentrated computing power can overpower the system. Another issue with permissionless blockchains is scalability. The data requirements of the blockchain limit the growth potential for this type of technology. In a permissionless blockchain, every node in the network needs to process every transaction. This is not efficient, especially with an increasing supply of transaction services (participating nodes).
- Permissioned blockchains are gaining traction within financial institutions and digital ledger-based startups. A financial institution must verify non-cash payments between individuals for the transaction to be complete. Financial institutions would understandably like the same degree of control over the verification and recording process of digital currencies in order to minimize risks. Transactions could possibly

[34] https://www.gov.uk/government/uploads/system/uploads/attachment_data/file/492972/gs-16-1-distributed-ledger-technology.pdf, Accessed 20 August 2016.

take less time and potentially be cheaper because the supply of transaction services will be smaller, resulting in a lower network hash rate and difficulty of the proof-of-concept solution, meaning that transactions are less expensive to vendors of transaction services.

The current form of blockchain applied to most digital currencies is a public, permissionless blockchain. There are security issues. Blockchains may be able to ensure that transactions and payment verification can occur without the existence of a centralized oversight, similar to a central bank or even just banking institutions. However, financial institutions and large companies must have guarantee concerning the security of outgoing and incoming transactions.

Main Potential Applications of Blockchain

It is possible to use blockchain as an open data affecting the interactions between financial institutions and third parties: agency networks, external vendors, and customers.

Distributed ledgers such as blockchain have numerous cross-industry use opportunities. These include distributed ledgers with limitations concerning verification, transaction recording, and access. While these major innovations affect who can view or verify transactions on any distributed ledger, they have little impact on the core engineering of the blockchain. The basic idea of the distributed ledger would still be essentially the same.

Blockchain is a very cost-effective method of facilitating the availability and exchange of data between many parties interested in financial services. It is a trusted utility service that boosts financial market competitiveness. Blockchain can affect portfolio management, administration of bonds and obligations, sales, and claims handling. In the financial world, it could give a powerful support to trade finance. Blockchain could help in setting up smart contracts with a distributed ledger solution. It could help in managing customer identities, reference data, and assets in a contract or order. In this way, it could increase secure visibility and ensure a seamless, reliable, and uninterrupted messaging service to the financial services market.

There has been a thorough analysis of the use of blockchain for virtual currencies (Antonopoulos 2014). There are several other potential applications of blockchain in the financial services industry (Pilkington 2016). Blockchain or distributed ledger technology will gain more traction when major financial participants (such as banks, exchanges, clearing houses, or funds) can trust the level of security and volatility of transactions. There must be an industry consensus concerning the engineering of the ledger and the methodology of the verification process. Financial institutions and other companies must feel that the technology has low risk to utilize it in their businesses. Table 4.5 lists some of the main applications of blockchain technologies.[35]

Aside from future challenges and opportunities, the main technical innovation of blockchain technology is represented by cryptocurrencies, such as Bitcoin (further details about Bitcoin will be given in the next section). Suffice it to say here that a cryptocurrency is a digital currency that makes use of cryptography for security reasons: it is then very difficult to counterfeit, and it is not issued by a central authority.

Table 4.5 makes clear the great potential of blockchain technologies in the financial services industry. A possible application for smart contracts would work in the following way (Deloitte 2015):

Table 4.5 Potential applications of blockchain technologies

Market	Government	IoT	Health	Business, Science
Currency	P2P bonds	Agricultural network	Health token	Community supercomputing
Payments	Tax receipts	Robotics	Smart property	P2P
Fintech	Voting	Drones	Databanks	AI
Insurance	Contracts Automation	Smart home Sensors	Universal EMR	Crowd analysis
Crowdfunding		Autonomous cars		
Banking		Connecting cars		Mortgage
Procurement				Smart contracts

[35] Swan, M. Blockchain Consensus Protocol, slideshare.net/lablogga/blockchain-consensus-protocols, Accessed 11 August 2016.

1. The process starts with writing an option contract between parties as code into the blockchain. The individuals involved are anonymous, but the contract is in the public ledger.
2. A triggering event, such as an expiration date or strike price, is hit and the contract executes itself according to the coded terms.
3. Regulators can use the blockchain to understand the activity in the market while maintaining the privacy of the individual actors' positions.

Microsoft, IBM, and other tech companies are launching in their cloud platforms interesting blockchain services. Known as "Blockchain-as-a-Service", they allow enablers to deploy their semi-public or private blockchains.[36]

Organizational Innovation: Social Networks

McKinsey sees a very bright future for social technologies. It defines social technologies as digital technologies used by people to interact socially and together to create, enhance, and exchange content (Chui et al. 2012). Social technologies distinguish themselves with the following three characteristics:

- They are enabled by information technology.
- They provide distributed rights to create, add, and/or modify content and communications.
- They enable distributed access to consume content and communications.

Social networks are more and more important as a way to connect people. In some cases (for instance, private communications), the number of messages through social networks has become even greater than

[36] http://dupress.com/articles/trends-blockchain-bitcoin-security-transparency/, Accessed 20 August 2016.

in traditional emails or SMS. Insurance marketing and sales can greatly benefit from the channel of social networks.

Social networks have proven to be a fertile ground for experimentation and innovation. Most people and companies think of social media first in terms of customer acquisition or customer service. There are several other ways in which financial institutions have or can use social media. These include[37]:

- Using onboard social media to create a platform for independent agents to come and share ideas, experience and expertise.
- Capturing feedback and input from customers for use in product design. This is an excellent way to gain insight into what customers want in terms of channel design, new products, and other features.
- Using off-board social media such as Facebook and LinkedIn to develop a recruiting presence, especially among younger individuals more likely to use these sites.
- Employing social media to complement call centers, helping reduce the number of incoming calls and, in effect, helping customers to answer other customers' questions thanks to the creation of communities.
- Putting a "person face" on the company by publicizing charitable activities, sustainability initiatives, and other initiatives not directly related to insurance sales.

Celent surveyed the state of insurance in many countries with respect to social networks (Monks and Michellod 2014). The survey found that 68% of American companies use Twitter versus 42% globally, and LinkedIn is used by 57% in the region, compared with 35% globally. Reflecting this higher level of use, 91% of companies monitor what customers say about their brands online and in social networks, against a global ratio of 75%. In Latin America, countries such as Colombia have

[37] See also http://www.slideshare.net/AccentureInsurance/mastering-a-social-media-strategy-in-insurance-in-four-steps, Accessed 20 August 2016.

leapfrogged many developed countries and now have more active social networks than London and Paris.

The same Celent survey found that differently from their global counterparts, Asian insurance companies are less likely to use social media and mobile tools to interact with customers and agents: 30% use mobile apps, lower than half the global ratio of 61%. Facebook use is much higher at 60%, but still short of the global percentage of 71%. The infrequent use of apps and social media may suggest that insurance companies do not want to rely on such tools for business purposes. Similarly, there is a lower use of online and social media monitoring (56%, compared with 75% globally).

A lack of interest in social media may reflect a more general reluctance to use digital tools to engage in customer dialogue, at least for some types of communication. Differently from their global counterparts, Asian insurance companies are more likely to interact digitally with customers at financial stages (for instance, quotes, transactions, and payments). For example, 83% of regional insurance companies provide online quotations and 70% offer online purchase/transaction capabilities (72% and 66% globally, respectively). In contrast, 82% provide company and product information, and 49% educate customers about their brand values, compared with 92% and 63% globally, respectively.

Social networks are becoming more and more important as a way for connecting people. In some cases (for instance, private communications), the number of messages through social networks has become even greater than the number of messages exchanged through traditional emails.

Lenddo

"We have been hardening the product and readying it for outside institutions. Now we are at the point where the data showed the algorithms worked and we could offer them to financial institutions."[38]—Jeff Stewart, CEO of Lenddo

[38] http://www.forbes.com/sites/tomgroenfeldt/2015/01/29/lenddo-creates-credit-scores-using-social-media/#1a1c5a243f79, Accessed 20 August 2016.

Lenddo (continued)

Lenddo, a FinTech Innovation Lab alum, also leverages social media to enable borrowing.[39] It provides loans of up to one month's salary to people in emerging markets based on the strength of their social contacts and has acquired more than 350,000 members globally.

Business Model Innovation

A business model describes the rationale of how an organization creates, captures, and delivers value (Osterwalder et al. 2010).

The economic literature has identified the primary dimensions of a business model in the V4 business model framework (see Fig. 4.7):

- The value proposition
- The value architecture
- The value finance
- The value network

This model, developed by Al-Debei and Avison (2010), clarifies the main dimensions of a business model. It is important to consider also a central element, labeled knowledge management, to coordinate and synchronize the four-value dimension.

In terms of innovation, any strategical and considerable change in the four components of the V4 business model framework, aimed at creating, delivering, or capturing more value, may be identified as a business model innovation. Today, the focus is on technology. This is even clearer within the financial services industry, especially when dealing with fintech initiatives. This is the reason why people talk about tech organizations (Lamberg and Närvänen 2015). These companies have leveraged on technology to achieve a competitive advantage, disrupting their market and revolutionizing the conception of the business.

[39] http://pfnyc.org/wp-content/uploads/2014/06/NY-FinTech-Report-2014.pdf, Accessed 20 August 2016.

On one hand, each of the fintech initiatives shows a business model innovation (see, for instance, Figs. 4.6 and 4.7). The extent to which these companies are disrupting their target markets is, in some sense, a measure of the innovation implemented in their business models. Some elements are of pivotal importance in fintech initiatives' business plans. For a better comprehension: for instance, how can a robo-advisor company target the mass market without a working, effective investment algorithm? How may it be possible for a P2P lending company to effectively operate without a well-designed online platform? These elements are strategic keystones and not simple innovations. Keystones will most likely be cascading through other types and forms of innovation, generating a virtuous circle that identifies a business model innovation (BMI) (Cantamessa and Montagna 2016).

On the other hand, some schools of thought refer to BMI in a stricter way. According to them, it is important to focus in the existent synergies between each of the innovations that involve different elements of the business model. In other words, innovation should use a BMI approach (Chesbrough 2010). In this way, it becomes a system not linked to a single element.

Therefore, innovating a business model means much more than innovating a product or a process. In fact, BMI should be "systematically cultivated, sufficiently supported, and explicitly managed in order to confer a competitive advantage. BMI goes beyond single-function strategies, such as enhancing the sourcing approach or the sales model. Innovation becomes BMI when two or more elements of a business model are reinvented to deliver value in a new way" (Lindgardt et al. 2009).

It is not easy to discern BMIs and single product or process innovation when dealing with fintech initiatives. Due to the high level of disruption that those companies are causing in the financial services industry, one tends to identify those companies as examples of BMI. Many times, they are "fast followers", meaning that they have managed to exploit an opportunity by following the business model of another company in a very short lapse of time. If examining, for example, the robo-advisor industry, it would be hard to understand which of them has shown a real and disruptive BMI. As a whole, fintech robo-advisor companies have introduced a radically new business model, based on ICT infrastructure and investment algorithms that have disrupted and disintermediated the market from financial institutions and other traditional organizations.

Financial institutions should thoroughly take into consideration their own BMIs in their business plans, this being even more important for traditional organizations. Implementing an innovative culture, and being inspired by changes and innovation, is their key to growth. In part, this reflects the interest of a certain number of banks for business labs, incubators, and accelerators assisting companies in the integration of external knowledge, narrowing the know-how gap.

Robots

A robot is a technology or technology-enabled process that can perform functions previously only performed by persons. More and more, robots are finding ways to provide support also for financial services. A research report published by the investment bank Morgan Stanley in November 2015 predicted that several European financial institutions would pilot robo-advisor (or simply robo), many collaborating with startups as the most cost-effective way to do this.[40]

Fintech companies have been disrupting the financial services industry with new products and services, but also with technological innovations able to revolutionize the traditional organizational paradigm. One of the main innovations in this field is virtual robotics. This technology, in its applications to the financial services industry, takes mainly the shape of financial robo-advisors. The *New York Times* defines robo-advisors as a definite class of financial advisors that provide online services with "minimal person intervention".[41] Even though robo-advisors could support wealth management services, until now they have been mainly used for portfolio management. Some US robo-advisor startups have already linked up with established companies. Investment giant BlackRock

[40] http://www.computerweekly.com/feature/The-rise-of-the-robots-in-financial-services, Accessed 20 August 2016.

[41] Financial Advice for People who aren't rich, The New York Times, Apr (2014).

bought FutureAdvisor,[42] while Betterment is collaborating with financial services group Fidelity on a service for institutional investors.[43]

On the other side, robots can help in process automation. This section analyzes these interesting developments for fintech startups and traditional financial institutions alike, called robotic process automation (RPA).

Virtual Robotics

"About 50% of today's service jobs will be taken over by computers"[44] This is a statement in one of their most recent reports developed by the consultancy company PricewaterhouseCoopers. A multitude of economics schools has looked, with some concerns, at organizational changes (Huberman and Miles 2013). This means a period when organizational structures, together with their own elements, undergo significant changes and transformations. It is necessary to open the mind in order to understand the implications of an organizational change within the boundaries of a business organization.

Robo-advisors

Today, mainly persons provide financial advice. Digital applications could provide advice. The complete underlying process—from its generation to the delivery—is radically different. Furthermore, the person brain will never be able to work as an algorithm (and vice versa), so the contents of the generated advices will seldom be the same, at least for the time being.

The key differentiation lies in another factor, that is, the underlying cost structure. Many economic scenarios suggest that the use of digital solutions may significantly reduce costs and, in some cases, be more effective. Robo-advisors could revolutionize the delivered value proposition.

---

[42] http://fortune.com/2015/08/26/blackrock-robo-advisor-acquisition/, Accessed 27 July 2016.

[43] http://www.businessinsider.com/betterment-announces-partnership-with-fidelity-2014-10?IR=T, Accessed 27 July 2016.

[44] PricewaterhouseCoopers (2015), ibid.

A financial services company could offer affordable services, reaching different markets and gaining new customers. This is a way to make mass services of private banking and insurance.

According to a report developed by the consultancy company EY,[45] the advice is indeed to go virtual. New entrants have been revolutionizing the market by simplifying user experience and lowering fees, contextually developing new models that allow them to reach uncharted patterns.

Robo-advisors in the Fintech Industry

It is interesting to analyze some of the most relevant fintech startups that have built their business upon robo-advisors and automatic procedures, managing to reduce costs and to gain a competitive advantage on traditional financial institutions.

Wealthfront

"We're not very concerned about the large companies being able to keep pace, They simply can't innovate and deliver features fast enough. Instead, we're focused on defining a better way to invest for this generation."—Adam Nash, CEO of Wealthfront[46]

Wealthfront is an American company that offers investment services by fully employing complex algorithms. The company bases its investment strategy on the identification of risk tolerance, of the investment goals, and the budget of the investor through a streamlined questionnaire. Afterward, it automates the process through a software designed to adjust automatically the customer portfolios, keeping them diversified and tax efficient while maintaining the target allocation.

[45] EY (2015), Advice goes virtual: How new digital investment services are changing the wealth management landscape, http://www.ey.com/Publication/vwLUAssets/Advice-goes-virtual/$FILE/EY-Digital-investment-services-Canada.pdf, Accessed 20 August 2015.

[46] Fintech 100 (2015), Leading Global Fintech Innovators, Reports, page 9, http://fintechinnovators.com/uploads/H2-Fintech-Innovators-2015.pdf, Accessed 07 August 2016.

Betterment

"We have built a service unlike any other, and it is a whole new way of thinking about investing"—Jon Stein, CEO of Betterment[47]

Betterment is an American company, based in New York, NY. It is a fully automated, robo-advisor company, providing automated investment advice at very low fees (aligned with fully automated companies, from 0.15% to 0.35%, depending on the exact account) (see also Fig. 4.6).

Personal Capital

"We became the first digital wealth-management company offering state-of-the-art tools and an unbiased advisory service."—Bill Harris, Co-founder and CEO of Personal Capital[48]

Personal Capital, formerly known as SafeCorp Financial Corp., offers wealth management services and financial software solutions to its customers. In 2016, they managed $2.6 billion.[49]

A free Personal Capital app is available for all the mobile devices using iOS and Android, furthermore providing a web version accessible from desktop computers. This app has three functionalities:

- Monitoring
- Analytics
- Planning

This company comes under what can be identified as advisor-assisted companies, actually combining robo-advisor algorithms and person capital with the aim of slightly elevating the level of the service in relation to fully automated advising companies. Comprehensibly, this implies higher fees: they oscillate from 0.49% to 0.89% of the assets managed per year.

Personal Capital mainly targets not only high-net-worth investors who significantly value personal advice but also those people who are only willing to make minor changes to their portfolio, relying on their personal advisor for the largest part of their activities. This class of investors is known as "hands-off investors".

[47] Fintech 100 (2015), Leading Global Fintech Innovators, Reports, page 28, http://fintechinnovators.com/uploads/H2-Fintech-Innovators-2015.pdf, Accessed 07 August 2016.

[48] Fintech 100 (2015), Leading Global Fintech Innovators, Reports, page 26, http://fintechinnovators.com/uploads/H2-Fintech-Innovators-2015.pdf, Accessed 07 August 2016.

[49] https://www.personalcapital.com/company/about, Accessed 20 August 2016.

MoneyFarm

"We want to allow people to take control of their finances and to autonomously manage them in a direct and simple way"—Paolo Galvani, Chairman and Co-founder of MoneyFarm[50]

MoneyFarm is an Italian advisor company, performing its business in the wealth management industry. It operates through the employment of robo-advisor algorithms, able to profile customers and suggest the best suitable investments. The pricing strategy consists of fees from 0.50% to 1.25% of the assets managed per year.

A New Business Model

Advising companies operating in the wealth management industry can be[51]:

- Fully automated: These companies digitally deliver their services through the employment of algorithms and software-based solutions. Their pricing strategy is based on low fees, usually 0.25–0.50% of the assets managed per year, furthermore targeting a price-sensitive, millennial customer.
- Advisor-assisted: These companies deliver their personal advice through digital channels. Their value proposition then comprises a digital platform together with a person advisor relationship. The applied fees are usually higher than the ones applied by fully automated companies due to the use of person capital and, consequently, a different cost structure (0.30–0.90%) on assets managed per year plus monthly fees per planning program. These companies' typical investor comes from the mass market, valuing both person guidance and technology.
- Traditional: These companies will continue to deliver their services utilizing an in-person relationship. They apply the highest level of fees

[50] https://www.moneyfarm.com/it/chi-siamo, Accessed 07 August 2016.

[51] EY (2015), Advice goes virtual: How new digital investment services are changing the wealth management landscape, http://www.ey.com/Publication/vwLUAssets/Advice-goes-virtual/$FILE/EY-Digital-investment-services-Canada.pdf, Accessed 20 August 2016.

(0.75–1.5%+ on assets managed per year). Their target market comprises high-net-worth customers who desire trusted and personal financial advisors. Furthermore, traditional companies are the ones providing advice on a bigger number of investment vehicles. According to EY, in this case, the management includes mutual funds, commodities, options, and structured products, in addition to the more common ETFs (exchange-traded funds) and stocks.

It is interesting, the reaction of the customers to robo-advisors. The customers tend to prefer a combination, robo-advisors and person advisors. In a survey in Italy, 60% of Italian investors were ready to use the robo-advisor, 49% would not use it without the support of a person consultant. According to a research conducted by Schroders Global Investor Study in 2016, only 11% of the sample were willing to rely autonomously on the robo advisor. They were part of the 60% of Italian investors which declares themselves ready to use immediately robo-advisors.[52] The remaining 40% of respondents were divided between

- those who, at the time, say no investment in robo-advisors, but leave an open window of opportunity for the future (31%); and
- those who categorically exclude cyber trading, feeling the need of direct contact with an advisor (9%).

It is not new that millennials (18–35 years) are most attracted by the new technology: 70% are prepared to rely on a robo-advisor. The percentage drops to 45% among investors over 55.

According to this survey, the robo-advisor is an opportunity for financial advisors, rather than a threat. The Italian consultants, in particular, enjoy a good level of confidence from investors. They take a more pragmatic and cautious approach relative to foreign colleagues, according to the research by Schroders on robo-advisors. They are, on average, more likely to sensitize their customers to a medium-term perspective, and more realistic in terms of achievable returns. Around 65% of respondents

[52] http://www.bluerating.com/banche-e-reti/178-consulenti/49046-robo-advisor-agli-italiani-piacciono-ma-con-il-consulente-vicino.html, Accessed 15 July 2016.

claimed to take a higher horizon of three years (47% of the global figure), while only 4% want to invest in one year (10% overall). What links then to get a return of 5.9% per annum from the investments of their clients, a full two percentage points below the global average?

The Future of Virtual Robotics

Robo-advisors are reshaping the financial services industry, especially in the wealth management and portfolio management areas. The reason why this is happening is simple: fintech companies have been leading the way of new business patterns, anticipating trends and putting their customers at the center of their strategies.

The approach followed by these companies is consistent with the model presented in this book. These companies have been largely showing a forward-looking attitude by implementing disruptive technologies, by focusing on digital channels, and by exploiting the use of appropriate automated resources.

These companies have reached an enlargement of the customer base by significantly reducing the costs of the delivered services, thanks to automation. They have also adequately enforced marketing campaigns with the aim of spreading the brand and the services toward new customers and markets.

The future developments of robo-advisor companies are clear. These business organizations are perfect examples of disintermediation, even though their customer base is still poor when compared with larger banks and wealth management branches. They can revolutionize the market through simple and direct actions, as shown in Fig. 4.9.

Traditional organizations are not passively observing the market. Some of them are continuously involved in activities aimed to narrow their technology gap. The tools are always the same: innovation labs, business incubators, business accelerators, and acquisitions (Fig. 4.10).

More than in other areas, fintech companies have been successful in disintermediating traditional financial organizations; this could be identified as one of the main reasons for which acquisition has been chosen by a multitude of financial institutions as the best way to fill the technological gap. In relation to this last element, one could expect a period of acquisitions

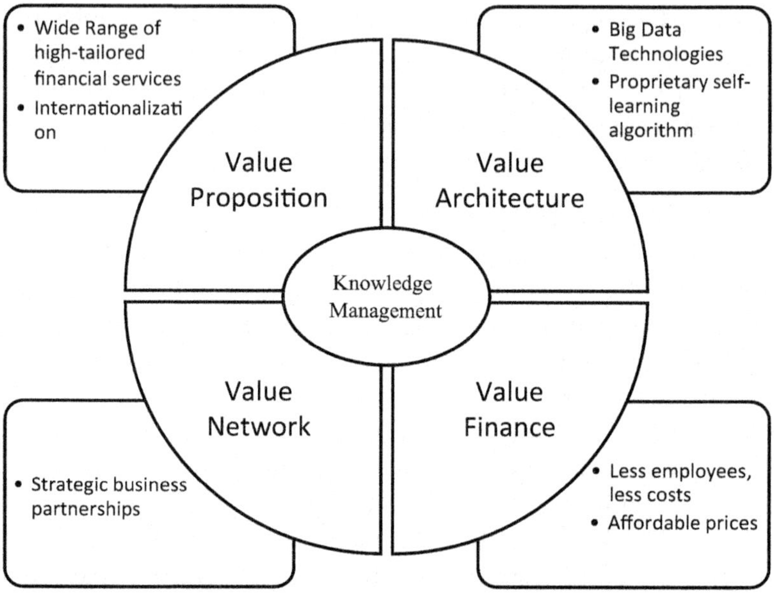

Fig. 4.9 The V4 business model framework for Kreditech

and partnerships. For instance, very recently, money management giant BlackRock has acquired Future Advisor, a fintech company delivering financial advice through the employment of investment algorithms.[53]

Even though automation is the future, robo-advisor companies should carefully take into consideration critical challenges. Not all customers prefer the automated nature of these solutions. Millennials, most likely, have often been target customers. Most of the traditional high-net-worth customers more likely prefer face-to-face relationships and meetings over fully automated processes, therefore continuing to choose the old and traditional methods.

The biases represent another issue. Modern economic theories are at the base of robo-advisor algorithms. Although they are still a valuable financial planning tool, there are still difficulties in the assessment of short-term strategies, even when they have their merits.

[53] http://www.notey.com/blogs/roboadvisors, Accessed 20 August 2016.

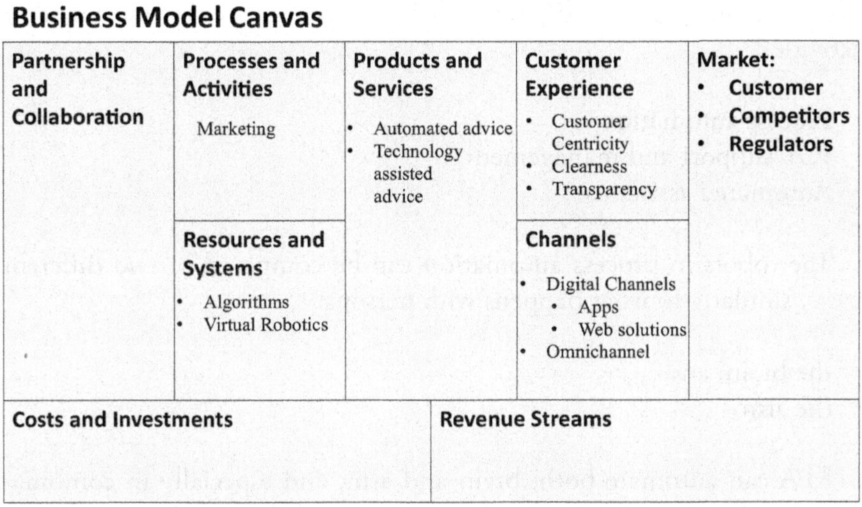

Fig. 4.10 The business model applied to robo-advisors

Fintech companies successfully countervail these challenges. Expect that fintech initiatives will compete with traditional companies with more and more advanced robots.

Robotic Process Automation

RPA is the application of technology that allows a company to configure computer software or a robot to capture and interpret existing applications for processing a transaction, manipulating data, triggering responses, and communicating with other digital systems (Fung 2014). In simple words, RPA aims to implement solutions which "sense-think-act" (Siegel 2003).

RPA is revolutionizing the way people think about and administer business processes, ICT support processes, workflow processes, remote infrastructure, and back-office work. RPA provides substantial improvements in accuracy, cycle time, and increased productivity in transaction processing while elevating the nature of work by removing people from simple, repetitive tasks.

The technology of RPA can provide a solution to a wide range of activities:

- Process automation
- ICT support and management
- Automated assistance

The robots in process automation can be composed of two different parts, similarly to what happens with persons:

- the brain; and
- the arm.

RPA can automate both, brain and arm, and especially in combination. It can get excellent results especially in activities where there is a need of:

- analysis/judgment: the "brain" part manages workflow and validation across many activities and workflow;
- complex data entry/rule-based decision: the "brain" part drives validation of the arm-driven automation;
- simple data entry that does traditional automation, use of macros, Optical Character Recognition (OCR)/Intelligent Character Recognition (ICR), and so on (the "arm" side).

This solution is particularly interesting for a financial services company whose general knowledge processes are manual intensive. On the other side, the combination of AI with the manual capabilities of a robot-like solution can bring big benefits. For instance, in the case of insurance companies, RPA is useful in several fields, such as:

- automated quotes and letter generation
- auto data extraction and presentation for the customer relationship center
- automatic claims processing, etc.

Genfour

"Users no longer have to go through complicated, long winded processes set out by IT. They could test something and give it a go."—James Hall, Founder and CEO, Genfour[54]

Genfour is a British company that specializes in automation of rule-based processes found in almost any organization, but especially in those with large volumes of transactional data from multiple sources.[55] These processes are common with teams and individuals that

- use structured, repeatable, computer-based tasks;
- do searching, collating, or updating of information;
- access one or more systems to complete a process; or
- perform simple or complex decisions and algorithms.

The Genfour approach can address all, or part, of an end-to-end business process, including

- workflow-enabled interaction with humans;
- skilled tasks such as approvals, reconciliations, and auditing;
- link into operational excellence projects and workflow systems.

Genfour claims to automate business processes quickly and cheaply. The economics are hugely compelling. An offshore Full-time Equivalent (FTE) costing $20,000 (total cost) can replace an onsite FTE costing $50,000. A digital worker can perform the same function for $5000 or less, without the drawbacks of managing and training offshore labor.

Magna

KPMG Magna is an integrated environment in which an ongoing picture of traders' behavior can be effectively, efficiently, and economical monitored to detect early warning, daily activity risk signs.[56] Using KPMG member

(*continued*)

[54] http://www.accaglobal.com/content/dam/ACCA_Global/Technical/fin/ea-robots-finance-shared-services-0909.pdf, Accessed 26 August 2016.

[55] http://genfour.net/robotic-process-automation/, Accessed 05 August 2016.

[56] http://kpmgkonduct.com/about-kpmg/, Accessed 11 July 2016.

Magna (continued)

companies' experience and understanding of the risks of trader misconduct (gained from hundreds of different fraud investigations), leading behavioral change technology, and user interface, KPMG helps customers to transform their compliance monitoring function. Doing this facilitates the prevention and early detection of unauthorized trading incidents, as well as reduces costs in reacting to internal investigations—which can be disproportionately high when there is regulatory scrutiny.

Virtual Currencies

A virtual currency or virtual money has been defined in 2012 by the ECB as "a type of unregulated, digital money, which is issued and usually controlled by its developers, and used and accepted among the members of a specific virtual community" (Simmons 2016). Bitcoin is one of the more famous virtual currencies. Bitcoin, thanks to the absence of a central authority, allows reduction in transactional costs. At the same time, it can minimize both time and fees to transfer money. In some cases, there might be transactional fees to get a speedier process. The chargeable transactions, paying higher fees compared with the others, most likely have priorities during validation. Bitcoin makes use of cryptography and digital signatures as security measures, making it almost impossible to alter maliciously the public ledger. Combined, these features generate an environment that recreates most of the key characteristics of a cash transaction (Deloitte 2015).[57]

The impact of Bitcoin is not limited to digital money. There is also an important innovation with the blockchain protocol. This solution is able to generate and establish technically trust among participants as never seen before. In a world where money and profits always occupy primary roles, this concept is potentially game changing.

As of mid-June 2016, the value of all blockchain-based currencies in circulation was $14.37 billion, and the price of Bitcoin was, as it has been

[57] http://www2.deloitte.com/content/dam/Deloitte/us/Documents/regulatory/us-advisory-bitcoin-regulation-dcrs.pdf, Accessed 20 August 2016.

historically, a leading driver of this growth. At June 2016 highs of $700, the price of Bitcoin had risen by almost $300 since the end of May 2016.[58]

Christine Lagarde, Managing Director of the International Monetary Fund (IMF), in an interview for the World Economic Forum (2015), has drawn attention to both the positive and negative impacts that such innovation could bring about.[59] The impacts are not only in reducing costs but also in providing better value and reaching the unbanked. There is a positive impact in reducing the influence of the size of the shadow-banking system (Lemma 2016). Negative impacts may have disrupting consequences, and not only for monetary policies. The points of strength might turn out to be a double-edged sword: the combination of trust and anonymity could perfectly fit the aims and the requirements of crime. Crime might actually benefit from a digital environment able "to recreate most of the key characteristics of a cash transaction" (Deloitte 2015). On the other hand, Bitcoin and blockchains may become tools used for illicit transactions, money laundering, tax evasion, and a potential threat to financial stability, being completely outside of a regulated environment.[60]

Virtual currencies, and in particular Bitcoins, are indeed pseudo-anonymous (IMF 2016).[61] Even though transactions are publicly recorded in the ledger, it is almost impossible to trace back the user's virtual identities to the user's real-world ones. As a consequence, regulatory and policy challenges are most likely the biggest issue for virtual currency holders.

A number of international bodies have both provided a forum to discuss issues related to virtual currencies and contributed to the debate through the issuance of reports, guidance, and manuals in their areas of expertise.[62] In particular, the Financial Action

[58] http://www.coindesk.com/rethinking-bitcoin-market-cap/, Accessed 28 July 2016.

[59] https://www.weforum.org/events/world-economic-forum-annual-meeting-2016/sessions/the-transformation-of-finance-8824a51b-91e1-4f29-88a2-abbfabb5fa8f/, Accessed 28 July 2016.

[60] "The Transformation of Finance. Fintech @ Davos World Economic Forum" Video YouTube, 5:30. Published by YouTube, January 21, 2016. https://www.youtube.com/watch?v=AsetntXCPRQ, Accessed 31 July 2016.

[61] International Monetary Fund, Virtual Currencies and Beyond: Initial considerations, Jan 2016. http://www.imf.org/external/pubs/ft/sdn/2016/sdn1603.pdf, Accessed 31 July 2016.

[62] Https://www.imf.org/external/pubs/ft/sdn/2016/sdn1603.pdf, Accessed 31 July 2016.

Task Force (FATF)—the Anti-Money Laundering (AML)/Combating the Financing of Terrorism (CFT) standard-setter—and the United Nations Office on Drugs and Crime (UNODC) have focused on the prevention and law enforcement response to the money laundering risks posed by virtual currencies. The Committee on Payments and Market Infrastructures (CPMI) has considered the implications of virtual currencies as a means of exchange and of distributed ledger technologies for central banks. Other institutions that have contributed to the debate include the Organisation for Economic Co-operation and Development (OECD), the European Banking Authority (EBA), and the Commonwealth Secretariat.

Customer protection is a challenge of virtual currencies. Customers are particularly vulnerable in the virtual currency's environment. In the worst-possible scenario (a disruption in the virtual currency protocol), the entire system would be paralyzed with a high probability of losses between virtual currency holders. Fraudulent operations, together with the overall absence of regulation, make the customer more vulnerable. It is possible to steal virtual currencies through hacking tools and fraudulent investment schemes. It is not only a matter of crime and illicit transactions. It is unclear in the case of a dispute: which national agency should regulate it. Currently, a lot of disparity and inconsistencies exist between jurisdictions, making coordination far more difficult. Traditional regulatory models may not apply to the virtual currency decentralized systems.

The irreversibility of the transactions is another big issue. Users, in the case of problems, do not have the right to reverse the charges.

The last issue relates to the monetary policy. It covers governments' and central banks' activities. Due to the relatively low amount of cryptocurrencies in the monetary system, they do not represent a problem. If they become more widely used, they would start to create concern in the public institutions in charge of managing monetary policies.

Virtual Currency and Fintech

The research developed in 2015 by H2 Ventures, KPMG, and Matchi (2016) may be instrumental in understanding how leading fintech companies are leveraging on blockchains and in particular on Bitcoins in their business.

Coinify

"Blockchain payments represent a new era of security on global transactions and it is only natural that Coinify implements new standards for compliance that cover this global mindset."—Christian Visti Larsen, CFO of Coinify[63]

Coinify is a blockchain currency service provider. With over $25 million of daily transactions in Bitcoin and other digital currencies, Coinify provides sellers from all over the world with a payment system that allows 16 virtual currencies (Bitcoin, Litecoin, Startcoin, TetherUS, Dogecoin, Peercoin, IXCoin, IOCoin, Mintcoin, Storjcoin, XNubits, Hypercoin, Novacoin, Digibyte, Quarkcoin, and Reddcoin).

In particular, Coinify makes transactions fraud-free and chargeback-free, furthermore giving business organizations the possibility to get paid in their local currencies while accepting virtual currencies as payment methods.

Colu

"This is a bitcoin-secured platform that empowers millennials and baby boomers looking for new ways to access online purchase and experiences."—Amos Meiri, Co-founder and CEO of Colu[64]

Colu is a fintech company that delivers a powerful solution for businesses and developers aiming to build blockchain-based applications. "From a mobile app that enables to store, send and receive digital assets just like texting your contacts, to the Dashboard which is a control panel for managing digital assets, to the Engine that handles all things blockchain in the backend using our API and SDK."[65]

---

[63] https://www.finextra.com/news/announcement.aspx?pressreleaseid=61456, Accessed 07 August 2016.

[64] http://fintechinnovators.com/company/524, Accessed 07 August 2016.

[65] https://startupxplore.com/en/startups/colu, Accessed 20 August 2016.

UBS

"You need a form of digital cash on the distributed ledger in order to get maximum benefit from these technologies."—Hyder Jaffrey, head of fintech innovation at UBS[66]

A consortium of institutes led by UBS Swiss, which now also includes the US Bank of New York Mellon and other European banks including Deutsche Bank and Santander, as well as ICAP broker, plans to launch a new virtual currency in 2018.[67] UBS is betting on this virtual currency initiative since 2015 with the support of a company specialized in blockchain technology, Clearmatics. The name of this new virtual currency is Utility Settlement Coin, or USC.

UBS counts on central banks and their open cooperation rather than challenging them. UBS designed this digital currency as an equivalent in cash for each currency guaranteed by central institutions, which are dollar and euro. It would therefore be convertible into a deposit in the currency considered due to the presence of as many assets in cash at the central bank. According to some estimates, each year, the financial sector spends between $65 and $80 billion to complete transactions that currently require several days.

Technology Acceptance Model

It is interesting in the case of fintech initiatives to analyze a model developed in the past for evaluating the acceptance of new solutions (technology acceptance model; TAM) (Davis 1989). A number of recent studies have adopted this model to study the acceptance of the internet and mobile-related technologies, such as mobile payments, digital insurance, and m-commerce (Kim et al. 2016; Chen et al. 2016). The base of the evaluation of TAM is on the premise that the fundamental determinants of the adoption and use of new technologies are

- the perceived usefulness (PU), which is the degree to which people think that using a particular system will enhance their performance.

[66] http://www.ft.com/cms/s/0/1a962c16-6952-11e6-ae5b-a7cc5dd5a28c.html, Accessed 26 August 2016.

[67] http://www.ft.com/cms/s/0/1a962c16-6952-11e6-ae5b-a7cc5dd5a28c.html, Accessed 25 August 2016.

The measures of PU include performance increase, productivity increase, effectiveness, overall usefulness, timesaving, and increased job performance.
- the perceived ease of use (PEOU), which is the degree to which a person believes that using a particular system requires little effort. The measures for PEOU include ease of control, ease of use, simplicity, clarity, and flexibility of use. PEOU has a significant and direct effect on the intention of uninsured people to adopt digital insurance services.

These two beliefs create a favorable disposition or intention toward the use of a technology and, consequently, affect its use.

Actually, there are other factors to take into account when considering digital insurance with respect to the basic TAM. Despite the unique benefits of digital insurance, overcoming trust issues is, for instance, a major challenge to the adoption of any digital insurance.

A complete model for TAM should include (Schierz et al. 2010; Nicoletti 2014a) (see Fig. 4.11):

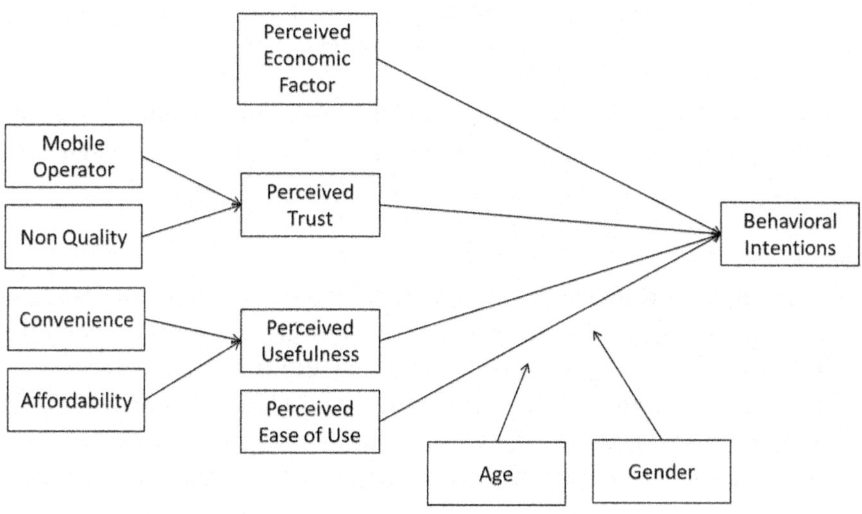

Fig. 4.11 The extended technology acceptance model

- behavioral intentions (BI), which is the propensity to adopt a new solution;
- perceived economic factor (PEF), which has a significant and direct effect on the intention of uninsured persons to adopt digital insurance services;
- PU, which has a significant and direct effect on the intention of the customer to adopt digital insurance services. It is determined by the level of convenience (CON) and affordability (AFF) derived from digital insurance services;
- perceived trust (PT), which has a significant and direct effect on the intention of un/insured persons to adopt digital insurance services;
- age and gender of un/insured persons, which affects their perceived ease of use of digital insurance services;
- Mobile Network Operator (MNO) characteristics; and
- the non-quality (NQ) of the service provided.

Conclusions

Fintech startups should maintain a customer-centric approach to their business. Most of them have managed to develop richer interactions with their users, in a goal-oriented and proactive environment where technology is at the service of customers.

Innovations, both pure and marginal, have played a vital role throughout the whole process of disintermediation. Therefore, fintech startups' innovative attitude is one important catalyst for their growth.

According to the analysis in this chapter (see also Table 4.5):

- Currently, customers see mobility apps mostly as payment "facilitators". Companies should leverage on mobility as soon as possible. These apps are going to turn mobile devices into digital advisors.
- Big Data Analytics allows significant cost reductions not by simply bringing cost advantages, but also by identifying new paths and ways of doing business. It brings about better decision-making processes, with reference to both time and quality. Decision-makers have the opportunity to analyze new sources of data in a faster way, which could

lead to the discovery of completely "uncharted oceans", as new markets, products, or services.
- Robots have been allowing the enlargement of the customer base, reached by significantly reducing the costs of the delivered services.
- Financial institutions should thoroughly take into consideration the innovation of business models in their business plans. This is even more important for traditional organizations introducing financial technologies. Implementing an innovative culture and being inspired, not feared, by changes and innovation is their key to growth.
- Blockchain technology has the potential to revolutionize many fields, not only the financial services industry, by ensuring traceability and trust between users of the same network.

The way that financial institutions need to pursue these innovations is through innovation projects. This is not easy, since traditionally insurers have bet on conservation rather than on innovation. The innovation discussed in this chapter might require an infusion of new blood in the management of traditional financial institutions.

References

ABI. (2013, May 9). *Internet of everything research service*. ABI Research Report.

Albright, S. C. W. C., Winston, W., & Zappe, C. (2010). *Data analysis and decision making*. Boston, MA: Cengage Learning.

Al-Debei, M. M., & Avison, D. (2010). Developing a unified framework of the business model concept. *European Journal of Information Systems, 19*, 359–376.

Anderson, J., & Rainie, L. (2014, May 14). *The Internet of things will thrive by 2025: Main Report: An In-depth Look at Expert Responses*. Pew Research Center, 1–66.

Antonopoulos, A. M. (2014). *Mastering Bitcoin: Unlocking digital cryptocurrencies*. Sebastopol, CA: O'Reilly Media.

Bhargava, A. (2014). *A dozen ways insurers can leverage Big Data for business value*. Tata Consultancy Services White Paper, 1–12.

Cantamessa, M., & Montagna, F. (Eds.). (2016). Business model innovation. In *Management of innovation and product development: Integrating business and technological perspectives* (pp. 115–135). London, UK: Springer.

Carlzon, J., & Peters, T. (1987). *Moments of truth*. Cambridge, MA: Ballinger.

Carter, P. (2011). *Big Data Analytics: Future architectures, skills and roadmaps for the CIO*. IDC Whitepaper, 1–16.

Cavanillas, J. M., Curry, E., & Wahlster, W. (Eds.). (2016). *New horizons for a data-driven economy*. Heidelberg, Germany: Springer Open.

Chandler, A. D. (1962). *Strategy & structure: Chapter in the history of American industrial enterprise*. Cambridge, MA: MIT Press.

Chen, M. C., Chen, S. S., Yeh, H. M., & Tsaur, W. G. (2016). The key factors influencing internet finances services satisfaction: An empirical study in Taiwan. *American Journal of Industrial and Business Management, 6*(06), 748–762.

Chesbrough, H. (2010). Business model innovation: opportunities and barriers. *Long Range Planning, 43*(2), 354–363.

Chui, M., et al. (2012). The social economy: Unlocking value and productivity through social technologies. *McKinsey Global Institute Report*, 1–184.

Christensen, C. (2013). *The innovator's dilemma: When new technologies cause great firms to fail*. Cambridge, MA: Harvard Business Review Press.

Cutroni, J. (2010). *Google analytics*. Luxembourg: Amazon Media EU S.à r.l.

Davenport, T. H. (2013). Analytics 3.0. *Harvard Business Review, 91*(12), 64–72.

Davis, F. D. (1989). Perceived usefulness, perceived ease of use, and user acceptance of information technology. *MIS Quarterly, 13*(3), 319–340.

Deloitte. (2015). *Financial services in the age of the internet of things*. Retrieved July 31, 2016, from https://www2.deloitte.com/content/dam/Deloitte/cn/Documents/about-deloitte/aff2015/deloitte-cn-aff-postcon-leaflet-en-150227.pdf

Desyllas, P., & Sako, M. (2013). Profiting from business model innovation: Evidence from Pay-As-You-Drive auto insurance. *Research Policy, 42*(1), 101–116.

Ernst and Young. (2016). *UK Fintech: On the cutting edge, Ernst and Young Report*. Retrieved July 31, 2016, from http://www.ey.com/Publication/vwLUAssets/EY-UK-FinTech-On-the-cutting-edge/$FILE/EY-UK-FinTech-On-the-cutting-edge.pdf

Fall, K. R., & Stevens, W. R. (2011). *TCP/IP illustrated, volume 1: The protocols*. Boston, MA: Addison-Wesley.

Feldman, R., & Sanger, J. (2007). *The text mining handbook: Advanced approaches in analyzing unstructured data*. Cambridge, UK: Cambridge University Press.

Fintech 100. (2015). *Leading Global Fintech innovators*. Report 2015. Retrieved August 24, 2016, from http://www.fintechinnovators.com/

Fung, H. P. (2014). Criteria, use cases and effects of information technology process automation (ITPA). *Institute for Robotic Process Automation, 3*, 124.

Gubbi, J., Buyya, R., Marusic, S., & Palaniswami, M. (2013). Internet of Things (IoT): A vision, architectural elements, and future directions. *Future Generation Computer Systems, 29*(7), 1645–1660.

Gulamhuseinwala, I., Bull, T., & Lewis, S. (2015). Fintech is gaining traction and young, high-income users are the early adopters. *Journal of Financial Perspectives, 3*(3), 1–20.

H2 Ventures, KPMG and Matchi. (2016). Fintech 100. *Leading Global Fintech innovators, Report 2015*. Retrieved July 31, 2016, from https://www.kpmg.com/FR/fr/IssuesAndInsights/ArticlesPublications/Documents/Etude-Fintech100-2015.pdf

Hey, T., Tansley, S., & Tolle, K. (Eds.). (2009). *The fourth paradigm*. Redmont, WA: Microsoft Research.

Huberman, A. M., & Miles, M. B. (2013). *Innovation up close: How school improvement works*. New York, NY: Springer Science & Business Media.

Hu, H., Wen, Y., Chua, T. S., & Li, X. (2014). Toward scalable systems for Big Data Analytics: A technology tutorial. *IEEE Access, 2*, 652–687.

Hussain, K., & Prieto, E. (2016). Big Data in the finance and insurance sectors. In J. M. Cavanillas, E. Curry, & W. Wahlster (Eds.), *New horizons for a data-driven economy*. Heidelberg, Germany: Springer Open.

IMF—International Monetary Fund. (2016). Virtual currencies and beyond: Initial considerations. Retrieved February 21, 2017, from http://www.imf.org/external/pubs/ft/sdn/2016/sdn1603.pdf

Kim, Y., Park, Y. J., & Choi, J. (2016). The adoption of mobile payment services for Fintech. *International Journal of Applied Engineering Research, 11*(2), 1058–1061.

Kipling, R. (2013). *Just so stories*. CreateSpace Independent Publishing Platform.

Kroll, J. A., Davey, I. C., & Felten, E. W. (2013). The economics of Bitcoin Mining or, Bitcoin in the presence of adversaries. *Workshop on the economics of information security*.

Kwon, J. (2014). TenderMint: Consensus without mining, 2014. Retrieved February 21, 2017, from http://tendermint.com/docs/tendermint.pdf

Lamberg, H., & Närvänen, E. (2015). Creating market orientation in a professional high-tech organization. *International Journal of Business and Management, 10*(5), 44.

Leavitt, H. J. (1965). Applied organizational change in industry: Structural, technical and humanistic approaches. In J. G. March (Ed.), *Handbook of organizations* (pp. 1144–1170). Chicago: Rand McNally.

Lemma, V. (2016). *The shadow banking system*. London, UK: Palgrave Macmillan.
Lindgardt, Z., et al. (2009). *Business model innovation. When the game gets tough, change the game*. Boston, MA: The Boston Consulting Group.
Lohit, N. (2013, July 5). Big data. *Bigger Facts*. Retrieved October 4, 2016, from http://blogs.sap.com/innovation/big-data/big-data-bigger-facts-098520
Lopez, J. C., Babcic, S., & De La Ossa, A. (2015). Advice goes virtual: How new digital investment services are changing the wealth management landscape. *Journal of Financial Perspectives, 3*(3), 1–191.
Manyika, J. M., Chui, M., Brown, B., Bughin, J., Dobbs, R., Roxburgh, C., et al. (2011). *Big Data: The next frontier for innovation, competition, and productivity*. Washington, DC: McKinsey Global Institute.
McKinsey. (2016, August). The CEO guide to customer experience. *McKinsey Quarterly*. Retrieved August 25, 2016, from http://www.mckinsey.com/business-functions/operations/our-insights/the-ceo-guide-to-customer-experience
Monks, K., & Michellod, N. (2014, September 12). Digital transformation in insurance: Differences across continents. *Celent Industry Trends Report*. Retrieved August 25, 2016, from http://celent.com/reports/digital-transformation-insurance-differences-across-continents
Ngai, J. L., Qu, J., & Zhou, N. (2016, July). What's next for China's booming Fintech sector? *McKinsey Review*. Retrieved August 25, 2016.
Nicoletti, B. (2012). *Cloud computing in financial services*. London, UK: Palgrave Macmillan.
Nicoletti, B. (2014a). *Mobile banking*. London, UK: Palgrave Macmillan.
Nicoletti, B. (2014b, Feburary). Using operational analytics to achieve a digitized, visible supply chain. *Inbound Logistics*, 1.
Nicoletti, B. (2016). *Digital insurance*. London, UK: Palgrave Macmillan.
Osterwalder, A., Pigneur, Y., Smith, A., & 470 practitioners from 45 countries. (2010). *Business model generation*. Self-published.
Pilkington, M. (2016). Blockchain technology: Principles and applications. In F. Xavier Olleros & Majlinda Zhegu (Eds.), *Research handbook on digital transformations*. Chaltenam, UK: Edward Elgar.
Porter, M. E. (1990). The competitive advantage of nations. *Harvard Business Review, 68*(2), 73–91.
Pricewaterhousecoopers. (2015). Consumer lending: Understanding today's empowered borrowers. Retrieved February 24, 2017, from https://www.pwc.com/us/en/consumer-finance/assets/pwc-consumer-lending-radar.pdf
PwC. (2016). Blurred lines. How Fintech is shaping financial services. Retrieved February 22, 2017, from https://www.pwc.com/il/en/home/assets/pwc_fintech%20global_report.pdf

Rivera, J., & van der Meulen, R. (2013, December 12). *Forecast: The internet of things, Worldwide*. Gartner Report. Retrieved August 25, 2016, from http://www.gartner.com/newsroom/id/2636073

Schierz, P. G., et al. (2010). Understanding customer acceptance of mobile payment services: An empirical analysis. *Electronic Commerce Research and Applications, 9*(3), 209–216.

Siegel, M. (2003). The sense-think-act paradigm revisited. *Robotic Sensing*, 1–5.

Simmons, R. J. (2016). *Blockchain explained: A technology guide to the Bitcoin and cryptocurrency Fintech Revolution*. Belle Isle, FL: Sparrow Publications.

Tiwari, R., & Buse, S. (2007). *The mobile commerce prospects: A strategic analysis of opportunities in the banking sector*. Hamburg, Germany: Hamburg University Press.

Troester, M. (2012). *Big Data meets Big Data Analytics: Three key technologies for extracting real-time business value from the Big Data that threatens to overwhelm traditional computing architectures*. SAS White Paper, 1–13.

Utterback, J. (1994). *Mastering the dynamics of innovation: How companies can seize opportunities in the face of technological change*. Thesis at the University of Illinois at Urbana-Champaign's Academy for Entrepreneurial Leadership Historical Research Reference in Entrepreneurship, Urbana, IL.

Woerner, S., & Wixom, B. H. (2015). Big Data: Extending the business strategy toolbox. *Journal of Information Technology, 30*(1), 60–62.

World Economic Forum. (2015). *The Future of Fintech : A paradigm shift in small business finance*. Geneva, Switzerland: World Economic Forum Publications.

Zeithaml, V. A., Berryh, L. L., & Parasuraman, A. (1996). The behavioral consequences of service quality. *Journal of Marketing, 60*, 31–46.

Zhang, L., Stoffel, A., Behrisch, M., Mittelstadt, S., Schreck, T., Pompl, R. et al. (2012). Visual analytics for the Big Data era—A comparative review of state-of-the-art commercial systems. In *Visual Analytics Science and Technology (VAST). 2012 IEEE Conference*, 173–182

Zhu, N. Q. (2013). *Data visualization with D3. js cookbook*. Birmingham, UK: Packt.

5

Critical Success Factors

Introduction

This chapter defines a model for critical success factors (CSFs) for fintech initiatives. Fintech refers to innovative financial services or products delivered via technology. With advancements in technology (such as mobility and the internet), coupled with their global widespread adoption, customers' expectations are changing. Many companies or startups are working on fintech-related products and major disruptions in financial services are expected. On the other side, launching and running a startup is not an easy job (Horowitz 2014).

CSF is a management term for an element that is necessary for an organization or project to achieve its mission. CSFs are critical factors or activities required for ensuring the success of an initiative (Heath and Heath 2008). The term was initially used in the world of data analysis and business analysis. An example of a CSF for a successful ICT project is user involvement (Rockart 1979).

Boynlon and Zmud (1984) provided a complete definition:

B. Nicoletti, *The Future of FinTech*,
DOI 10.1007/978-3-319-51415-4_5

"Critical success factors are those few things that must go well to ensure success for a manager or an organization, and, therefore, they represent those managerial or enterprise area, that must be given special and continual attention to bring about high performance. CSFs include issues vital to an organization's current operating activities and to its future success."

It is particularly important to evaluate the CSFs of fintech initiatives since the investors and the executives are very much interested in making the venture successful. The definition of success criteria is in connection with the initiative and the objectives. KPIs can measure them.

The differences between CSFs versus KPIs are as follows:

- CSFs are elements that are essential for a strategy to be successful. Managers should ask themselves: "Which value is our product/service adding to the customers?" The answer is normally a critical success factor.
- KPIs are measures that quantify management objectives, along with a target or threshold. They make possible the measurement of the strategic performance of an organization, or a project, or an activity.

The Critical Success Factors

Many authors have examined the subject of CSFs for ICT initiatives normally not in connection with specific financial services.

Martin Pieterse (2012) investigates CSFs for ICT projects. His intention was to identify a set of factors that would increase the probability of an ICT project succeeding. The author investigated IT in the business environment to understand ICT project success. The systems and components that comprise ICT can provide the business organization with significant competitive advantage. The development of ICT systems follows a process known as the software development life cycle and is normally managed as a project. A project is a grouping of related activities that consume some of the limited resources of an organization for a fixed period and that has a measurable objective as its goal. Projects normally follow the same path, from project concept initiation, planning, plan development, execution through to project closeout. A project is deemed to be successful if it delivers the objectives stated for the project, is delivered on time, within the cost estimates, to expected quality, and if it is profitable for the stakeholders. Despite the competitive advantage that ICT can provide the business and the fact that projects are well defined, more than half of ICT projects still fail.[1] There are, however, a number of reasons that can contribute to the failure of ICT projects. The main factor contributing to ICT project failures is the lack of management and leadership in projects.

Investigation reveals that a number of factors do exist that are critical to ICT project success. These factors are customer involvement, a positive attitude toward project success, flexible project tools, defined criteria for success, keeping to schedules and budgets, and team management and communication (Lencioni 2002; Nicoletti 2016).

Kiioh (2015) examined why so many projects continue to fail despite the huge investment and use of established project methods and tools. The root cause is the lack of leadership competency. A project's success or failure is in part contingent on effectively managing the constraints of scope, time, costs, and quality expectations. In order to achieve this, it is essential that the project manager possesses and displays appropriate project management leadership. The aim of Kiioh's study was to add to the existing body of leadership research on project management by examining the influence of leadership aspects on ICT projects. Kiioh's study identified four aspects of leadership, which include skills, experience, control, and style, and investigated their influence on the performance of ICT projects at a fintech company in Kenya. The study concluded that there was a significant relationship between the leadership of project management and the performance of ICT projects. The study recommends that all the project staff acquire effective leadership skills. It is necessary to give emphasis to the experience of the project staff to ensure that projects are effective in fully meeting the set objectives. The study recommended that the evaluation of the performance of ICT projects should be from the perspective of leaders and team members using their style to demonstrate concern, care, and respect to other employees. This attitude

[1] http://jamia.oxfordjournals.org/content/16/3/291.short, Accessed 29 July 2016.

increases the employees' interest in their work, thereby affecting their job satisfaction positively, enabling them to put up better performance.

Nicoletti (2010, 2013) examined lean thinking initiatives. These initiatives focus on improving business processes by using statistical methods, team involvement, and manual approaches. The results tend not to be effective in the frequent situations where there is an intensive use of ICT systems. Nicoletti's work aims to define a project management methodology to streamline and digitize business processes and reduce waste by using a novel approach labeled "Lean and Digitize". All the papers mentioned before present a framework based on empirical experiences and field implementations. The digitization of a business process that is not streamlined can generate problems, slowing down the process and increasing errors. A map of the process highlights waste and low quality. The CSF of a project is to optimize it, taking also into account the potential ICT support for re-engineering and digitizing. The project in this way will digitize only value-added activities for the users and the organization.

Clarysse and Yusubova (2014) examined business accelerators as a relatively new type of incubating startups. Accelerators help nascent companies succeed in the early stage of development by providing support services. Success factors of accelerators can minimize the startup teams' failures. This research discusses three main factors of success: selection process and criteria, business support services, and network. This study uses the lens of institutional theory to propose that success factors help accelerators acquire legitimacy in the eyes of their stakeholders. Legitimacy plays a key role in business accelerators' survival and growth. The stakeholders' needs and requirements drive the variety of business accelerators. Following this, this study also emphasizes different types of accelerators: generic, specific, private, and public. The empirical evidence in this paper comes from multiple case studies representing 13 accelerator programs in Europe (Paris, London, and Berlin).

Chuen and Teo (2015) identified some of the factors that can lead to the success of fintech initiatives. They termed the factors the LASIC (Low margin, Asset light, Scalable, Innovative, and Compliance easy) principles. They explained the LASIC principles and then used them to discuss two examples of successful fintech companies (Alibaba and

M-Pesa). Fintech will lower business costs and increase profit margins. The authors also discussed in the final section of their paper the benefits of investing for financial inclusion. In order to remain sustainable and profitable, enterprises need to expand their business by embracing financial inclusion. There is an estimated 38% of the world population that has no formal bank accounts and another 40% underserved by financial institutions, providing a huge potential market for financial institutions.

The Model

This chapter defines a model for the CSFs for a fintech initiative. The name of the model is CLASSIC from the initials of the list of the CSFs. This model expands the LASIC components presented by Lee and Teo (2015): (1) Low margin, (2) Asset light, (3) Scalable, (4) Innovative, and (5) Compliance Easy. This new model modifies one factor of the LASIC model, Asset light, to Agility. It adds two essential CSFs, mentioned in the initials C and (second) S. They are Customer centricity and Security management. The new initials add up to CLASSIC.

The following sections describe the components of this new model. These components can successfully harness fintech initiatives to reach the objective of creating a sustainable financial technology business.

Customer Centricity

Drucker (1954) introduced the concept of customer centricity in *The Practice of Management.*[2] He stated that it is the customer who determines what a business is, what it produces, and whether it prospers (Levitt 1986, 2004). He proposed that companies should not focus on selling products but rather on fulfilling customer needs. According to a 2003 Gartner Group report, "By 2007, fewer than 20 percent of marketing organizations among Global 1000 enterprises will have evolved

---

[2] Drucker, P. F. (1954). *The Practice of Management: A Study of the Most Important Function in America Society*. Harper & Brothers, New York, NY.

enough to successfully leverage customer centric, value-added processes and capabilities" (Marcus and Collins 2003). The same report states: "by 2007, marketers that devote at least 50 percent of their time to advanced, customer-centric marketing processes, and capabilities will achieve marketing ROI that is at least 30 percent greater than that of their peers, who lack such emphasis."

Customer centricity means creating a positive customer experience at all the physical or virtual contact points with the organization and adding value to the organization. A customer-centric approach can add value to a fintech initiative by enabling a differentiation from competitors that do not offer the same experience.

Low-Profit Margin

Schwartz and Moon (2000) report that, depending on the chosen parameters, the value of an internet share may be rational if growth rates in revenues are high enough. Even with a real possibility that a company may go bankrupt, if the initial growth rates are sufficiently high and if this growth rate contains enough volatility over time, then valuations can reach a level that would otherwise appear very high.

Profit margin is part of a category of profitability ratios calculated as net income divided by revenue, or net profits divided by sales (Troy 2008). Low-profit margins are a characteristic of successful fintech initiatives. Most of the web accesses are available free. Fintech customers tend to have low willingness to pay for services providers of any type. High network effects exhibited in such technologies require an initial phase of critical mass accumulation (Lee and O'Connor 2003). This is a costly process. It requires much marketing efforts. When achieved, it can reach the objective of a very low marginal cost (Rifkin 2014). Once a critical mass is built, monetization becomes possible through channels such as advertising, subscription fees, or customer data analysis. Over a long period, the initial margins appear low. They increase over time thanks to different sources of revenue. In synthesis, it is important for fintech initiatives to apply the concept of customer lifetime value rather than a short-term one (Venkatesan and Kumar 2004).

Agility

The Advanced Research Program Agency (ARPA) and the Agility Forum provide a definition of agility. It is the ability to thrive in an environment of continuous and often unanticipated change (Sarkis 2001). Agility is also the ability to detect and seize market opportunities with speed and surprise.

Agility is vital for innovation and the competitive performance of companies in the contemporary business environment (Sambamurthy et al. 2003). It is an imperative for business services. Fintech initiatives, which are agile, have a competitive tool. They can grasp on the opportunity for competitive actions in their markets. With agility, a fintech initiative can continuously improve the processes of creation, capture, and competitiveness introducing innovations in products, services, processes, organizations, and business models adapting to a changing environment.

Agile businesses are able to be innovative and scalable since they do not need to incur in large fixed costs on assets. This allows relatively low marginal costs, which in turn allows low-profit margins, as mentioned in the previous sections. One can add on to an existing system (such as the mobile phone) that depreciates quickly but offers an alternative revenue source (such as an internet phone messaging service) at low marginal costs. Riding on existing infrastructure allows minimizing fixed costs and initial setup costs.

Agility is preferred to asset light, used in the LASIC model by Lee and Teo (2015), for two reasons:

- It is an objective, not a mean.
- It generalizes anyway also the concept of asset light.

A corporate debt that has less than the usual amount of collateral, which is normally 30% or more of the company's value, is "Asset light". With asset-light debt, that number is much lower, with many companies' collateralized debt percentage falling far below their previous standards. It can sometimes even be at zero (Manyika et al. 2011).

Scalability

Scalability is the capability of a system, network, or process to handle a growing amount of work or its potential to be enlarged in order to accommodate that growth (Bondi 2000). For example, it can refer to the capability of a system to increase its total output under an increased load when resources (e.g., hardware) are added.

Staykova and Damsgaard (2015) argued that the timing of an expansion is of equal importance as the timing of entry. If the expansion does not take place within the optimal time, there is a reduction in the previously gained competitive advantages.

Any fintech business may start small but needs to be scalable in order to reap the full benefits of the network effect (Hagiu and Rothman 2016). It is important that such a business be capable of developing new technology that it needs to be able to increase in scale without compromising the effectiveness, efficiency, and economics of the initiative. Moving online reduces the need for physical outlets. This makes businesses easier to scale, since it is necessary to invest mainly in a central location, possibly located in a low-cost position. However, developers need to be mindful and ensure that the technology itself is scalable. One negative example is the Bitcoin protocol. It is innovative, but the protocol's architecture implementation is not simple to scale, as it is unable to manage a massive amount of transactions at an instantaneous speed. This is also hard to change because of the way the protocol was designed and implemented.

Security Management

Security management is the identification of an organization's assets (including information assets), followed by the development, documentation, and implementation of policies and procedures for protecting these assets.[3]

An organization uses such security management procedures as information classification, risk assessment, and risk analysis to identify threats,

[3] http://www.dell.com/learn/us/en/555/software-it-security-management?c=us&l=en&s=biz&pcat id=by-need-security-management, Accessed 29 July 2016.

categorize assets, and rate system vulnerabilities so that it can implement effective controls. Focardi and Martinelli (1999) presented a uniform approach for the definition and the analysis of various security properties. The general idea is that a security property should be satisfied even in the presence of a hostile environment. These authors identified some general conditions that permit to check a property only against a "most powerful" intruder. The results of this theory are applicable to a number of existing security properties. This shows the generality of the approach. It permits to find some interesting relations among properties proposed for different security issues.

Security is by far the main concern of the customers using the internet and mobile applications (Nicoletti 2014). This applies even more in the case of financial systems. Companies generally must maintain reasonable but very effective procedures to protect sensitive information. It is mandatory for each fintech initiative to build a secure, trustworthy service, regardless of geography and local regulations.

One way to comply with this CSF is to adhere to the Framework for Improving Critical Infrastructure Cybersecurity. US Department of Commerce's NIST prepared this framework with input from the private sector.[4] The framework represents an effort to develop a voluntary how-to guide for key organizations with critical infrastructure to enhance their cybersecurity. The framework is a key part of President Obama's Executive Order on "Improving Critical Infrastructure Cybersecurity" that he announced in the 2013 State of the Union address. To help organizations charged with providing financial, energy, health care and other critical systems of the United States better protect their information and physical assets from cyber-attacks, the NIST released a Framework for Improving Critical Infrastructure Cybersecurity. The framework provides a structure that organizations, regulators, and customers can use to create, guide, assess, or improve comprehensive cybersecurity programs.

The framework allows organizations—regardless of size and the degree of cyber risk or cybersecurity sophistication—to apply the principles and best practices of risk management to improve the security and resilience of critical infrastructure.

[4] http://www.nist.gov/cyberframework/, Accessed 29 July 2016.

Organizations can use the framework to determine their current level of cybersecurity, set goals for cybersecurity that are coordinated with their business environment, and establish a plan for improving or maintaining their cybersecurity. It offers a methodology to protect privacy and civil liberties and to help organizations incorporate those protections into a comprehensive cybersecurity program.

Innovation

The research of Rao et al. (2001) strongly suggests that technical progress, the embodiment of innovation, is the fundamental determinant of longer-term productivity performance, and hence of international competitiveness, living standards, and quality of life.

Successful fintech businesses need to be innovative in their products, processes, organization, and business model. With the increasingly widespread use of mobile phones and internet services, much innovation can be made in new technologies, such as mobility, Big Data, Analytics, IoT, social networks, cloud computing, and AI in the fintech space.

The aims of innovation ("successfully advancing" and "competing and differentiating") reflect both the overall strategic aim of innovation and the potentially diverse social and environmental contexts in which innovation occurs (Baregheh et al. 2009). Innovation needs to take into account its different aspects, products, processes, organization, and business models. All of these aspects must be integrated, and consistent diagrammatic and textual definitions, which seek to subsume and supersede earlier definitions with their specific disciplinary biases, recognize that an all-embracing definition of innovation needs to encompass a number of aspects of the essence of innovation.

Ease of Compliance

Financial institutions' regulations are increasingly complex and potentially costly, especially for fintech startups. It would be particularly important that compliance with regulations would not be difficult. Modifications in regulatory and legal framework conditions have a significant influence on the dynamics of innovations (Blind 2012).

In general, compliance means conforming to a rule, such as a specification, policy, standard, or law. Regulatory compliance describes the goal that organizations aspire to achieve in their efforts to ensure that they are aware of and take steps to comply with relevant laws and regulations.

Compliance with legal financial regulations is not optional, but mandatory. Almost every nation has its own individual financial regulation based on its distinct culture, financial system, and historical experiences. When fintech initiatives operate in several markets, they need to comply with complex multilevel regulations undertaken by different regulators. Due to the increasing number of regulations and the need for operational transparency, organizations are increasingly adopting the use of consolidated and harmonized sets of compliance controls. This approach can ensure compliance with all necessary requirements without the unnecessary duplication of effort and activity from resources.

Stakeholders, industries, and government demand greater accountability and increased respect for data privacy. Civic criminal liabilities are on the rise. The number of regulations, policies, laws, and standards that organizations must adhere to continues to grow and will continue in the near future.

Organizations that are not subject to high-compliance regimes are able to be innovative and require lower capital requirement. While financial stability and consumer protection are important for a market to function, a tight regulatory environment has its trade-off. Besides the benefits of a "compliance easy" environment, organizations that receive subsidies or incentives aided by social, financial, and economic inclusion agenda brought about by an anti-income/wealth inequality regime have the added benefits. The main benefit of operating in a lightly regulated environment is that lesser resources need to be spent on compliance activities and this encourages innovation.

Some regulators are shifting to a forward-looking, from a retrospective, approach with respect to fintech companies (Arner et al. 2015). This should allow markets to become more efficient and competitive.

Eventually, this will yield benefits for customers and the economy. It is possible to use different approaches. There is a potential for common international approaches to fintech initiatives' regulations. The objective is to maximize market opportunity while setting best practices for managing risks to financial stability and customer protection. These regulations would be similar to those applied in the context of payment systems and other forms of regulation by international standard-setters.

Metrics

In order to compare different fintech initiatives from the point of view of CSFs, it is possible to use a radar chart. This is a chart and/or plot with of a sequence of equiangular spokes, called radii. Each spoke represents one of the variables. The data length of a spoke is proportional to the magnitude of the variable for the data point relative to the maximum magnitude of the variable across all data points. A line connects the data values for each spoke. This gives the plot a star-like appearance. In this way, it is possible to compare the CLASSIC CSFs for a specific fintech initiative with the ideal ones (see example in Fig. 5.1).

Conclusions

This chapter presents a method to identify and measure CSFs for a fintech initiative.

Fintech companies, especially startups, are in fashion. Their number is growing by the day (or the hour). A very large amount of money has been invested in them and will likely be invested in the future. It is very important to define criteria for an early identification of the probability of success or failure of a fintech initiative.

This chapter generalizes a previous model for defining CSFs for a fintech initiative. This chapter labels the criteria identified, for mnemonic reason, as CLASSIC from the initials of the main factors:

- Customer centricity
- Low-profit margins

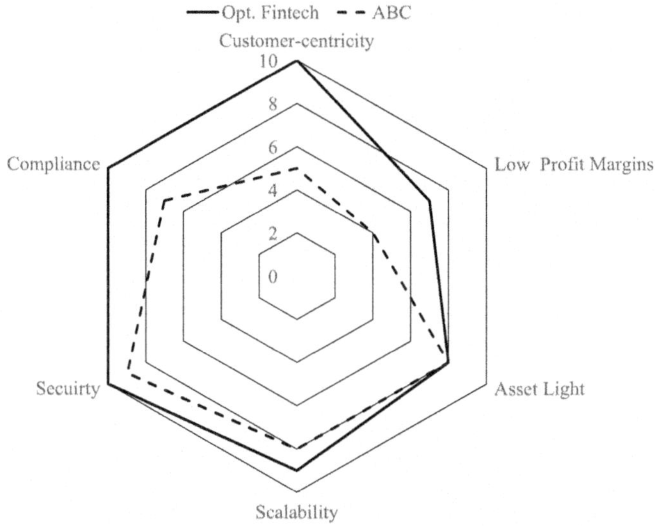

Fig. 5.1 Evaluation of critical success factors for a fintech ABC

- Agility
- Scalability
- Security management
- Innovation
- Compliance easy

The chapter substantiates the choice of the factors because of the previous single research that highlighted the importance of each of these factors.

References

Arner, D. W., Barberis, J. N., & Buckley, R. P. (2015, October 1). *The evolution of Fintech: A new post-crisis paradigm?* University of Hong Kong Faculty of Law Research Paper No. 2015/047, 1–44.

Bareghe h, A., Rowley, J., & Sambrook, S. (2009). Towards a multidisciplinary definition of innovation. *Management Decision, 47*(8), 1323–1339.

Blind, K. (2012). The influence of regulations on innovation: A quantitative assessment for OECD countries. *Research Policy, 41*(2), 391–400.

Bondi, A. B. (2000). Characteristics of scalability and their impact on performance. *Proceedings of the Second International Workshop on Software and Performance—WOSP '00*, 1–9.

Boynlon, A. C., & Zmud, R. W. (1984). An assessment of critical success factors. *Sloan Management Review, 25*(4), 17–27.

Chuen, D. K., & Teo, E. G. (2015). *Emergence of Fintech and the LASIC principles*. doi:10.2139/ssrn.2668049.

Clarysse, B., & Yusubova, A. (2014, October 23). Success factors of business accelerators. *Technology Business Incubation Mechanisms and Sustainable Regional conference. Toulouse Business School*, Toulouse, France, 1–19.

Drucker, P. (1954). *The practice of management*. New York, NY: HarperCollins.

Focardi, R., & Martinelli, F. (1999). A uniform approach for the definition of security properties. In J. Wing, J. Woodcock, & J. Davies (Eds.), *FM'99* (Vol. I, LNCS 1708, pp. 794–813). Berlin, Heidelberg, Germany: Springer-Verlag.

Hagiu, A., & Rothman, S. (2016). Network effects aren't enough. *Harvard Business Review, 94*(4), 65–71.

Heath, C., & Heath, D. (2008). *Made to stick: Why some ideas take hold and others come unstuck*. New York, NY: Random House.

Horowitz, B. (2014). *The hard thing about hard things: Building a business when there are no easy answers*. New York, NY: Harper Business.

Kiioh, L. K. (2015). *Influence of project management leadership on performance of information technology projects: A case of fin-tech Kenya*. Doctoral dissertation, University of Nairobi.

Lee, Y., & O'Connor, G. C. (2003). New product launch strategy for network effects products. *Journal of the Academy of Marketing Science, 31*(3), 241–255.

Lee, D. K., & Teo, E. G. (2015). *Emergence of FinTech and the LASIC principles*. SSRN 2668049.

Lencioni, P. M. (2002). *The five dysfunctions of a team: A leadership fable* (vol. 13). New York, NY: Wiley.

Levitt, T. (1986). *Marketing imagination*. New York, NY: Simon and Schuster.

Levitt, T. (2004). Marketing myopia. *Harvard Business Review, 82*(7/8), 138–149.

Manyika, J. M., Chui, M., Brown, B., Bughin, J., Dobbs, R., Roxburgh, C., et al. (2011). *Big Data: The next frontier for innovation, competition, and productivity*. Washington, DC: McKinsey Global Institute.

Marcus, C., & Collins, K. (2003). Top-10 marketing processes for the 21st century. *Gartner Group Report* SP-20-0671.

Nicoletti, B. (2010). Lean and digitize project management. *Proceedings of the 24th IPMA World Congress* (pp. 1–6).

Nicoletti, B. (2013). Building an executive dashboard for a project portfolio. *PM World Journal, 2*(8), 2–6.

Nicoletti, B. (2014). *Mobile banking*. London, UK: Palgrave Macmillan.

Nicoletti, B. (2016). *Digital insurance*. London, UK: Palgrave Macmillan.

Pieterse, M. (2012). *Critical success factors in information technology projects*. Retrieved March 9, 2016, from https://scholar.google.it/scholar?cluster=110970802498518962 32andhl=itandas_sdt=0,5

Rao, S., Ahmad, A., Horsman, W., & Kaptein-Russell, P. (2001). The importance of innovation for productivity. *International Productivity Monitor, 2*, 11–18.

Rifkin, J. (2014). *The zero marginal cost society: The internet of things, the collaborative commons, and the eclipse of capitalism*. London, UK: Palgrave Macmillan.

Rockart, J. F. (1979). Chief executives define their own data needs. *Harvard Business Review, 57*, 81–93.

Sambamurthy, V., Bharadwaj, A., & Grover, V. (2003). Shaping agility through digital options: Reconceptualizing the role of information technology in contemporary firms. *MIS Quarterly*, 237–263.

Sarkis, J. (2001). Benchmarking for agility. *Benchmarking: An International Journal, 8*(2), 88–107.

Schwartz, E., & Moon, M. (2000). Rational pricing of internet companies. *Financial Analysts Journal, 56*(3), 62–75.

Staykova, K. S., & Damsgaard, J. (2015). The race to dominate the mobile payments platform: Entry and expansion strategies. *Electronic Commerce Research and Applications, 14*(5), 319–330.

Troy, L. (2008). *Almanac of business and industrial financial ratios*. Englewood Cliffs, NJ: Prentice-Hall.

Venkatesan, R., & Kumar, V. (2004). A customer lifetime value framework for customer selection and resource allocation strategy. *Journal of marketing, 68*(4), 106–125.

6

Responses of Traditional Players

Introduction

This chapter analyzes the responses of large traditional players and examines the various strategies that are open to them. Incumbent companies and new entrants are creating links that could offer a foretaste of the future structure of the financial sector.

The traditional financial institutions have not remained idle in the face of the rising threat from fintech startups. Their digital strategy can be summed up in one simple question: make or buy? This section considers both alternatives and then describes a third path, midway between the other two: "partner". The latter could form the basis for a new business model, whereby traditional players combine their skills in core financial service systems with the agility of new entrants (what was termed CLASSIC in the previous chapter).

Many market and media commentaries have emphasized the threat to established banking models, and the opportunities for incumbent organizations to develop new partnerships aimed at better cost control, capital allocation, and customer acquisition are growing. McKinsey's most

B. Nicoletti, *The Future of FinTech*,
DOI 10.1007/978-3-319-51415-4_6

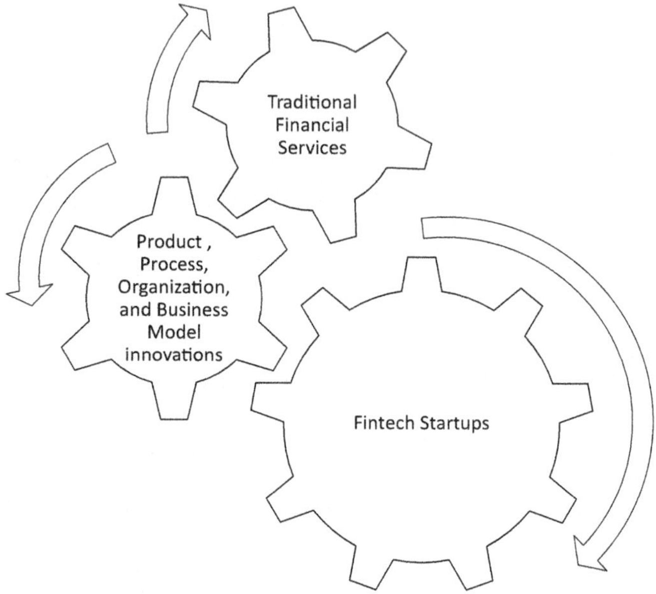

Fig. 6.1 Fintech and financial services partnership

recent analysis suggests that the structure of the fintech industry is changing and that a new spirit of cooperation between fintech startups and incumbents is developing (Dietz et al. 2016) (see also Fig. 6.1).

Fintech and Financial Services

The financial services industry plays a crucial role in the global economic scenario. This relevance has been growing since the aftermath of the global crisis, which started in 2008. Governments and regulation entities directed much attention toward this sector. This has underlined its absolute centrality in the economy, recognizing the need for an almost continuous overhaul of the governance of the phenomenon.

The financial services industry is a merger of two words: finance and service. Finance deals with money. Service, together with goods, is one of two macro-categories of things that money can buy. One aspect (among other ones) of services that is particularly important is its intangibility.

Therefore, it is vital to distinguish financial services from financial goods: the former could be considered as the process of acquiring the latter.

The core area of the financial services industry is intermediation. In particular, companies operating their businesses in this area deal with savings, lending, investing, trade finance, capital markets, insurance in its various types, and so on. Abstracting from a detailed overview (see, for instance, Greenbaum et al. 2015), financial services are essentially information agents between owners, financial users, and providers. These services alleviate information problems through different functions. Chapter 10 on the future of these services examines this consideration in details since it can provide interesting insights on future developments.

Although the oldest and most prevalent type of financial service institutions is the bank, other providers are included in the industry. Their overall weight has varied in the last decade due to the increasing importance of fintech initiatives and startups operating independently from traditional financial services (see Fig. 6.2).

New and external knowledge and technology are generally not easy to implement in traditional organizations such as banks or insurance companies. This is mostly due to internal resistance to change. Actually, for organizations used to working in specific ways for years and constantly managing to be profitable, it may be difficult to change. Old routines never overhauled and rigid business models may make it more difficult to innovate or to bring new knowledge into the organization (Koen et al. 2011; Teece 2010).

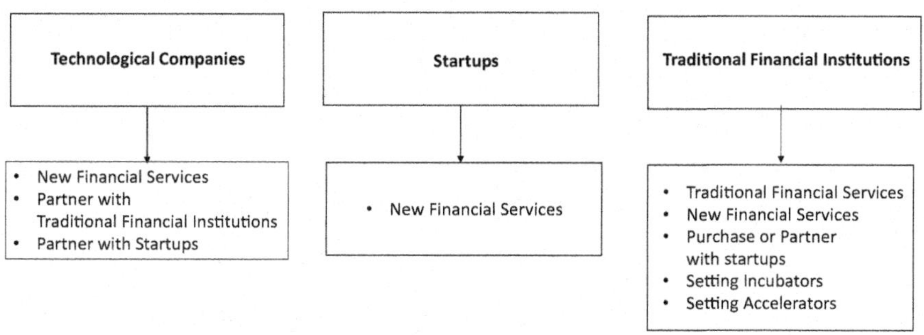

Fig. 6.2 Structure of fintech initiatives

Times are changing; the so-called traditional organizations operating in the financial services industry are experiencing a digital transformation, or even revolution (Accenture Research 2014; Skan et al. 2014), that has brought new entrants into the industry, new business models, and changed needs of the customers. These business organizations are trying to compensate for this innovation lag by leveraging on their large (or very large) economic base. In short, they are both acquiring innovative startups and participating in business incubators, alliances, and innovation labs, gaining access in this way to new advanced and innovative solutions.

The European insurance company Assicurazioni Generali has declared that it will invest up to €1.25 billion in financial technology through these channels.[1] Other organizations are following the same path, such as AXA, that in 2015 launched a venture capital fund of €200 million.[2] Barclays, in the last New York Accelerator Program, has signed up eight direct investment agreements. They are in the areas of cloud computing, videoconferencing technology, e-signatures, cybersecurity measures, and loan information metrics.[3] Just like Barclays, all the major financial institutions have a startup program.[4]

The Challenges

Challenges of Make

The previous chapters discussed in depth the digital transformation currently changing the face of the financial industry. As in other industries, market newcomers, and not incumbents, fuel this revolution. In the

[1] http://www.generali.com/it/investors/investing-in-generali/targets-and-achievement.html, Accessed 26 July 2016.

[2] https://us.axa.com/news/2015/axa-announces-venture-capital-fund-launch.html, Accessed 26 July 2016.

[3] http://www.newsroom.barclays.com/r/3245/barclays_signs_contracts_with_eight_companies_from_new, Accessed 26 July 2016.

[4] http://banknxt.com/53302/banks-startups-together/, Accessed 20 August 2016.

financial industry, in particular, fintech companies have a competitive advantage due to the technical debt accumulated by traditional players, notably the financial institutions. The concept of technical debt links with that of financial debt. Developing an ICT system generates future costs, which are similar to a form of interest payment, and the total amount of these costs makes up the technical debt. The more complex a system becomes, the more frequently it needs to be upgraded and the higher is the associated technical debt. A good example of this is a large banking group created through the merger of several different financial institutions. The overall information system has to integrate various pre-existent components; as a result, it reflects the history of the bank and the major stages in its construction, but it is never as efficient as a comprehensive ICT system, built to cover the current scope of the bank's activities. Asset management is another good example. Financial innovation has created increasingly complex tools, requiring the development of more and more sophisticated storage and control systems. The introduction of tighter regulations has also had a similar effect. Indeed, the vast majority of the ICT resources deployed in recent decades have been in response to these two phenomena. Today's ICT systems are like a *millefeuille*, built in multiple versions layered on top of each other as new financial innovations or regulations have emerged. For a long time, this complexity was a barrier to entry for new participants. Fintech initiatives now have access to technical solutions enabling them to integrate the impact of financial innovation and regulation from the outset, all at a much lower cost. There seems to be no holding them back. In contrast, incumbent companies have more limited room for maneuver due to their technical debts, leaving fintech startups ideally placed to take the lead.

The industry incumbents have responded by trying to expand the technical skills of their ICT teams and by changing the ways they are structured. The digital transformation has led to changes in the management of projects, with large groups adopting development methods and more agile ICT. These changes are similar to the ones used by tech startups. It is still important to know the business, notably due to its regulatory complexity, but the key factor now is the ability to develop interactive tools that match new user habits. Traditional players have all the elements they need to succeed in this transformation: knowledge of the business, a network, a record of accomplishment in CRM, transaction security, and financial resources. It is easy, therefore, to imagine them launching a digital version of their conventional banking model, drawing on their existing industry expertise to offer a different customer experience. A number of traditional players have already tried this, albeit with mixed results. There are various reasons why they have struggled: fear of cannibalizing their existing activities, the failure of previous attempts or difficulties in effectively mobilizing staff—all these can explain why traditional players have been reluctant to invest massively in the digital transformation. Financial institutions only succeed if they can encourage their staff to adopt new working methods, while capitalizing on their main strength: knowledge of their customers. This transformation is not easy to implement.

Challenges of Buy

Traditional banking and financial players have not been very active when it comes to investing in or acquiring fintech companies. Indeed, financial institutions have made almost no investments at all in this segment, despite regularly taking indirect capital stakes in startups via investment funds. The few cases where they have taken a stake have been for a set purpose: to modernize an existing service offering, acquire a new technology, or foster the development of a specific fintech initiative. Indeed, for fintech startups, having a financial institution as a stakeholder can reassure the regulators and make it easier to get a license for their activity.

Acquisitions of fintech startups by traditional players are even rarer. Financial institutions seem to be afraid that they will slow their target's momentum, or will struggle to merge the new entity with their existing development teams. The main motive for purchases by incumbent companies seems to be, again, to acquire a new technology or development team that can help them upgrade their offering as quickly as possible. Combining a fintech startup with conventional banking services is a way of developing new services in the short term. It also makes it easier to shift traditional customer relationships toward a more interactive and personalized model.

Aspects to Consider

Traditional financial institutions and fintech startups are vastly different types of organizations. While a partnership between the two may seem to make sense, it helps to understand the differences.

Fintech startups should consider the following aspects before collaborating with traditional financial institutions[5]:

- Fintech firms should never forget or compromise on their long-term vision, no matter how tempting the short-term benefits might be. If the goal is to change the status quo, a fintech company may find it more difficult to do so by collaborating with a financial institution and becoming part of the very system and status quo they set out to disrupt.
- Collaborating with an existing financial institution can decrease the time to market and the costs substantially by leveraging not only the financial institution's existing customer base but also its skilled and experienced sales teams.
- Fintech companies must consider how many parts of the value chain they need to capture in order to be successful. In the case of those developing new technology for specific parts of a more extensive value chain, the proposition of collaborating with a financial institution makes much sense.

Traditional financial institutions should consider the following aspects before collaborating with a fintech startup:

- The banking industry needs to look at the bigger picture and properly access the long-term impacts of a partnership or acquisition.
- When considering collaborating with a fintech startup, financial institutions should consider the "make vs. buy" options. Financial institutions need to be careful and realistic about their internal capabilities

[5] http://bit.ly/digital_banking_report_242_personalizationhttp://bit.ly/digital_banking_report_242_personalization, Accessed 19 July 2016.

and need to account for the time and cost required to produce a high-quality partnership. This should add value to both parties.
- One important area where fintech firms are especially good at, and traditional financial institutions have difficulties with, is iterating a product until finding the right solution that fits market needs. For most traditional financial institutions, a product tends to launch only after a long build process. The traditional financial institutions should be prepared to a test-and-change attitude.
- Due to the ephemeral nature of many startups, financial institutions should also evaluate the record of accomplishment of the teams they are looking to collaborate with on many levels.

A Cooperation Model

A third method of collaboration is emerging, specifically in the banking and financial sector. In order to sell their financial services and products, fintech startups need to have access to partners that know how to operate a core banking system; financial institutions, in turn, can provide this service and can sell the startups' products to third parties in unbranded form. A number of financial institutions have opted for this solution in order to create ties with fintech startups. This is a way for traditional financial institutions to position themselves as a service provider and provide guidance on their core banking business to startups. Some payment fintech startups, for example, operate using existing platforms. A number of platforms for the distribution of savings products sell solutions constructed using traditional financial institutions' products. In return, the partner institution can directly observe how the customer relationships evolve and adapt its offering to suit the needs of the fintech startups, and ultimately of the final users.

The Accelerator Programs and the Incubators

The financial services industry is significantly changing, especially due to the digital transformation that has forced new and old organizations to renovate their value propositions, their internal processes, and especially the engagement of their customers. For traditional organizations, such as banks and insurance companies, this has turned out to be a double-edged sword. On one hand, they certainly have the economic strength to innovate and/or renovate their businesses without needing to take into consideration the magnitude of its impact on their economic statements. They have the possibility to consolidate their competitive advantage within the boundaries of a high-regulated industry where entry barriers are difficult to pass through. On the other hand, financial institutions often are stuck in old business models that make it more difficult to implement new knowledge and capabilities in their organization. In short, traditional organizations have difficulties in innovating (Koen et al. 2011; Teece 2010).

In order to properly deal with the relationships between fintech startups and traditional organizations operating in the financial services industry, it is important to emphasize the changed need of adaptation that is now affecting the latter. Financial institutions should keep in consideration three aspects in order to adapt their business models:

1. The developments brought by new disruptive organizations
2. More openness to changes
3. More attention to other ways to innovate[6]

With the aim of realigning the business model of traditional organizations with the new needs of the market, it becomes important to gain access to the ecosystem of the entrants. To stimulate innovation, by developing new knowledge and skills, recent studies have corroborated the importance of a collaboration or a partnership with rapidly growing entrants (Clarysse et al. 2014).

This happens often through the participation in business incubators. A business incubator provides startups with an environment that support them in three areas: knowledge development, funding, and network

[6] Ensor, B. (2013), Making Leaders Successful Every Day, http://docplayer.net/12163899-Making-leaders-successful-every-day.html, Accessed 31 July 2016.

Table 6.1 Characteristics of accelerators and incubators (Cohen and Hochberg 2014; Hoffman and Radojevich-Kelley 2012; Miller and Bound 2011; Slaats 2015)

Characteristic	Value in accelerators	Value in incubators
Duration	3–4 months	1–5 years
Cohort based	Yes, approximately 10 startups	No
Equity	Yes, around 5–8%	No
Participation fee	No	Minimal
Startups phase	Minimal beta-product	Low to medium
Education and technical assistance	Different seminars	Ad hoc. HR/Legal
Working space	Yes	Yes
Final	Demo day	Ongoing
Business model	Mainly investment	Rent, non-profit

resources (Van Huijgenvoort 2012). Founders and investors constitute generally the ownership structure of fintech startups due to forms of funding that require financing organizations to exchange capital for equity. Nevertheless, financial institutions carefully select startups. They do not simply choose the ones with the highest potential based on business plans and pitches. They actively organize and join business incubators with the aim of further developing the ideas of innovative startups (Table 6.1).

The table shows that it would be better to define these growing environments as business accelerators, rather than as business incubators. These two expressions are interchangeable and a real overlap exists. There are some elements that could differentiate them. Business accelerators and business incubators are both providing mentorship and guidance to companies, ensuring the right support to help their growth. Business accelerators provide medium- and short-term businesses (not necessarily in a seed phase) with a service similar to the one offered by traditional consultancy services, in a very short period of time, with the aim of ensuring a fast and rapid growth. On the other hand, business incubators may last longer periods and help companies to "stand and walk" in the very first years of the firm's life cycle.

Financial institutions tend to prefer accelerator programs for obtaining new knowledge regarding emerging technologies by means of cooperating with groups of startups in a relatively short period of time (Clarysse et al. 2014; Spelier 2014; Cohen 2013). Accelerators are also important from the point of view of open innovation (Chesbrough et al. 2006). Rapid technological changes and highly agile, innovative entrepreneurial ventures pose serious threats to established firms, which are often sluggish and not much radically innovative. The literature on external corporate entrepreneurship has demonstrated that incumbents have identified the value of startups as a source for external knowledge. Corporate accelerators, which foster a collaborative and mutual learning relationship between incumbent and startups, are very interesting. Moschner and Herstatt (2016) analyzed the new type of external corporate entrepreneurship activity as a means of overcoming the innovator's dilemma by drawing on open innovation literature and conducting six case studies with incumbents operating such programs. Their findings indicate that a close collaboration with potential young competitors is favorable for the incumbents scouting for new trends. Established firms can learn from technological as well as methodological expertise of the entrepreneurial mindset of young ventures, thereby breaking down traditional thought patterns and scrutinizing sluggish corporate processes.

Particularly useful is the designation of a liaison manager. He or she is responsible for building contacts between corporate employees and startups in order to foster direct and personal collaboration. Such aspects are important to generate and sustain knowledge transfer benefits. Consequently, corporate accelerators seem to be a meaningful way for incumbents to keep their potential competitors close and learn from them.

In the use of accelerators initiatives, two phases are important:

1. Production of new knowledge
2. Implementation of new knowledge

In order to accept startups in an accelerator program, they must meet some criteria. Apart from psychological and organizational aspects such as enthusiasm, resilience, and the right and multidisciplinary knowledge, the startup team must show a remarkable potential relative to the proposition value they would like to deliver. The team must be ready to cede a part of the shares to the incumbents in exchange for participation (Slaats 2015).

Traditional financial institutions generally meet most of the difficulties in the second phase due to a general high internal resistance and an overall large cognitive distance between them and the startups. Financial institutions generally may decide between implementing the knowledge internally or externally, depending on the extent of the two phases previously explained.

Discussed at the end of this chapter, the business model presented in Chap. 3 helps to better understand how fintech startups and financial institutions should manage their relationships. This chapter also presents best practices along with a new model.

Large financial institutions, leveraging on their financial strength, aim to reach a win-win collaboration with them: fintech startups may gain access to funding, resources, and experienced consultancies. On the other hand, financial institutions may gain innovative knowledge and fresh ideas that they can convert into new products or markets.

FreeFormers

"Barclays recognized, very early on, that they needed to help their customers be more digital, help their branches be more digital, and to be a digital workforce. In order to do that, they needed to take enthusiastic, passionate staff and give them that digital expertise. That's where we came in."—Emma Cerrone, Co-founder and CEO of FreeFormers[7]

One example of an advantageous collaboration is the one provided by FreeFormers, a London startup that has demonstrated how to develop a win-win partnership with financial institutions.[8] In more detail, FreeFormers is specialized in supporting enterprises in their path toward digital transformation. FreeFormers works with Barclays' employees with a double-fold aim: transforming them into a digital workforce and supporting them in teaching digital skills to their customers.

As an additional signal of this trend, suffice it to know that global financial institutions, such as Barclays, Standard Bank, and AIB, are therefore signing up to an online "matchmaking" service called "Matchi", with the aim of joining forces and efforts with financial technology startups.[9] Matchi is a digital platform that acts as a portal, connecting large

---

[7] Fusionwire interview, 10 September 2015. http://www.fusionwire.net/insiders/forget-disruption-collaboration-is-the-key-to-fintech-innovation/, Accessed 20 August 2016.

[8] https://freeformers.com/, Accessed 05 August 2016.

[9] http://www.ft.com/cms/s/0/919e0168-4f08-11e5-b029-b9d50a74fd14.html, Accessed 26 July 2016.

Table 6.2 Potential relationships between fintech and traditional financial institutions

	Domestic bank	Large innovative bank
Enabler startup	Mild	Synergetic
Disruptive startup	Disruptive	Collaborative

financial institutions with selected digital innovators chosen on a global basis. However, several financial technology startups with leading-edge technology have already consolidated into larger fintech players or larger financial institutions and insurance companies. In this way, newcomers were able to save on lead generation or fund availability, therefore allowing quick scaling of the technology they are delivering to the market.

According to the Global Fintech Report developed by PricewaterhouseCoopers,[10] a small number of CEOs (26%) disagree on putting fintech initiatives at the heart of their strategy. Around 14% do not agree or disagree.

Certainly, establishing a partnership with a traditional financial institution may not be the right choice for all the organizations due to the nature of both the fintech startup and the institution itself. It is then better to distinguish financial institutions in large fintech-oriented financial corporations and domestic financial institutions. The latter, threatened by the growing influence of startups on their target market, may be very aggressive. It is possible to categorize fintech startups into disruptors or enablers depending on the nature of their business model (see Table 6.2).

Unicredit

"Ours is the result of a choral work."—Paola Garibotti, Head of Country Development Plans of Unicredit[11]

(continued)

[10] PwC (2016), Blurred Lines, How Fintech is shaping Financial Services. https://www.PwC.com/il/en/home/assets/PwC_fintech%20global_report.pdf, Accessed 20 August 2016.

[11] http://www.economyup.it/startup/3828_unicredit-start-lab-2016-i-progetti-e-le-scadenze.htm, Accessed 25 August 2016.

Unicredit (continued)

Considering the growing financial technology trend over the past few years and the importance of establishing a position in it, in October 2014, Unicredit launched its Start Lab Financial Technology Accelerator program.[12] Unicredit managers mentored some selected fintech startups. Some of them benefitted from investor support. In a co-working space in the heart of Milan, there were meetings with internal and external experts. There were also presentations for commercial agreements with the network of partners of Unicredit. Four companies achieved extremely strong results and collaborated with Unicredit to integrate their solutions into the latter's systems. The program terminated in January 2015.

Commercial Bank of Africa

"[My six-year-old son] will never use a plastic card or checkbook to pay for anything (and likely no cash either) and he'll interact with hundreds of computers that don't have a mouse or keyboard."—Brett King, writer (King 2016)

One example of a successful partnership between a bank and a fintech startup comes out of Kenya, where fintech company M-Pesa opened up money accounts by allowing credits on mobile phones (King 2016). Since 2006, financial inclusion in Kenya has grown to 85% as a result. At first, the banks in Kenya fought to get M-Pesa shut down, but the Commercial Bank of Africa decided to work with M-Pesa. In 2012, the bank began offering a savings account linked to M-Pesa. In the three years that followed, there was an increase of 4.5 million customers, which added $2.2 billion in deposits. The key was to make the process as frictionless as possible for the customer to open the account.

Open Innovation

The cooperation between traditional financial institutions and fintech startups is an example of open innovation. Open innovation is the use of purposive inflows and outflows of knowledge to accelerate internal innovation and expand the markets for external use of innovation, respec-

[12] https://www.unicreditgroup.eu/content/dam/unicreditgroup-eu/documents/en/sustainability/reporting-and-metrics/integrated_report/Intellectual_Capital_BI2015.pdf, Accessed 26 July 2016.

tively (Chesbrough 2006). Open innovation is a paradigm that assumes that firms can and should use external ideas as well as internal ideas, and internal and external paths to market, as they look to advance their technology. Open innovation processes combine internal and external ideas into architectures and systems. Open innovation processes utilize business models to define the requirements for these architectures and systems. The business model utilizes both external and internal ideas to create value while defining internal mechanisms to claim some portion of that value. Open innovation assumes internal ideas can also be taken to market through external channels, outside the current businesses of the firm, to generate additional value.

This type of relationship is raising fundamental questions about the way the distribution of financial products is currently structured. It is possible to imagine a new distribution model with financial institutions operating as product design platforms, selling unbranded solutions to captive, or non-captive fintech startups, and capable of adapting more readily to changes in the user needs. In this case, acquiring a fintech startup as a subsidiary would make sense, as it would enable financial institutions to secure their distribution channels. The risk with this model is that the fintech startup, which is in charge of the customer relationship, might outgrow the platform supplying the financial products. The question thus is if financial institutions really have the capacity to keep pace with fintech startups' growth.

Conclusions

Up to now, traditional financial services have responded largely by collaborating with fintech startups rather than seeking to acquire them. As a result, a number of partnerships have emerged between major institutions and newcomers, a trend that could shape the future of the financial services sector.

Financial institutions need to develop partnerships with fintech companies for several reasons such as to retain customers and innovate, whereas fintech startups need partnerships with financial institutions for several other reasons, including the availability of funds.

There are many challenges in such a partnership, but it is a "wedding made in heaven". The task to make it successful is hard but achievable.

To do this, financial services providers and regulators will have to work together to figure out how to allow more access to the financial system to bring customers into the regular circuits. This is the subject of the following chapter.

References

Accenture Research. (2014). *A disruptive value stream for banks*. Retrieved February 21, 2017, from https://www.accenture.com/_acnmedia/Accenture/Conversion-Assets/DotCom/Documents/Global/PDF/Dualpub_21/Accenture-AS-Bank-Customer-Value-Ecosystem-POV.pdf.

Chesbrough, H. (2006). *Open innovation: The new imperative for creating and profiting from technology*. Cambridge, MA: Harvard Business School Press.

Chesbrough, H. W., Vanhaverbeke, W., & West, J. (2006). *Open innovation: Researching a new paradigm*. Oxford, UK: Oxford University Press.

Clarysse, B., Wright, M., Bruneel, J., & Mahajan, A. (2014). Creating value in ecosystems: Crossing the chasm between knowledge and business ecosystems. *ERC Research Paper, 22*, 1–45.

Cohen, S. L. (2013). What do accelerators do? Insights from incubators and Angels. *Innovations: Technology, Governance, Globalization, 8*(3–4), 19–25.

Cohen, S., & Hochberg, Y. V. (2014). Accelerating startups: The seed accelerator phenomenon. *SSRN Electronic Journal*, 1–16. doi:10.2139/ssrn.2418000.

Dietz, M., Moon, J., & Radnai, M. (2016, July). Fintechs can help incumbents, not just disrupt them. *McKinsey Review*. Retrieved August 24, 2016, from http://www.mckinsey.com/industries/financial-services/our-insights/fintechs-can-help-incumbents-not-just-disrupt-them

Ensor, L. (2013). Big business lags on empowerment, says Davies. *Business Day –Live*. Retrieved August 14, 2016, from http://www.bdlive.co.za/business/2013/10/17/bigbusiness-lags-on-empowerment-says-davies.

Greenbaum, S. I., Thakor, A. V., & Boot, A. W. A. (2015). *Contemporary financial intermediation* (3rd ed.). Amsterdam, The Netherlands: Elsevier Academic Press.

Hoffman, D. L., & Radojevich-Kelley, N. (2012). Analysis of accelerator companies: An exploratory case study of their programs, processes, and early results. *Small Business Institute Journal, 8*(2), 54–70.

King, B. (2016). *Augmented: Life in the smart lane.* Singapore: Marshall Cavendish International (Asia) Pte Ltd.

Koen, P. A., Bertels, H. M. J., & Elsum, I. R. (2011). The three faces of business model innovation: Challenges for established firms. *Research-Technology Management, 54*(3), 52–59.

Miller, P., & Bound, K. (2011). *The startup factories: The rise of accelerator programmes to support new technology ventures* (pp. 1–40). London, UK: Nesta.

Moschner, S. L., & Herstatt, C. (2016, July 3–6). *Overcoming the innovator's dilemma by keeping your enemies close—How incumbents can learn from entrepreneurial ventures.* R&D Management Conference 2016 From Science to Society: Innovation and Value Creation, Cambridge, UK

PwC. (2016). Blurred lines. How Fintech is shaping financial services. Retrieved February 22, 2017, from https://www.pwc.com/il/en/home/assets/pwc_fintech%20global_report.pdf

PwC—Price Waterhouse Coopers. (2016). *Global FinTech survey.* Retrieved February 20, 2017, from http://www.pwc.com/gx/en/industries/financial-services/fintech-survey/report.html.

Skan, J., Lumb, R., Masood, S., & Conway, S. K. (2014). *The Boom in global Fintech investment* (pp. 1–16). Accenture Report, London, UK.

Slaats, L. H. M. (2015). *Learning from Accelerator programs, a framework to analyse the success of FinTech Accelerator Programs for traditional banks.* Master Thesis, University of Utrecht, Utrecht, The Netherlands.

Spelier, P. (2014). Rabobank biedt Fintech startups een podium om zich door te ontwikkelen. *Finno.* Retrieved July 31, 2016, from https://finno.wordpress.com/2014/03/19/rabobank-biedtfintech-startups-een-podium-om-zich-door-te-ontwikkelen/

Teece, D. J. (2010). Business models, business strategy and innovation. *Long Range Planning, 43*(2–3), 172–194.

van Huijgevoort, T. (2012). *The 'business accelerator': Just a different name for a business incubator?* Utrecht School of Economics. Retrieved February 21, 2017, from http://www.dutchincubator.nl/uploads/Documents/49.pdf.

7

Regulations

Introduction

Fintech initiatives are now more and more in the spotlight. Their flurry of activities raises questions over what kind of financial landscape will emerge because of the digital transformation. The critical questions are regarding the role that traditional financial institutions will play, but especially regarding the new risks that the new initiatives create for the customers of financial services.

This chapter addresses some of these issues. It looks at the challenges faced by regulators. It explores different approaches they could adopt to ensure a level-playing field for incumbent companies and newcomers and, at the same time, protect the customers of financial services. This chapter considers how financial regulations can contribute to supporting fintech initiatives in order to foster innovation. Most of this chapter follows the approach used by Dareolles (2016) in his paper.

B. Nicoletti, *The Future of FinTech*,
DOI 10.1007/978-3-319-51415-4_7

The Role of the Regulators

The financial services sector is undergoing big transformations. In this situation, it is important that regulators

- continue to assure a reasonable protection of the customers and of the system;
- avoid overprotection of the incumbents by building barriers to entry for newcomers. Doing so would discourage financial innovation in the economy and stifle competition in the sector they are supervising; and
- choose instead to favor newcomers by possibly regulating them less stringently than incumbents.

A couple of examples are useful to clarify these challenges and their dangers: customer identification in internet payments and in bank account aggregation services (Dareolles 2016).

For online and mobile payments, customers have access to a range of different options. The trend is to use simpler and more user-friendly identification solutions than the standard login-and-password approach. These solutions are very different from the traditional approaches used by financial services. The European directive on access to banking information covers the range of new uses and innovative services positioned between the financial services and their customers.[1] Under this directive, new payment service providers are subject to the same rules as other payment institutions (Górka 2016). There might be concerns about security.

Bank account aggregation services create a similar problem. These applications need to retrieve information from the financial institutions on their customers' banking activity. The customer needs to send credentials for his/her different accounts to the aggregator. The aggregator, in turn, uses them repeatedly to construct an overview of the customer's finances. Financial institutions are constantly receiving requests for data using customer identification codes, without knowing whether they come from the customer or a potentially unauthorized third-party operator. The nec-

[1] http://eur-lex.europa.eu/legal-content/EN/TXT/?uri=COM%3A2015%3A630%3AFIN, Accessed 05 August 2016.

essary first step is to improve the traceability of these connection requests. Financial institutions believe that actions that are more protective need to be in place. They also ask for the use of strong identification systems. In this case, third-party operators would need to request authentication each time they send a request to the financial institution's systems. This situation would not appeal to the customers. In fact, an account aggregator would need to ask its customers to re-enter their credentials each day, for each of their accounts. There are issues connected in this way with security. Regulators can respond by issuing recommendations on the security of cashless payment systems or online access to bank accounts. At the end, the customers should decide whether to adopt a solution or not. Financial institutions are obliged to give service providers access to information on their customers. This means, for example, that a financial institution cannot stop an aggregator from accessing its customers' details by advising the latter not to give a third-party access to their accounts. This raises the question on who should pay for the infrastructure needed for this type of interconnection and the resolution of any issue of interconnectivity. The most critical issue it raises is that of security, since the sharing and use of customer identification details increases the threat of cyber-attacks. If a payment services provider is hacked, it could unintentionally propagate the attack to all its customers' financial services. Traditional financial institutions ask for tighter security regulations for new entrants. They raise concerns about the authentication systems they use.

Equal Treatment and Competition

These examples demonstrate the difficulties regulators face in reconciling innovation and security. This is true for all the countries, but the responses of the regulators are different. China, for instance, has an open, supportive regulatory environment (Ngai et al. 2016). In fact, in 2013, the People's Bank of China explicitly expressed support for tech companies to promote internet finance.[2]

[2] https://www.mckinsey.it/idee/whats-next-for-chinas-booming-fintech-sector, Accessed 20 August 2016.

Regulators have a difficult role to play, as their decisions have both a direct and an indirect impact on competition between incumbent companies and newcomers. They need to provide a level-playing field for all participants. At the same time, they should foster an innovative, secure, and competitive financial market.

It is interesting to examine what the Swiss regulator did against money laundering. The Financial Market Supervisory Authority, or FINMA, has modified its Anti-Money Laundering Ordinance to reflect directly changes in technology.[3] The revised version covers internet payments and identification procedures. The regulator allows online authentication. FINMA has defined specific thresholds below which customers do not need to identify themselves formally. This is a good example of how regulators can take into account the needs of innovation without affecting security.

Regulators need to look more generally at the incentives offered to market agents and the way these incentives can modify their behavior.[4] They also need to keep a harmonized set of rules in place. There is resistance to apply different regulations to different categories of players. This would create silos in the financial industry with different obligations to comply with. In this way, it is possible to prevent the emergence of new players and discouraging financial innovation. Keeping newcomers out distorts the market in favor of existing players. Authorities might tend to regulate existing players more tightly, as they know their business well. They might take a laxer stance toward market entrants whose activities are new, and who have not been through sufficient crises to evaluate completely the risks they pose. Regulators face a difficult task in finding the right balance, on one side, allowing existing players to survive, and on the other, to facilitate innovation by new entrants.

It is interesting to outline some general principles (Dareolles 2016):

- Maintain a neutral stance with regard to technological advances. Regulations should foster healthy competition between institutions,

---

[3] https://www.finma.ch/en/#Order=4, Accessed 29 July 2016.

[4] http://www.fca.org.uk/static/channel-page/business-plan/business-plan-2015-16.html, Accessed 20 August 2016.

regardless of whether they offer conventional approaches or use new technological solutions.
- Keep in place a harmonized set of rules. These rules should cover all players at the same time, rather than treating players differently according to their characteristics. Whether the financial institution is using an online or a conventional method for processing transactions should not affect how the regulators see them.
- Protect the customers of the financial system as well as the system itself. Regulators must act in the interests of customers, protecting them in a changing environment that can pose new, unanticipated risks. At the same time, they should assure that the system is functioning well and is stable from a financial point of view.

The respect of these principles is not easy. An example is as follows. In terms of customer authentication, there are several technologies to simplify this step. Each one of them entails very different risks. Rejecting the notion of online identification outright would make it more difficult to innovate. It would stifle innovation and prevent new solutions from emerging to tackle problems already identified. In contrast, allowing online identification for transactions below a specific threshold would encourage the development of new solutions. It would eventually give rise to more efficient tools that limit the risks of fraud. This approach would allow regulators to meet two of the above-listed principles, despite them being hard to reconcile. This is already happening in other financial fields. For instance, there is now a threshold for credit cards payment authorization which, when done using the fast approach of Near Field Communication (NFC) reading, do not require a lengthy signature from the customer.[5]

It is also difficult to see how it is possible to treat fintech initiatives, which sometimes are highly specialized, in the same way as traditional players. The latter are much more generalists with respect to the former. The solution for regulators could be to create new categories of financial intermediary, subject to less stringent requirements than financial services. This would allow relaxing some rules under specific conditions, for exam-

[5] https://usa.visa.com/dam/VCOM/download/merchants/card-acceptance-guidelines-for-merchants.pdf, Accessed 20 August 2016.

ple if there is no exposition to liquidity mismatch for the new entities in question. A market newcomer does not really qualify as a bank if it has no liquidity mismatch. In that situation the risk for its customers is much less. Therefore, new entrants that respect these conditions do not need to be fully compliant with the regulations valid for traditional institutions.

European Regulations

Since 2007, the European Union Payment Service Directive has established non-bank payment service providers (so called, payment institutions) enjoying lighter authorization and stability requirements. They might be taken into account whenever fintech entrepreneurs operate in the area of payments.

The Payment Service Directive 1 (PSD1) is not fully equipped to deal with new technologies and fintech companies. Topics such as supervision, security, and data protection are important for the customers to trust these new companies and their technology. In order to accommodate these developments and companies, the European Commission (EC) initiated the revision of the PSD1. The EC created the Payment Service Directive 2 (PSD2).[6] The PSD2 legally justifies fintech companies to deliver some new and innovative services based on financial data. The PSD2 legally forces banks to give third parties access to bank accounts of their customers. This access, which is currently only available to banks, will make financial data and the ability to initiate transactions available to the fintech industry on a large scale.

Banks are referred to as account servicing payment service providers (AS-PSPs). The companies delivering the services are called third-party payment service providers (TPPs). The services they provide consist of the use of customer data, also referred to as account information services (AIS), and the ability to initiate a payment, also known as payment initiation services (PIS). Together, they are commonly referred to as payment accounts access services (PAAS).

[6] Reijers, J., Jacobs, B.P.F., and Poll, I.E. (2016). Payment Service Directive 2. Master Thesis, Radboud University Nijmegen, the Netherlands.

By allowing TPPs to enter the market for certain financial services, currently dominated by banks, the EC expects more economic growth and, thus, welfare in the EU. More players allow more competition. This would translate into a positive effect on the types and pricing of financial services. This development supports innovation and allows for more diversity of services provided to customers and in that way, providing more choices.

The Risks to Consider

Technical progress fosters innovation. It also brings new risks. At the same time, the primary mandate of regulators is to protect the customers and the investors of financial services, and assure the stability of the financial system. This section analyzes three risks on which regulators need to focus:

- The threat of cyber-attacks
- The risks related to the outsourcing of certain traditional financial services activities
- The issues with Big Data Analytics

Financial services are prime targets for cyber-attacks. The emergence of online and mobile services, designed to be simple and interactive, only makes these risks more likely. In a worst-case scenario, it is possible to imagine a series of concerted attacks triggering a liquidity squeeze in the markets and threatening the solvency of a specific institution. It is not simple to know how to evaluate these new risks. There is no history to use for constructing realistic scenarios. Regulators could take a pragmatic approach. They can define possible attacks and test the defense mechanisms put in place by companies. The problem is that innovation is continuously opening up new possibilities of attack. Only the availability of in-depth expertise in this field can make regulators able to fulfill their role.

The outsourcing of certain activities is another source of risk. In the past, a large number of financial institutions carried out internally almost all activities in the value chain. Therefore, only one overall entity was subject to regulation. More and more these days, the situation has completely changed, both for conventional players and especially for startups. In the case of traditional financial services, cost pressures are pushing companies to outsource some traditional activities, such as computerized transaction processing, onto external service providers. In the case of activities with a high technological content, it is interesting to find a trend toward outsourcing them to specialized and more agile players, who are better at using new technologies and are more likely to be cost-effective, thanks to volume scale. The value chain is a responsibility partially of the regulated financial institutions and partially of other players that are not necessarily subject to the supervision. This makes it hard to predict how the relationship between financial institutions and their outsourcers would evolve if a crisis threatened an institution's solvency. It is not clear if the service provider would agree to continue to process transactions if the financial institution were in trouble. Although economically viable in normal times, outsourcing raises a new risk of coordination in times of crisis. Similarly, a default by a service provider with a monopoly or oligopoly position could create a new systemic risk.

The question of outsourcing concerns especially startups. Many fintech startups use the services of traditional financial institutions in core banking systems or even their licenses. In some cases, this helps them in starting to provide financial services immediately. It also allows them to concentrate on adding value, via CRM, without having to pay to develop their own service operation components. These new players are therefore highly likely to use outsourcing. Being in today's sharing and virtual economy, they feel the pressure to look for efficient and low-cost solutions to handle the least profitable and non-core specific activities in the value chain. For regulators, outsourcing has many different consequences and, in this case, the challenges of technological innovation affect both historical and new market players. It is particularly important for the customers and regulators to verify the resilience of the outsourcers and extend to them their supervision (Nicoletti 2016).

Regulators should devote attention to the use of Big Data Analytics, not only at institutional level but also at commercial level. The objective should be to avoid negative consequences that are discriminatory against groups of individuals. Regulators should be vigilant in three main directions:

- Data collection must not infringe the privacy of individuals.
- The classification of risks must not become a constraint in the market.
- The use of information about the personal life should not be a discrimination tool.

Barnard-Wills (2016) wrote an interesting book that can provide more insights on this subject.

Regtech

To close this chapter on a positive note, there are fintech companies that can help in complying with regulations. They are called regtech. They apply innovation to provide solutions to the complex challenges of achieving compliance with regulatory requirements. The FCA describes them as a subset of fintech initiatives that focuses on technologies that may facilitate the delivery of regulatory requirements more efficiently, effectively, and economically than existing capabilities.[7]

The objectives of regtech companies in supporting financial institutions include:

- New regulations: The introduction of new regulations presents a series of challenges from understanding the regulations, scoping for individual organizations, strategic and operational planning of resources for implementing modifications or new applications. The time to respect the new regulations is normally rather short.

[7] https://www.the-fca.org.uk/firms/project-innovate-innovation-hub/regtech, Accessed 18 July 2016.

- Existing regulations: Financial institutions need to assure continuous compliance that may be in the form of reporting, audits, respect of governance requirements, and so on.

Regtech initiatives provide the following solutions[8]:

- Compliance and conduct analytics: conduct risk assessment matrices
- Regulatory compliance automation.
- Regulation-specific on-demand service documentation and audit
- Employee surveillance: behavioral assessment, voice and electronic communication screening
- Fraud prevention: anti-money laundering (AML), transaction monitoring, and fraud detection
- Reporting and fraud detection: on-demand, user-tailored compliance risk reporting
- Compliance data warehouse and case management

EY categorize regtech solutions with respect to what they offer[9]:

- Fraud prevention
  - These solutions monitor transactions in real time to identify gaps, issues, and trends in financial malpractices. Prevention can reduce the risks and associated cost of loss funds due to fraud.
  - Companies can use analytical capability for examining a very large number of different data points to identify potential threats to financial security.
  - Solutions can support, in real time, verification of decisions for their compliance. In this way, regtech solutions can also help in the operational field.

[8] http://www.ey.com/Publication/vwLUAssets/EY-Innovating-with-regtech/$FILE/EY-Innovating-with-regtech.pdf, Accessed 18 July 2016.

[9] http://www.ey.com/Publication/vwLUAssets/EY-Innovating-with-regtech/$FILE/EY-Innovating-with-regtech.pdf, Accessed 18 July 2016.

- Regulatory compliance automation
  - Regtech platforms can potentially support interpreting regulations, and include upcoming changes.
  - Several regtech initiatives are addressing the key challenges to build a converged regulatory risk and controls management framework.
  - Robotics can perform routine compliance monitoring and testing processes.
  - Robo-advisors use sophisticated algorithms to provide customers with automated advice without human intervention.
- Conduct and culture
  - Solutions to behavioral profiling and behavior-driven risks to indicate potential misconduct and map out company culture
  - The quantification of the impact of cultural change initiatives
- Predictive analytics
  - Analytics can support in forecasting organization-specific operational and regulatory risks.
  - Analytics can help in finding the root causes of previous regulatory breaches. It can use them to predict potential risk areas and disruptive events in the financial markets. It can also support possible remediation.

The one single biggest benefit of regtech solutions is in supporting a multiregulatory environment. Many regulations have in common the same data, processes, or governance structures. This often leads to multiplication of efforts for financial institutions. The implementation of a regtech solution can allow financial institutions to avoid such duplication or multiplication. It can empower them to achieve organizational effectiveness, efficiencies, and economics.

Regtech solutions are interesting for professional organizations that currently provide personnel to do the job. In this way, they can move from providing services to providing products. High-end professional service firms that work for corporate clients have a clear upside. Because they provide specialized expertise, their offerings can be very lucrative. There is a downside. If a consulting company wants to double its revenue, it has to double its staff of consultants. Technology offers these companies a way out. They can leverage the power of algorithm-driven automation and data analytics to “productive” aspects of their work. They can increase their margins as they grow while offering better service to their customers at prices that competitors cannot match (Sawheny 2016). An interesting solution for example for compliance professional services is to move to regtech solutions.

There is a large amount of activity in the field of regtech initiatives. There will be more such activity in the future with the availability of better and effective solutions and the expected need to comply with more regulations. The idea of regtech itself presents an excellent opportunity to financial institutions. It can help to address the heavy and time-consuming activity of regulatory compliance.

An interesting development is the use of AI in regtech initiatives. This means not only automation of ordinary activities associated with compliance (Svärd 2012). It would also mean using robo-advisors or neural networks for performing complex activities that currently require professionals.

Examples of regtech companies[10]

Examples of Irish regtech companies include:

FundRecs—creates reconciliation software for the funds industry

Silverfinch—creates connectivity between asset managers and insurers through a fund data utility in a secure and controlled environment

Trustev—prevents online fraud by scanning transactions in real time to determine whether they are fraudulent

TradeFlow—provides trade data tracking and risk alert-based technology

Vizor—creates software to support the supervision of companies by a supervisory authority, such as a central bank, financial regulator, or tax authority

Corlytics—creates software that analyzes compliance risks in financial institutions

AQMetrics—delivers high-quality integrated regulatory risk and compliance management solutions

[10] http://www2.deloitte.com/content/dam/Deloitte/ie/Documents/FinancialServices/ie-regtech-pdf.pdf, Accessed 05 August 2016.

FundApps

"Firms that have embraced modern solutions in regard to infrastructure, including best-of-breed cloud-based technology, have already reaped the rewards of lower overall costs with greater scalability and efficiency. More importantly, the industry is only beginning to realize how technologies that have actually been around for some time are highly complementary in a world where regulation is changing constantly."—Karl Schindler, Head of Content, FundApps[11]

London-based FundApps is an example of a regtech company.[12] Founded in 2010, FundApps, had two very simple aims for its compliance monitoring and reporting solution:

1. Make it cloud based
2. Maintain a team of compliance experts who can update the platform as new regulations emerge

Core to the company's success was the solution's ability to scale and flex as new regulations emerged. This would not only be beneficial to the company's overall cost and client servicing model but also help in reducing the regulatory burden its clients faced and in increasing its overall value proposition to them. The ways to get these results were cloud technologies, accessible development capabilities, and an ecosystem at the TechHub in London that powered its growth.[13]

Hogan Lovells

"Cost and management time devoted to becoming and being authorized are a major investment for any business. We know that the FCA has gone a long way to help with their regulatory accelerator program but we also know

(continued)

[11] https://www.fundapps.co/blog/karl-schindler-featured-by-regtech-summit, Accessed 26 August 2016.

[12] https://www.fundapps.co/, Accessed 20 August 2016.

[13] http://www2.deloitte.com/content/dam/Deloitte/ie/Documents/FinancialServices/ie-regtech-pdf.pdf, Accessed 20 August 2016.

Hogan Lovells (continued)

that this is not available for everyone, so we have created our own tool to address the challenges we see fintech clients facing on a daily basis."—Rachel Kent, Global Head of Hogan Lovells' financial institutions sector[14]

Hogan Lovells has launched an online tool to help fintech startups gain a better understanding of FCA regulations.[15] The law company will be providing the tool free to businesses that take part in regulated activities in the United Kingdom.

The company has launched its regulatory accelerator to help fintech companies understand FCA regulations when starting up and to address the challenges of scaling their business. The accelerator consists of tools and resources to help businesses

- understand the FCA application process;
- whether or not they need to be an authorized company; and
- whether they are conducting regulated activities or are making financial promotions.

The tool helps fintech startups enter the market in an easier, quicker, and less expensive way.

Conclusions

The current regulatory approach is subject to significant political economy and coordination costs. Therefore, this makes it hard to deliver structural change (Philippon 2016). Fintech initiatives, on the other hand, can bring deep changes, but they are likely to create significant regulatory challenges.

Up to now, traditional financial services have responded largely by collaborating with fintech startups rather than seeking to acquire them. The digital transformation offers a huge growth potential for the financial

[14] http://www.gtreview.com/news/global/hogan-lovells-launches-fintech-regulatory-accelerator/, Accessed 26 August 2016.

[15] http://www.lsbf.org.uk/blog/news/accountancy-finance/law-firm-launches-online-tool-fintech-startups/100716, Accessed 06 August 2016.

sector. It is essential that the necessary regulatory changes do not make it difficult to innovate while providing the stability the system needs to meet customer expectations, and reduce risks and hassle for them.

Regtech initiatives could support with new and interesting solutions.

References

Barnard-Wills, D. (2016). *Surveillance and identity: Discourse, subjectivity and the state*. London, UK: Routledge.

Dareolles S. (2016). The rise of Fintechs and their regulation. *Financial Stability Review*, *20*, 85–92.

Górka, J. (Ed.). (2016). *Transforming payment systems in Europe*. Heidelberg, Germany: Springer.

Ngai, J. L., Qu, J., & Zhou, N. (2016, July). China's innovation engine picks up speed. *McKinsey Review*. Retrieved August 25, 2016, from http://www.mckinsey.com/business-functions/strategy-and-corporate-finance/our-insights/chinas-innovation-engine-picks-up-speed

Nicoletti, B. (2016). Resilience and outsourcing. *PMWORLD*, *2*, 16.

Philippon, T. (2016). *The Fintech opportunity*. CEPR Discussion Paper No. DP11409.

Reijers, J., Jacobs, B. P. F., & Poll, I. E. (2016). *Payment Service Directive 2*. Thesis for the Degree of Master of Science in Information Sciences at the Radboud University Nijmegen, The Netherlands.

Sawheny, M. (2016), Putting products into services, *Harvard Business Review*, 82–89.

Svärd, C. (2012). *Methods for automated design of fault detection and isolation systems*. PhD thesis dissertations, Linköping Studies in Science and Technology, Linköping Studies in Science and Technology, Linköping University, Linköping, Sweden.

8

A Business Model for Insurtech Initiatives

Introduction

Fintech companies are reshaping the financial services industry, providing the market with innovative value propositions, backed by forward-looking strategies and cutting-edge business models.

The previous chapters focused on the analysis of this highly heterogeneous fintech environment. They provided insights about the behavior of those companies that populate it. The classification provided in Chapter 3 supports the comprehension of the big picture.

This chapter considers an important subject, relative to "insurtech", the insurance-specific branch of fintech.[1] Such companies are rethinking the insurance value chain by means of technology. The insurance industry is ripe for technological disruption. The results might not be pleasant. Fintech startups have relentlessly targeted some areas of financial services, mainly in payments. Now it is the turn of insurance companies. Nine out of ten insurance executives polled by the consultant company

[1] PwC (2016), Insurtech: A golden opportunity for insurers to innovate. http://www.PwC.com/us/en/insurance/publications/assets/PwC-top-issues-insurtech.pdf, Accessed 31 July 2016.

B. Nicoletti, *The Future of FinTech*,
DOI 10.1007/978-3-319-51415-4_8

PricewaterhouseCoopers reckon that at least part of their business is at risk over the next five years—a greater proportion than in any other area of finance.[2]

According to CB Insights, in the first quarter of 2016, insurtech companies received $650 million in funding, showing off twice the transactions of the same period in 2015.[3] This chapter focuses on the application of the model presented in this book to insurtech. This chapter gives insights about the way it could overcome some of their current challenges.

A word of caution on this chapter is important. This chapter examines insurtech initiatives. The final part of this chapter tries to overcome the dichotomy that banking and insurance are two completely different and segmented subjects. More and more cross-fertilization and communication in products, processes, organizations, and business models is happening and will happen even more in the future. An example is Bancassurance. Unit-linked policies are another one (Koller 2012).

Drivers of Disruption

Each company must allocate part of its budget to technology investments. An important question is on the amount that should be invested and in which technology. These two questions help in understanding the peculiarities of the environment in which each business organization operates, and, first and especially, that no one-rule-fits-all exists. A certain degree of uncertainty is always modifying and changing the outcomes of a company's action. Mathematical models often comprise exogenous parameters able to reflect the impact of uncertainty on their outcomes. Still their effectiveness is not always guaranteed.

Insurtech companies, as well as all other business organizations, have a limited control on their external environment, which has recently shown

[2] http://blogs.reuters.com/breakingviews/2016/07/13/fintech-bigger-and-dicier-for-insurers-than-banks/, Accessed 29 July 2016.

[3] http://www.insuranceup.it/upload/images/07_2016/160721131117.pdf, Accessed 29 July 2016.

some interesting developments. These developments display a clear technological connotation.

It is interesting to examine two aspects:

- To deepen the comprehension of the elements that have significantly changed the insurance sector after years of technological stalemate
- To better analyze the levers on which insurance companies should rely in the immediate future

The insurance industry, as a whole, may be positioned two to five years behind on the digital maturity curve when compared with the financial services industry altogether. However, going away from these mere technological issues, an interesting point to analyze deals with the changed expectations and needs of the customers.

The New Customers' Needs and Expectations

Customers have radically changed their way of conceiving the nature of the relationship with financial institutions. Therefore, financial institutions should not be tempted to remain static on their positions. They should look forward and try to anticipate their own competitors. Certainly, this is not as easy as it seems. Companies should be able to understand why their customers are changed, and how they can leverage on this in order to find more effective approaches in enhancing their interactions and in building trust-based relationships.

Within the boundaries of their business plans, insurtech initiatives should include the delivery of personalized value propositions to their customers. Several technologies may support this step. Suffice it to think about IoT: having already dealt with it in Chapter 4, it should be now clear how it helps businesses in the delivery of personalized propositions. An easy example is wearables, such as fitness wristbands. By tracking and monitoring the main health indicators, these devices could send that information to an insurance company, which may be then capable of providing better and tailored services, such as proposing simple incentives to decrease premiums.

The nature of customer interactions has changed, thanks to technology. Currently, insurance companies mainly focus on pushing for new deals and contracts, with customers who are passively recruited and are not fully aware of what they are signing up for. This is a clear symptom of the so-called information asymmetries (Binks et al. 1992). Customers are pursued by agencies and brokers. They have been the main players in what has been identified as a "sales heavy" model.[4]

The changing course is consequently moving toward an environment where the weight of customers is much more relevant. Insurance companies are getting more and more aware of this. Therefore, they are moving to a much different relationship and a much more interactive engagement. Relationships are developing toward "interaction", where customers are becoming active and central players in an environment that is becoming day by day more "customer-pull".

Eventually, things are also changing for what concerns policy and underwriting processes. Customers are now expecting completely different approaches, mainly supported by tech innovations, such as Big Data Analytics and online portals.

The Impact of Technology

Technology is one of the most important elements to consider when dealing with the ongoing development of the insurance industry (see Fig. 8.1[5]). Insurtech companies are completely aware of the strategical benefits of this lever: Startupbootcamp has analyzed over 1000 companies with the aim of identifying the areas where technology is supposed to have its major effects.[6]

ICT has been important for insurance companies. Still, ICT has not been important in insurance companies as it has been in banks.

---

[4] http://web.bi.no/forskning/papers.nsf/0/b723c0570c4026eac12575b0004a329a/$FILE/2009-04-Jensen.pdf, Accessed 20 August 2016.

[5] Startupbootcamp (2015), "So, what is an Insurtech startup?" http://www.startupbootcamp.org/blog/2015/october/so-what-is-an-insurance-startup-infographic.html, Accessed 20 August 2016.

[6] http://www.ey.com/Publication/vwLUAssets/EY-UK-FinTech-On-the-cutting-edge/$FILE/EY-UK-FinTech-On-the-cutting-edge.pdf, Accessed 23 August 2014.

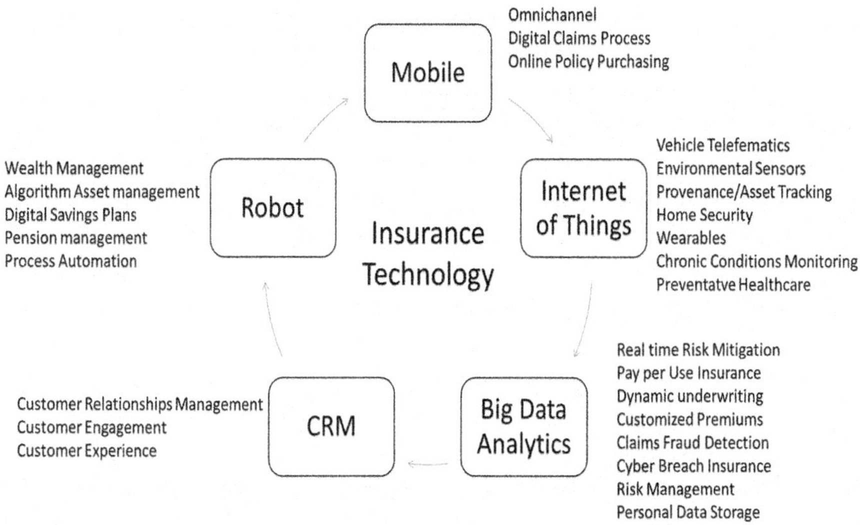

Fig. 8.1 Technology impact on insurance industry

ICT is becoming more and more important for insurance companies. There are several reasons why this is happening. Several forces can drive innovation:

- Markets (3 Cs: Customers, Competition, Compliance)
- Technology
- Design
- Compliance

This chapter examines the contribution of technology. ICT is in continuing development. Several new solutions are important for the fintech:

- Mobility
- Big Data Analytics
- IoT
- Social media
- Robots and AI
- Blockchain
- Cloud computing

It is interesting to examine the technologies more visible to customers (which are also a driving force).

Mobility is expanding at very high rates even in the presence of the current economic crisis, which is still affecting many economies in the world. The use of smartphones and tablets is expanding. The total number of mobile phones is almost equal to the world population. The sales of smartphones and tablets are expanding faster than traditional dumb phones and PCs. Mobile is influencing heavily the sales of insurance products. In some cases, it is the ideal solution. An example is travel insurance.

Big Data Analytics are technologies that are very important for insurance companies. Two uses stand out among the many: marketing support and risk management. These two technologies promise to move ICT from being a system of records to a system of engagement.[7] In other words, ICT can move from being a big archive to the operational support of decisions in insurance companies, such as the decision to accept re-insurances, decide on the premium on new risks, and so on.

IoT is particularly relevant in the case of insurance companies due to the possibility to base on it customized services for customers, such as the pay-per-use or based on your health fitness and life style.

The following sections give further insights about these areas when they focus on the application of the business model presented in this book. Nevertheless, it should be now clear how much potential might be unleashed by a massive use of technology within the insurance industry.

Insurance and Technology: Insurtech

PriceWaterhouseCoopers defines insurtech as the insurance-specific branch of fintech initiatives.[8] In particular, insurtech initiatives are actively leveraging on technology for providing innovative value proposi-

[7] http://www.forbes.com/forbes/welcome/?toURL=http://www.forbes.com/sites/joshbersin/2012/08/16/the-move-from-systems-of-record-to-systems-of-engagement/&refURL=https://www.google.it/&referrer=https://www.google.it/, Accessed 20 August 2016.

[8] PwC, "Insurtech: A golden opportunity for insurers to innovate", March 2016. http://www.PwC.com/us/en/insurance/publications/assets/PwC-top-issues-insurtech.pdf, Accessed 20 August 2016.

tions to their target markets, thus addressing their efforts in the achievement of a competitive advantage.

The insurance industry, according to PricewaterhouseCoopers, has not shown relevant changes for, more or less, 100 years.[9] During the last 10 years, technology has fostered transformation and innovations in every sector, carrying around exciting applications and cutting-edge business models (Nicoletti 2016). The size of its investments, if compared with fintech initiatives for the banking and payment sectors, follows pretty much the same pattern. This is an important indicator of the external appeal of the sector.

Technology is not the unique driver of disruption. Changes and additional developments in the financial services industry have also affected insurance companies. Customers have significantly changed and so have their expectations and needs.

Therefore, insurance companies should be able to fit this changed environment by adapting their business models to it, putting the costumer at the center of their strategies and being active, and not reactive, to changes and innovations.

Customer expectations are just one among all the elements relevant in the analysis regarding the drivers of disruption. Technology has had an impact on the so-called tech barriers, too, relevantly lowering them and allowing access into the insurance industry to several new players (Barry et al. 2011). The diffusion of open-source frameworks, development on demand, and cloud computing are others examples of technology facilitators for the new entrants. The results are causing unexpected disruptions and turbulences in the financial services market that was, by its very nature, stable and stationary in all its components.

Chapter 4 has analyzed some of the most important and unsettling innovations that are causing disruption in the financial services industry, most of the times referring to "fintech" altogether as their main recipient and beneficiary. Insurance companies, as part of fintech, may be identified as one of the branches of this industry where technology may have its best results as the example which is discussed in Chapter 4 relative to the application of Big Data Analytics.

[9] PwC, "Insurtech: A golden opportunity for insurers to innovate", March 2016. http://www.PwC.com/us/en/insurance/publications/assets/PwC-top-issues-insurtech.pdf, Accessed 20 August 2016.

The following sections analyze in detail the main drivers of disruption, trying to understand the possible developments of this industry and eventually suggesting a tailored implementation of the model developed in Chapter 3.

Application of the Model to the Insurance Industry

It is important to underline that the insurance universe is too large to allow building a model capable of fitting each of the organizations considered. In particular, the value proposition, the market, and the structure of revenues and costs are intrinsic aspects of every organization; however, they are not discussed in this chapter. Anyway, it is interesting to apply the business model presented in this book to the insurtech initiative (see Fig. 8.2).

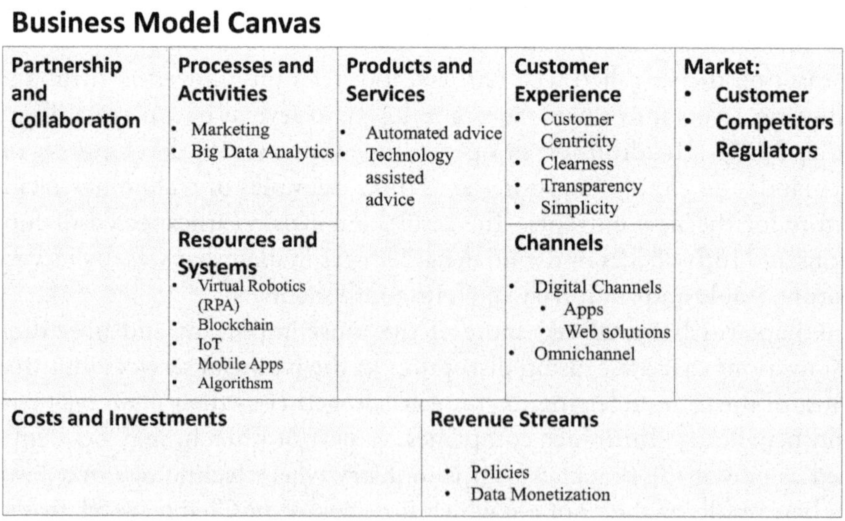

Fig. 8.2 Insurtech business model

Insurance and insurtech companies have several points in common. Although the financial base of the former, in some cases, is significantly greater than that of the latter, insurtech is the natural evolution of insurance: according to Darwinian principles of evolution (Darwin 1859), insurtech is the outcome of a still ongoing process of adaptation and mutual influence with regard to the external environment.

By cautiously adopting this perspective, a possible interpretation is as follows: the model aims to provide each company operating in the insurance industry with general and practical guidelines to becoming a successful organization.

The previous section dealt with the drivers that have disrupted the insurance industry, which McKinsey (2016) describes in the following paragraphs (Fig. 8.3):

- Poor engagement: "Life insurers have long struggled to engage prospective customers and nurture relationships with existing ones. The prod-

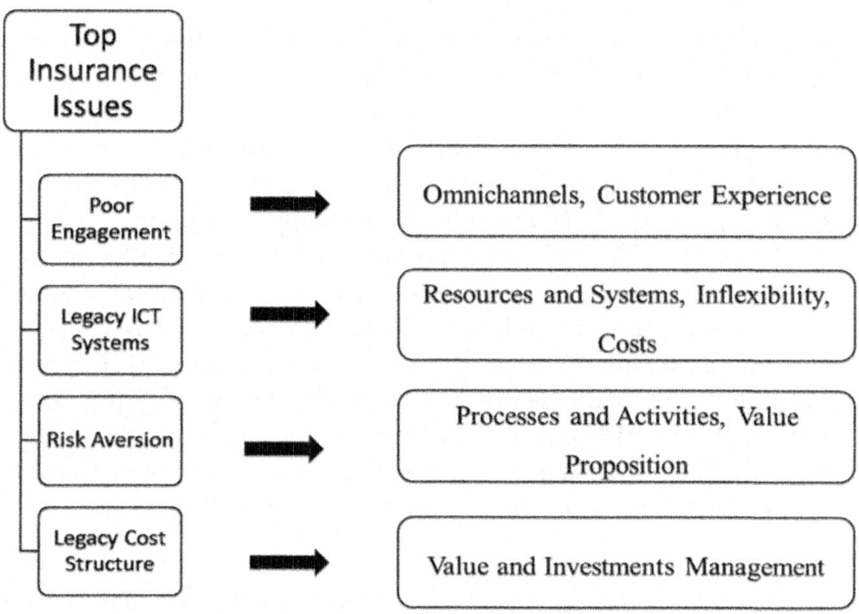

Fig. 8.3 Insurance issues and business model

uct purse high customer interest but low engagement, leading to significant untapped demand" (McKinsey 2016). The high degree of intermediation between insurers and consumers does not help in reducing their distance, this being due to agencies, banks, independent financial advisors, and brokers vertically operating within the distribution channels. The low digitalization of the whole industry does not match the expectations of the new generation of customers, such as the millennials. These customers do not rely on their private sphere, as family or friend, to get information. They prefer online reviews or social communities such as specialized forums and other online platforms. With the drastic diffusion of smartphones and other mobile devices, millennials affect the behavior of the old generation of customers. This is known as the "equalizing effect" (McKinsey 2016). Its aftermath may constitute a serious issue for a static and low digitized industry that has always been targeting a market predominantly populated by non-digital natives. The organizations that have shown a management mindset, a forward-looking attitude, and a digital firepower are relatively few, leading to opening the door to agile, digital-oriented innovators: insurtech startups.

- Legacy cost and investment structures: New startups have the possibility to deliver leading-edge propositions without incurring in transformation costs for incumbent organizations. This is not true in the case of traditional life insurance companies. They most likely have policies stipulated 20, maybe 30, years ago, implying an inflexible set of customers and policies that are difficult and costly to transform.
- Legacy ICT systems: Still referring to life insurers, the rigidity of their stock of policies and customers goes hand in hand with the employment of old processes and ICT systems. McKinsey (2016) suggests that the combination of legacy cost structures and legacy ICT systems has caused the total expense ratio to decline by only 0.5 percentage points (2000–2013) in key European markets.[10]
- Risk aversion: The insurance industry has often been static, averse to change and innovation: high product development cycles, low ICT

[10] Average expense ratio (expense per Gross World Product (GWP)) from 2000 to 2013; unweighted average expense ratios of Austria, Belgium, France, Germany, Ireland, Italy, the Netherlands, Portugal, Spain, Sweden, and the United Kingdom (McKinsey Global Insurance Pools).

investments, and slow delivery decisions have been serious bottlenecks for many insurance companies trying to grow. Somebody has labeled insurers as "slow fishes", operating in a "sea" built on stability and risk reluctance.

Figure 8.3 emphasizes the linkages between the main issues affecting the insurance industry and the model presented. It can provide insights into the factors that have or could create difficulties for the whole sector. It is interesting to consider the different paths within the model presented in this book. If it is possible to single out the adverse factors, it should be possible also to consider the possible remediation.

As a first step, it is interesting to position the four main issues identified by McKinsey in the associated area. This is the macro-area of the business model that is supposed to affect (positively or negatively) the issue taken into account (Fig. 8.4).

Chapter 3 describes a model with the objective to fit whichever fintech startups. For better fitting the insurance industry, it is necessary to make some adaptations. In particular, every startup should address its focus toward the following important elements:

(a) Market—focus on targets
(b) Products and services—focus on value added

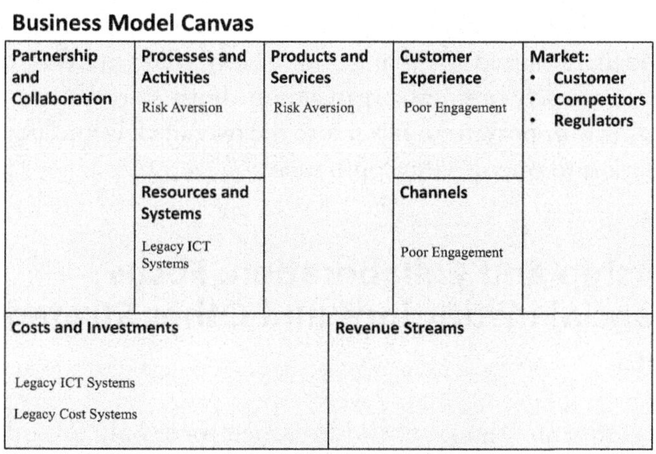

Fig. 8.4 Top insurance issues and business model

(c) Channels—focus on social and omnichannel
(d) Customer experience—focus on customer-centric approach
(e) Revenue—focus on customer lifetime value
(f) Processes and activities—focus on marketing
(g) Resources and systems—focus on technology
(h) Partnership and collaboration—focus on financial institutions
(i) Costs and investments—focus on risks

This framework better fits the new environment for a startup operating in the financial services industry. Considering different classes in fintech initiatives, the difference would be the weight of the different items in the list, together with their specific aims and objectives. Considering the "partnership and collaboration" area, for instance, the weight of financial institutions is quite different when referring to an insurance company or a marketplace lending company; this being the reason why here the focus in not on "financial institutions", but rather on "financial institutions and other strategic partners".

It is interesting to analyze which kind of organization mostly benefits from the business model presented in this book. Even though this model is mainly applicable to new entrants and to those companies that are willing to transform drastically their business, every organization that is performing its business in the insurance industry can benefit from the insights given in this chapter. Setting the stage for innovation and contextually being inspired by change are clearly elements that must lead the mindset of each business organization, both startups and seasoned companies. It is important to never lose the overall view and not limit the transformation to one specific component.

Partnership and Collaboration: Focus on Financial institutions and Other Strategical Partners

Insurtech companies should not address their focus only toward financial services. Still, this chapter deepens this type of relationship, since it is one of the most relevant.

Today, more than ever, insurance industry has been experiencing significant changes in its structural components, exposing business organizations to new risks and challenges. It is in this new scenario that insurance companies need to find vigor with the aim of more effectively pursuing competitive advantages. Cooperation is a powerful tool that, if well managed, allows companies to produce more revenues while minimizing costs.

Partnerships between financial institutions and insurers may not be identified as a recent trend; several business models have indeed been thought of in order to more effectively extract value from this type of relationship: most of them are encompassed by the bank insurance model (BIM), a new insurance branch which provides for new ways of doing business (Saunders 2004).

One potential first step for an insurance company is to establish a partnership with a bank. Figure 8.5 lists the most important elements to consider in a partnership.

Once, based on these elements, the insurance company has opted for a single or multiple partners, different scenarios are possible:

- The insurtech company has a leading position.
- The bank has a leading position. Or
- A joint venture is created.

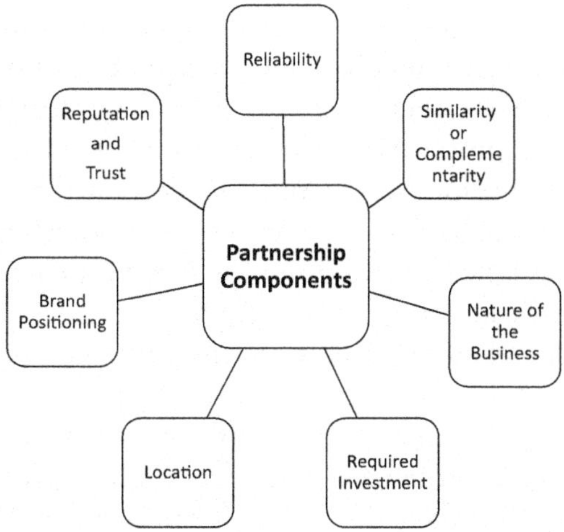

Fig. 8.5 Partnership components

This differentiation (Oliynyk and Sabirova 2013) aims to explain the strategical rationale behind every choice. Practically speaking, it gives interesting clarifications about the reason why financial institutions and insurers establish business relationships in each of the three scenarios.

Cooperation between financial institutions and insurtech companies is a necessary step capable of bringing about significant benefits to both the organizations:

1. Economies of scale and costs reduction
2. Market share growth
3. Diversification
4. Achievement of synergies

Financial institutions and insurers decide to undertake cooperation with the aim of increasing revenues while reducing costs, therefore being able to raise profits. This objective is the engine of any decision-making process: managers have to figure out thoroughly the impact of their decisions, contextually adopting the necessary mindset, which has to be forward-looking but always cautious.

Analytical components may affect two elements: revenues and costs, whereas combining and balancing these components is part of the decision-making process.

The first benefit that usually companies take into consideration is the enlargement of their customer base. Both financial institutions and insurers may actually merge their customer bases, contextually maintaining their own one. This process is usually structured on a fee basis. Insurance companies apply a fee for every transaction generated between their own customer base and the bank partner (and vice-versa), whereas the amount of the applied fees strictly depends on the bargaining power of the business organizations taken into consideration.

Sometimes, the relationship between insurance companies and financial institutions goes a little beyond the enlargement of the customer base, providing for the synergic development of new financial products and services. This may generate a competitive advantage.

Leveraging on a partnership with a financial institution also has its effects on the allocation of risks, whereas the same concept remains valid for the geographical diversification. It allows avoiding the concentration of risks in specific areas, while increasing the customer base through the penetration of different markets.

Economies of scale, instead, produce effects in the cost area, allowing organizations to generate a cost advantage by means of an increased output, thanks to the scaling of volumes.

The Empowerment of Customers

This section aims to clarify how insurtech startups and incumbent insurance companies that are willing to bring about serious changes to their business plans should deal with the general empowerment of their customers, at the same time, leveraging on them to achieve a competitive advantage.

Practically speaking, this section deals with three of the areas shown in the model presented in this book:

1. Processes and activities—focus on marketing
2. Customer experience—focus on customer-centric approach
3. Channels—focus on social and omnichannel

These three areas are very much interconnected. This interconnection justifies a combined presentation.

The main issues that are negatively influencing the market, especially incumbent organizations are:

- Poor engagement
- Risk aversion

Whereas for new entrants and recent startups, it may be easier to design their businesses in accordance with this model, incumbents must face severe transformation hurdles, which could end up with negative consequences if not well managed.

This book does provide guidelines on processes. It underlines a clear line capable of linking insurance companies with their objectives, to design a pattern. At the same time, it is important to remember that the ways through which these changes and innovations are implemented, and in which extent, are out of the aim of this book.

A European-wide study[11] commissioned by Fujitsu may support in perceiving the scale of the shift concerning the interaction between insurance companies and their customers.[12]

In particular, this study underlines the following facts[13]:

- More than a third of European customers would move out of banks or insurers if they did not offer up-to-date technology to aid interaction.
- Nearly a third are already embracing mobile payments. A fifth are already using wearables and cryptocurrency to pay.
- Almost a fifth would buy banking or insurance services from challengers such as Google, Facebook, and Amazon.

Specifically dealing with insurance companies, a Fujitsu press release (2016) states:

"Across Europe, 97% of those surveyed said they were happy for financial institutions or insurers to use their data to offer them a wider range of services; a huge shift in consumer mindset.

- Almost three in five (59%) would be happy for their bank or insurer to use their data to lower their mortgage premium.
- Nearly half (47%) of consumers would allow financial institutions or insurers to use their data to recommend relevant products and services.

[11] Fujitsu EMEIA (2016), Banking on Change: Consumers Drive Digital Charge in Financial Services, May. http://www.fujitsu.com/fts/about/resources/news/press-releases/2016/emeai-160504-banking-on-change-consumers-drive-digital.html, Accessed 20 August 2016.

[12] Around 7000 online consumer across the United Kingdom, France, Benelux , Spain, Germany, Switzerland, and Eastern Europe to understand consumers' habits and their views and opinions on current financial services.

[13] Fujitsu EMEIA (2016), ibid.

- More than two in five (44%) want their data used by financial institutions or insurers to keep them informed of their spending habits and offer relevant advice.
- More than a third (36%) would like their data used by financial institutions or insurers to amend their credit rating."

Based on this survey, the way that goes towards digital appears as a natural evolution of the insurance industry.

The following paragraphs give further insights about the application of some new technologies; suffice it to say that going digital is not an as easy as it seems: companies have to build their ICT systems, make changes to their business model, renovate their culture, adapt their structure to the new business, and so forth.

This section examines the way through which insurtech companies have leveraged on technology to deliver disruptive products and services to the market, with the aim of achieving a competitive advantage. Chapter 4 analyzes most of those innovations, without entering too much in detail as far as insurance industry is concerned.

Some of these innovations are game-changing elements for all those companies that perform their business in this field, and for all those companies that are based on information management for the delivery of their products and services.

Insurers can achieve growth by leveraging on several trends[14]:

1. Mobility
2. Channels
3. Big Data Analytics
4. IoT
5. Blockchain

[14] Classification modified by the author with respect to Vertafore (2013), 7 Technology Trends Transforming the Insurance Industry: How insurers can achieve growth, http://www.vertafore.com/~/media/Vertafore-Media-Library/Resources-Liabrary/Brochures/7-Trends-Transforming-the-Insurance-Industry-062513_v2b.ashx, Accessed 20 August 2016.

Mobility in Support of Insurance Companies

The current development of the insurance industry is bringing about changes to its products (Nicoletti 2016). Similarly to what is happening to fintech, insurance is moving toward what may be identified as "Insurance 2.0". This stage would be characterize by just-in-time products and services delivered through mobile devices providing immediate underwriting processes.

Moving toward a mobile approach does not simply mean to put at disposal of the customer base a mobile app to download. One should consider the fact that providing the company with mobile functionalities implies the implementation of internal processes that aim to enhance the customer experience through mobile tools, consequently changing, where necessary, the old routines in favor of new, re-engineered ones.

A company can use mobile apps also for its employees in order to enhance the customer experience. For instance, insurer employees may have the possibility to write an interactive performance report during a site visit with a customer, or may provide, in real time, marketers with the information they need for making their own analysis.

Other opportunities come from the underwriting area and from mere mobile functionalities, such as geolocation.

Knip

"With just one click, they can open the entire insurance policy, so every important information is always at hand. Furthermore, our insurance consultants help users find the insurances that best fit their needs."—Dennis Just, Co-founder of Knip[15]

Knip is basically an insurance manager. Covering the 29th position in the report developed by H2 Ventures, KPMG, and Matchi (Fintech 100, Leading Global Fintech innovators, Report 2015), Knip is one of the Swiss companies that has better put in place a business where the mobile delivery perfectly fits the changed needs of customers.

[15] https://techcrunch.com/2015/10/26/knip/, Accessed 07 August 2016.

In particular:

- No papers are involved.
- Customer can access their data anywhere and anytime through their mobile devices.
- There is a high level of personalization.
- There is optimization of the insurance coverage.

Trov

"Trov is dedicated to reinventing insurance by making it simple, flexible and transparent. With a simple swipe on your phone, you can easily protect just the things you want, exactly when you want. Whether you're at home or on the go, your things are protected against accidental damage, loss or theft. Easily report a claim with a few taps on your phone and have it processed in minutes, not days or weeks."[16]—Fintastico website

The American company Trov delivers an insurance service to those customers who are willing to protect single items or possessions, even for a short period. Streamlined processes back the final delivery, allowing the final customers relevant savings in terms of time (both in researching the best suitable policy and in administration procedures). In particular, it provides:

- Tracking
- Price information
- On-demand, micro-duration insurance coverage for single items

The recommendation of this book is to embrace mobility as soon and as much as possible. With mobility becoming one of the preferred financial services tools, it becomes critical for insurtech companies to provide mobile functionalities to their customers. The driver should be "enriching the customer experience", with a focus on retaining customers rather than attracting prospective ones, first and especially due to the costs of

[16] https://www.crunchbase.com/organization/trov#/entity, Accessed 07 August 2016.

acquisitions that are continuing to rise. Developing the right mobile skills for enhancing mobile functionalities and making better use of them has to be a primary step, followed by the creation of KPIs to measure the effectiveness, the efficiency, and the economics of the pre-existing and new apps in order to avoid unnecessary and waste costs.

Big Data Analytics

Getting a good handle on data should be one of the primary focuses of the insurance industry. Extracting value from data is central in this business: the assessment of risks is done based on statistical models underpinned on large datasets that over time have become more and more complex to manage.

Insurance companies have essentially three main imperatives:

- Profitable growth delivered through profitable customer acquisition and retention, cross-selling, and upselling. For this element, it is very important to delight the customer and manage the channels.
- Risk management delivered through capital efficiency and operational risk management. For this element, a strict cooperation between risk and finance is essential.
- Operational efficiency delivered through cost reduction, claims management, and productive strategies. The use of resources is particularly important for this element.

Big Data Analytics can help in fulfilling all these three imperatives (Boobier 2016).

Meanwhile, the diffusion of ICT and other solutions has renewed the interest toward data management across the insurance industry. Insurers have always engaged in the investigation of new ways and methods that can better and more accurately assess risks.

An effective, efficient, and economical data management is critical for properly setting policy premiums. In performing such activity, premium should be based on:

1. Coverage, taking into account the characteristics of the person/object insured: The insurer, or the agent, or the robo-advisor should consider and propose any possible cross-selling.
2. Assessments of the risks: The price of the premiums should be set at a level that actually covers the insured risk.
3. Potential margins: Significantly connected to (2), the potential margin depends on the cost structure of the insurance company taken into consideration.
4. Target market: Fitting the budget of customers is a key point for insurers, which, especially in high-competition markets, should thoroughly underline the centricity of the value added to the customers in their pricing strategies.

The following paragraphs underline some best practices for insurtech initiatives.

As mentioned previously, the massive volumes of data generated in the last decades have shifted the attention of insurance companies to the data management area. The companies' focus is on those voluminous, complex data that come from a variety of sources, such as documents, videos, photos, emails, and so forth. These data are unstructured data but have considerable value for the companies. Unlike structured data, which reside in a fixed field within a record or a file,[17] as a spreadsheet or as a database, it is much more difficult for a business organization to gain insight from unstructured ones. Contextually, companies should not miss the opportunity to analyze also unstructured data, which may be able to provide them with a considerable advantage against their competitors.

Different data need different management tools. To manage structured data, programmers use a specific programming language, called structured query language (SQL), used to manage definite classes of databases, called relational database management systems. Without entering into technical details (Zhu 2013), these systems are very effective as far as structured data are concerned. When it comes to unstructured data, these systems begin to struggle, showing all their limitations.

[17] http://www.webopedia.com/TERM/S/structured_data.html, Accessed 20 August 2016.

Those companies that are willing to leverage on Big Data Analytics should then look to other types of systems: to manage unstructured data, programmers need to use "non-relational databases" (see Table 8.1). This technology deploys leading-edge technologies able to manage large sets of unstructured data. D3.js is an example of the new technologies. It underlines the importance of data design in documents and supports the so-called Internet of Data.

Chapter 9 provides further insights, analyzing a fintech company by applying the model presented in Chapter 3. Nevertheless, general guidelines are provided in this chapter for understanding which elements could help in Big Data Analytics.

According to Bharal and Halfon,[18] the suggested approach for insurance companies is the hybrid one, a combination of relational and non-relational databases with the aim of pushing the old paradigm to the limit while leveraging Big Data Analytics with leading-edge technologies.

Rapidly emerging technologies for open data are becoming enablers to creating competitive advantages (B. Nicoletti, in press).

Meanwhile, the diffusion of ICT and other technologies is providing support to data management across the insurance industry.

Table 8.1 General Big Data Analytics guidelines

Traditional databases	Non-relational database	Hybrid systems
Data is mainly structured	Data is mainly unstructured	Need to leverage on both structured and unstructured data
Majority of tasks where fast analysis is critical	Majority of tasks where fast analysis is not needed	

[18] Bharal, P. and Halfon, A. (2013), Making Sense of Big Data in Insurance, http://www.marklogic.com/resources/making-sense-of-big-data-in-insurance/resource_download/whitepapers/, Accessed 05 August 2016.

The use of Big Data Analytics has a certain number of risks.[19] There might be problems of customer privacy, since the collection of data, with the advent of digital technology, is based on potentially invasive tools. There is also the risk of an increase in the concentration of market power and customer discrimination in a few companies that have the knowledge and the funds available to exploit Big Data Analytics, which require also relatively big investments. The information from the insured persons and the new processing technologies can be entry barriers for new entrants. Companies already operating in the market would benefit from such a barrier. The barrier would penalize the companies that are not able to compete in terms of collection and use of the data. One of the consequences could be the difficulty of companies not using these technologies to carry out an adequate advertising exploiting the direct contact with customers. In the case of non-mandatory policies, companies could take advantage of Big Data Analytics also to select the best customers, with the negative impact of marginalizing the market of less attractive customers (the so-called cream skimming).

Internet of Things (IoT)

"By 2025, IoT will be pervasive, with connected 'things' driving a data explosion with sensors embedded in cars, buildings, and wearable devices—so much so that a family of four could have more than 100 connected devices."—A.T. Kearney (2014)[20]

Insurtech companies are now experiencing a significant shift in their environment. This involves the nature of the environment itself (regulation, new entrants, and boundaries), the nature of risks, and eventually the needs of customers. Business organizations have to adapt to the new rules that are now part of the financial services industry.

---

[19] http://www.corrierecomunicazioni.it/digital/42773_come-cambiano-le-assicurazioni-ai-tempi-dei-big-data.htm, Accessed 30 July 2016.

[20] A.T. Kearney (2014), The Internet of Things: Opportunity for Insurers. https://www.atkearney.com/documents/10192/5320720/Internet+of+Things+-+Opportunity+for+Insurers.pdf/4654e400-958a-40d5-bb65-1cc7ae64bc72, Accessed 05 August 2016.

One of the most important changes is the change in the nature of customers. In particular, IoT technology stands as a new approach to the business: consumers have now become always-connected consumers, continuously exchanging information between each other and demanding more and more digitally sophisticated products and services.

Insurtech companies may benefit from IoT in several areas:

- Innovation in the value proposition
  - New sources of revenues
  - New customer services
- Improving economics
  - Better risk management
  - Less risky behavior (e.g., vehicle driving)
  - Better fraud detection
- Innovation in prevention solutions
  - New ways of avoiding losses (e.g., alerts)
  - Advanced monitoring (e.g., of health)

Insurtech organizations should develop a specific approach of "Improve and Expand". The overall proliferation of data generated by sensors and devices could support a more effective decision-making process, streamlining procedures and operations.

The challenges span in the following connected areas (Kearney 2014):

- Value and impact
- Processes and policies
- Services
- Applications
- Infrastructure
- Sensors and devices

The suggested approach is as follows:

- Improving stands for increasing the quality level of the current business. Considering connected vehicles, for instance, telematics allows usage-

based insurance (UBI). These offerings definitively change the customer perception on vehicle insurance. Improving means also adapting to all those technologies and features (such as Advanced Driver Assistance Systems (ADAS)) that will be widely implemented in the near future.
- Expanding refers to one of the most effective benefits previously explained: new value propositions. Companies should be able of identifying new behaviors and needs of the customers, therefore delivering new tailored products and services.

In this context, it is important to understand how the IoT changes the collection, analysis, and distribution of large amounts of data (Big Data Analytics) to make them convertible into information to support activities and business decisions. Everything should be in compliance with the rules established by current legislation and the opinions expressed by the authorities for the protection of personal data.

Some of the opportunities for insurance companies are as follows[21]:

- The pricing model will be increasingly customized and no longer be based solely on actuarial evaluations (backward-looking) but on the analysis of behavioral predictive (forward-looking). In this way, it is possible to move from static to dynamic prices updated with increasing frequency based on the evolution of the risk profile of the customers. In addition, it is possible to move the focus from pricing to the customer service model.
- The distribution model should follow the same approach in terms of the delivery of service customization, prevention and risk reduction, and improvement of claims management, with a more accurate reconstruction of the dynamics of claims and reduction of fraud and the litigation. This will allow their traceability, thanks to the connection of objects increasingly possible. It would allow also the analysis of the data that they express for each individual. It will, in short, make possible to extend the black box utilization for the vehicle insurance (for example, reduce the prize to the customer if he/she agrees to install it the vehicle) to the insurance models for other objects and to even for the persons.

[21] http://www.agendadigitale.eu/infrastrutture/come-cambieranno-le-assicurazioni-nell-internet-delle-cose_2384.htm, Accessed 30 July 2016.

From the point of view of the application of more customized rates, the consequences are:

- Higher initial costs for the evolution of tariff models
- A cannibalization of the existing portfolio
- The risk of potential distortion in insurance due to the absence of the principle of mutuality

One aspect that is particularly interesting is the possibility for insurance companies to change the service model. The change could be in the direction of offering new services to improve the attractiveness of their insurance policies. In the case of a vehicle accident or theft, there might be a prompt intervention in support or an offer of a replacement vehicle, an automatic message to the default number or e-mail address, and so on. The insurance service would become a kind of virtual assistant. In this way, there could be an increase in the retention of the best-performing customers. The black boxes installed in the vehicle could help in the reconstruction of how an accident happened. It would be possible to cross the data of those involved to better understand the dynamics, also analyzing social networks and other connections to highlight any fraudulent behavior networks.

A similar approach could be replicated for home automation (the so-called domotics), or the ability to make a home, an office, a shop, a department of a factory, and so on a technologically assisted place. It would be possible to insert smart sensors that can provide alarms or single out repetitive behaviors that may affect the likelihood and possible losses in case of occurrence of the accident for which the customer subscribed the policy. The insurance in this way provides a monitoring system. The continuous risk management interconnected with sensors in security systems would be able to detect, in real time, fires, water leaks, intrusion attempts, power cuts, and so on.

It is possible to imagine offering the same service to make it possible to detect accidental falls or other aspects related to the vital signs of the elderly or others who need a form of home care and so on.

Social Media

As far as collaboration is concerned, the consultancy company EY suggests helping distribution partners to develop digital capability by sharing resources and expertise.[22]

Insurtech initiatives should privilege customer centricity in every aspect: all the contacts with customers should be thoroughly managed, integrated, and made consistent. Agents and intermediaries should then be provided with all the necessary analytics, tools, and services for making the customer experience unique and, consequently, for increasing sales.

All these actions should instill in the organization what McKinsey (2016) names "customer empathy":

"Real empathy allows designers to respond to true underlying needs, not superficial, stated interests. By doing this, it spurs breakthrough innovation. In fact, we believe it is the only way an incumbent insurer can be sure of delivering more than a 'me-too' customer experience."

Insurtech initiatives have been excellent at recognizing the value of social media for their own business. Unfortunately, this is not true as far as traditional organizations are concerned. The latter are still investing a large amount of resources in traditional customer engagement solutions.

Therefore, it becomes a primary step to recognize the value and the overall benefits of social media for each typology of organization within the ecosystem.

Social networks are becoming more and more important as a way to connect people. In some cases (for instance, private communications), the number of messages through social networks has become even greater than in the traditional emails. Insurance marketing and sales can greatly benefit from the channel of social networks. It is very important to be consistent and integrated in all the channels (omnichannel).

[22] EY Report, Insurance in a digital world: time is now, 2013. http://www.ey.com/Publication/vwLUAssets/EY_Insurance_in_a_digital_world:_The_time_is_now/$FILE/EY-Digital-Survey-1-October.pdf, Accessed 20 August 2016.

Social media benefits are as follows (Fig. 8.6):

- Insights of the customers
- More efficient dissemination of services, news, and conditions
- More effective engagement with younger generations
- More effective education of customers
- Low costs

The suggestion of this book is to establish different profiles in all main social media sites, monitoring them regularly and promptly responding to any brand-damaging act from unsatisfied customers. It might be useful to consider guerrilla actions, mostly in the first phases of the firm's life cycle (Hutter and Hoffman 2011). Companies may therefore consider

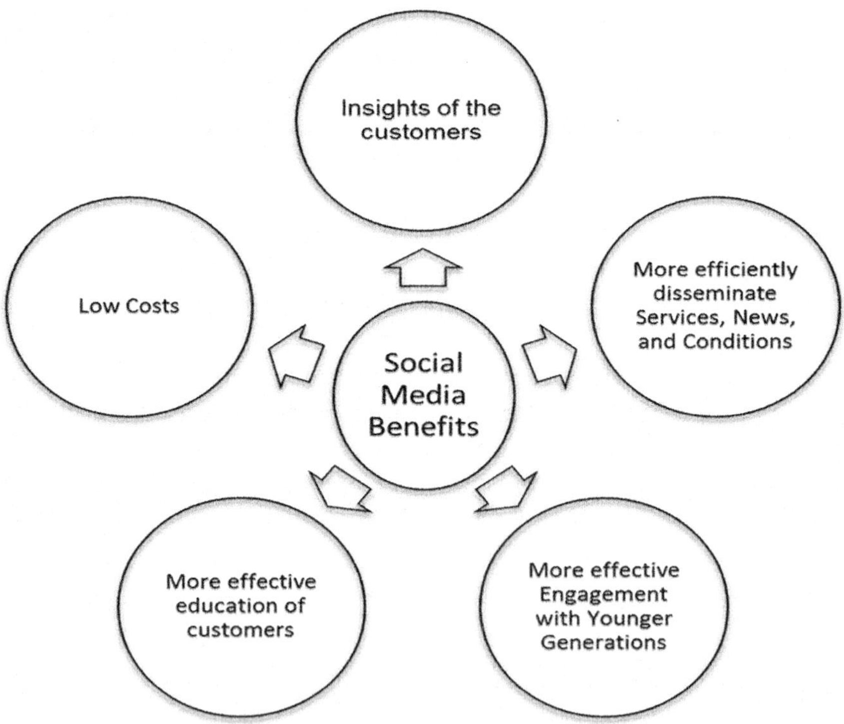

Fig. 8.6 Social media benefits

posting articles in order to spread out the brand image they want to instill in customers.

Marketing campaigns through social media, if well planned and implemented, may be highly effective, especially when unsatisfied or simply unreached customers do not know much about innovative and potentially disrupting products and services.

Amodo

"Telecom operators are offering their customers an increasing range of connectivity and IoT related products and services, such as 'connected home' and other solutions. Working with us, they are able to branch out into insurance services as well, and for us this is essentially a distribution channel."—Marijan Mumdžiev, CEO of Amodo[23]

Amodo is a Croatian startup, active also in the United States and other countries. With Amodo's Connected Customer Platform, insurers can properly address the needs and lifestyle of the new connected generation. Amodo collects data from smartphones and a number of different connected consumer devices in order to build holistic customer profiles, providing better insights into customer risk exposure and customer product needs.

Following the analysis, risk prevention programs, individual pricing, as well as personalized and "on the spot" insurance products can be offered to customers, increasing their loyalty and lifetime value. Throughout the entire process, the insurer has the means to engage proactively its customers. Customers enjoy a continuous positive experience with the insurer.

Robots

Robots and AI could be particularly relevant in the insurance industry. Robo-advisors could suggest the best policy to adopt for a specific customer. Robot process automation could help in the several activities that require the combination of manual and logical actions.

Robo-advice capabilities offer benefits to insurance companies as a way of expanding their presence in wealth management while allowing agents to maintain their focus on insurance sales.[24]

[23] http://www.amodo.eu/, Accessed 23 August 2016.

[24] https://www.accenture.com/_acnmedia/PDF-2/Accenture-Wealth-Management-Rise-of-Robo-Advice.pdf, Accessed 20 August 2016.

Ladenburg

"With $ymbil, we are helping advisors address the growing demand for wealth management services that harness the combined benefits of automation and human insight."—Adam Malamed, Chief Operating Officer (COO) of Ladenburg[25]

Ladenburg Thalmann Financial Services Inc. is a publicly traded diversified financial services company based in Miami, Florida. The company launched $ymbil℠, a self-service investment platform that matches clients of Ladenburg-affiliated advisors to a diversified portfolio consistent with their personal risk tolerance. Requiring a minimum investment of $500, $ymbil allows clients to fund their accounts and start investing in minutes. $ymbil℠ uses proprietary scoring methodology to recommend portfolios in multiple risk categories. The portfolios use globally diversified asset allocations and tactical decisions to capitalize on market conditions and unique investment opportunities.

Blockchain

There are several possible applications of blockchain in all sectors of insurance. Figure 8.7 shows the typical high-level processes of an insurance business. Blockchain could be useful along the entire cycle.

It is possible to use blockchain at the time of the subscriptions of new policies to verify the identity of the customers or to limit the risks of fraud.

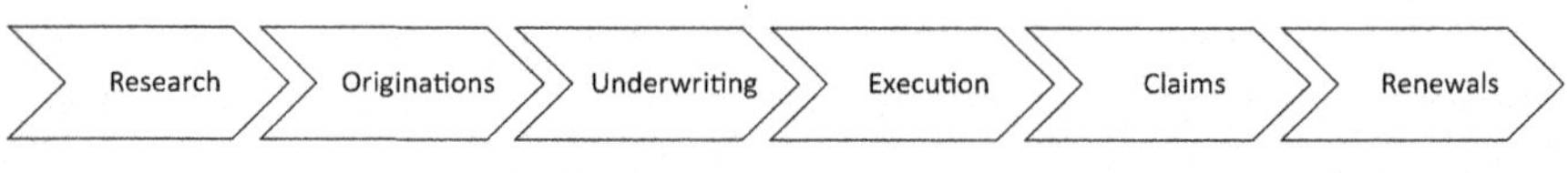

Fig. 8.7 High-level processes of an insurance business

[25] http://www.businesswire.com/news/home/20160321005351/en/Ladenburg-Thalmann-Launches-ymbil---Robo-Advisor-Platform, Accessed 20 August 2016.

Tradle

"Every bank can access this network and eliminate the number of KYC checks that they do today. But even before the network is born, within one bank there is inter-product KYC checks; inter-divisional, inter-location, inter-subsidiary. Those KYC checks are not shared. KYC costs are very high."—Gene Vayngrib, Founder of Tradle.[26]

Bancassurance underwriting can use blockchain. This is the case for the fintech company Tradle. This American startup support the storing of personal information with a very high resilience to potential hackers and cyber-attacks.[27] By allowing the partner financial institutions to share data about their customers, such as documents' identity, the partner company of financial institutions can offer a very quick and streamlined process for subscribing to a product without asking for data already available. Blockchain could save and guarantee document exchange and communications. This data certification would be in full compliance with European data laws.

SafeShare

"Insurance for the sharing economy needs to be flexible and responsive to customer needs. Our distributed ledger approach, developed by Z/Yen Group, offers the opportunity to coordinate the provision of products between counter-parties in near real-time and to radically cut the cost of this coordination."—Alex Steinart, Co-founder of SafeShare Global[28]

SafeShare, a British company provides another example of advanced underwriting. It uses Bitcoin's underlying blockchain technology to confirm counterparty obligations. Blockchain technology facilitates the delivery of a flexible and a responsive product to customers at a reasonable price.

The application of blockchain to the automation of contracts allows a reduction in administration costs for reconciliation and error. Smart contracts powered by a blockchain could provide customers and insurance companies with ways to manage claims in a transparent, responsive, and irrefutable manner. The process would be (Deloitte 2015)

[26] http://www.newsbtc.com/2015/08/24/tradle-integrating-blockchain-technology-with-kyc-requirements/, Accessed 26 August 2016.

[27] https://www.munichre.com/en/reinsurance/magazine/topics-online/2016/04/automated-life-insurance/index.html, Accessed 30 July 2016.

[28] http://www.metrognomo.com/pressrelease_mar2016/.

- an option contract and related claims between parties are written as code into the blockchain. The individuals involved are anonymous, but the contract is in the public ledger;
- a triggering event such as an expiration date or a ceiling value is hit and the contract executes itself according to the coded terms, validated by the network, ensuring that only valid claims are paid;
- regulators can use the block chain to understand the activity in the market while maintaining the privacy of individual actors' positions.

Blockchain could be even used for the automatic discovery of claims. Everledger, for example, uses blockchain to create a distributed ledger that records details of precious stones such as diamonds.[29] This ledger allows insurance companies (as well as potential purchasers) to check the history of any individual stone, including previous claims. In this way, it helps insurance companies to prevent, detect, and counter fraud.

It is possible to use blockchain together with connected devices: the vehicle's black box, a wearable or an installed device in the house sensor to detect an anomaly, sends an alarm. A blockchain would end up in the workflow associated with the complaint, pre-complaint, or automatic problem detected by the connected device.

Another example of a possible application of blockchain technology is the "peer to peer" insurance. This is a business model in which groups of individuals insure each other by sharing the premium, similar to what Friendsurance does.[30] A portion of the premiums paid goes to the company for the coverage of greater gravity claims, the remaining part remains in a fund of mutuality to take care of lower claims. Each participant signs a commitment to contribute to the fund of mutuality. The blockchain will store it in a safe way. The award is not paid immediately but "preserved" in the blockchain. The contributions from each individual are transferred only in the event of a claim.

Insurance companies are laggards with respect to the banking world in the examination of potential use of blockchains. However, there are exceptions. Lloyds is considering the redesign of its operating model

---

[29] https://www2.deloitte.com/content/dam/Deloitte/ch/Documents/innovation/ch-en-innovation-deloitte-blockchain-app-in-insurance.pdf, Accessed 30 July 2016.

[30] http://www.friendsurance.com/, Accessed 30 July 2016.

with blockchain. A real impact of this technology on insurance will take several years, even if the life cycles of new technologies are becoming shorter.[31] Another trend noted in the previously cited report is that some insurers, such as Aviva, Allianz, and MetLife, are bringing fintech and other technology firms together in innovation labs in an effort to engage customers in ways that are more meaningful across online and mobile platforms and improve policy handling and claims-payment processes.[32]

Cloud Computing

Cloud computing is the use of ICT resources on demand, through the internet, paying by the use and with a self-service mode. Cloud computing frees companies from fixed-location data centers. Therefore, it combines very well with previous technologies, based very much in the internet. For instance, the re-insurance business becomes much easier, thanks to cloud computing.

Nationwide

In the last 80 years, Nationwide has grown from a small mutual auto insurance company owned by policyholders to one of the largest insurance and financial services companies in the United States, with more than 38,000 employees. Headquartered in Columbus, Ohio, this Fortune 500-listed company is the number one provider of public-sector retirement plans and the seventh largest auto insurance company in the United States. Nationwide's 3000 distributed servers were inefficient and costly. To increase business agility and halt growing costs, Nationwide started a virtualization journey that ultimately led to the Cloud.[33] They consolidated their distributed server landscape to Linux virtual servers running on mainframes, creating a multi-platform private cloud optimized for all its different workloads. This cloud deployment reduced power, cooling, and floor space requirements by 80% and reversed expenditure on a distributed server landscape, saving an estimated $15 million over the first three years.

[31] Kumar, S., & Phrommathed, P. (2005). *Research methodology* (pp. 43–50). Springer US. New York, NY, and http://www2.deloitte.com/content/dam/Deloitte/dk/Documents/finance/CIOs-struggle-to-stay-ahead-POV.pdf, Accessed 05 August 2016.

[32] http://www.insurancenetworking.com/news/innovation/insurtech-companies-are-the-new-fintech-leaders-37470-1.html, Accessed 23 August 2016.

[33] http://www.enisystems.com/eninew/latest/blue/news/IBMSystem_z_Software_Virtualization_Virtualization_Server_Smarter_Computing.pdf, Accessed 25 April 2015.

Digital Wholesale Insurance

The digital revolution is spreading around the world. Insurance is no exception and there are recent studies that aim to create and describe a model for digital insurance. The spread of digital insurance is following the path of the so-called ICT consumerization (Nicoletti 2016). In the past, businesses were the first to use ICT innovations. Nowadays, more and more, consumers get priority in introducing ICT innovation. This took place with physical products, such as smartphones and tablets. Initially, the target was the consumer market. Later, also the businesses started to use them. Something similar is happening in financial services, such as in banking, where mobile banking was initially introduced mainly in retail banking. Only now, solutions are introduced also for corporate and small- and medium-sized firms.

It is now time to rethink this approach and better understand how to use fintech initiatives also for the wholesale insurance services. Some startups are already moving in this direction. More and more will come. Wholesale financial services are essentially operators which provide coverage for risks outside of the risk preference of admitted carriers or which provide specialized capabilities.

In order to analyze how digital insurance could support this sector, it might be interesting to refer to a sentence of Rudyard Kipling from his book: *The Little Elephant.*[34] Kipling considered the description of a problem complete if it is possible to answer six questions, each starting with an interrogative character: five Ws and one H. In the case of digital wholesale insurance, this would mean answering the following questions:

- Why: The reason to go digital could be defensive for wholesale insurers: startups might be able to invade their markets and introduce disruptive innovations. As a matter of fact, to go digital could also help established players in the wholesale insurance sector to become more effective, efficient, and economical.

[34] Kipling R. (2013), Just So Stories, CreateSpace Independent Publishing Platform.

- Where: Globalization, thanks to cloud computing, can expand easily the reach of concentrated markets, certainly fueling competition but also increasing the size of markets.
- What: Big Data Analytics can help in improving the analysis of risks. It can be applied to capital markets, security, customer insight, channel marketing, and for providing new datasets for risk pricing and tracking.
- Who: AI and robotics can help in selecting the best alternatives. The use of social media, now spreading in financial services, does not seem suitable for wholesale insurance. On the other side, comparators' websites could help customers to pick up worldwide their most convenient insurer. Some similar "marketplace" could also help to find the best solution for the requirements of a specific customer in the wholesale insurance market.
- When: Mobile technologies can help in reducing the time to take decisions and, especially, in taking decisions when the operator wants.
- How: Another opportunity connected with new technologies is blockchain. It could also change, in a radical way, the wholesale insurance environment. Blockchain is a technology introduced along with the virtual currency, Bitcoin. It is an interesting technology in itself. It is based on an online, distributed ledger technology. Blockchain could help in setting up smart contracts with a distributed ledger solution. It could help in managing customer identities, reference data, and assets; increasing visibility in a secure way; and ensuring a seamless, reliable, and uninterrupted messaging service to the insurance market. It could also serve as a cost-effective method of facilitating the availability and exchange of data between insurance business partners, and a trusted utility service that boosts insurance market competitiveness. PricewaterhouseCoopers is working on a Long Finance research project that looks into the potential of blockchain technology in wholesale insurance.[35]

[35] https://www.finextra.com/pressarticle/64838/PwC-preps-research-into-blockchain-tech-for-wholesale-insurance, Accessed 20 August 2016.

Fintech companies are not only a way to improve the processes of wholesale insurers. They can support the introduction and improvement of new products. Insurance for cyber risk would be an example (Klahr 2016). Cyber risk insurance covers the losses relating to damage to, or loss of information from, ICT systems and networks. Cyber risk policies generally include significant assistance with and management of the incident itself, which can be essential when faced with reputational damage or regulatory enforcement. A UK government survey estimated that, in 2014, 81% of large corporations and 60% of small businesses suffered a cyber breach. The average cost of a cybersecurity breach is £600,000–£1.15 million for large businesses and £65,000–115,000 for SMEs.[36]

In this new fintech ecosystem, there is the need of new business models. These models could foster, for instance, a much closer collaboration and partnership between wholesale insurers and brokers. The latter could greatly benefit from digital technologies. Brokers are not always able to invest in them due to their normal small size or the lack of the necessary knowledge.

Conclusions

This chapter analyzes insurtech, the insurance-specific branch of fintech initiatives, which are actively leveraging technology in support of insurance businesses.

During the last ten years, technology has fostered changes and innovations in every sector, carrying around exciting applications and cutting-edge business models. A large set of elements are now also disrupting the insurance industry. The most critical driver of disruption is the ongoing process of customer empowerment. Businesses should not remain static in their positions. They should look forward and try to anticipate the moves of their competitors. This is not as easy as it seems. Insurance com-

[36] https://www.abi.org.uk/Insurance-and-savings/Products/Business-insurance/Cyber-risk-insurance, Accessed 03 August 2016.

panies should be able to understand why their customers have changed. It is important to understand how companies can leverage on this in order to

- find more effective approaches;
- enhance their interactions; and
- build trusted relationships.

The insurance sector has not yet worked out a consistent approach to disruption. It is time for executives to think forward, putting innovation at the heart of their strategies. They need to decide how, and not if, to participate in the insurtech ecosystem. To embrace insurtech initiatives, incumbents should take the following concrete steps[37]:

- Exploration: Well-informed incumbents are actively monitoring new trends and innovations. Some of them are establishing a presence in innovation hotspots (for instance, Silicon Valley) where they can learn about the latest developments directly and promptly.
- Strategic partnerships: Some incumbents collaborate with startups and build pilot solutions to test in the market. Ensuring a design environment ("sandbox") helps in boosting creativity so as to produce tools and resources for designing potential prototype solutions.
- Insurtech involvement: Traditional insurance companies' involvement in startup programs such as incubators, accelerators, mechanisms to fund companies, and strategic acquisitions may result in insurers' readiness to address specific problems, especially those that otherwise might not be tackled in the short term.
- New product development: Involvement in insurtech initiatives could help traditional insurance companies to discover emerging coverage needs and risks that require new insurance products and services.

While the insurance industry has been slow to change, insurers also increasingly need to work to develop POC initiatives around analytics,

[37] PwC (2016), Opportunities await: Global Fintech Survey, June. http://www.PwC.com/gx/en/financial-services/assets/fintech-insurance-report.pdf, Accessed 15 July 2016.

wearables, the IoT, blockchain, and other solutions to offer more customer insights. This is a way to start a more effective insurance marketing and operations, and engage millennials.

The expectation is that investments in the next few years in insurance technology will significantly outweigh investments in banking and capital markets, much of which would be regulatory driven.[38]

References

Barry, C., Hogan, M., & Torres, A. M. (2011). Low-cost carriers and high-tech barriers: User views on questionable web design practices in Ireland. *Irish Journal of Management, 31*(1), 43.

Binks, M. R., Ennew, C. T., & Reed, G. V. (1992). Information asymmetries and the provision of finance to small firms. *International Small Business Journal, 11*(1), 35–46.

Boobier, T. (2016). *Analytics for insurance: The real business of Big Data.* New York, NY: Wiley.

Darwin, C. (1859). *On the origin of species by means of natural selection, or the preservation of favoured races in the struggle for life* (1st ed.). London, UK: John Murray.

Deloitte. (2015). *Financial services in the age of the internet of things.* Retrieved July 31, 2016, from https://www2.deloitte.com/content/dam/Deloitte/cn/Documents/about-deloitte/aff2015/deloitte-cn-aff-postcon-leaflet-en-150227.pdf

Fintech 100. (2015). *Leading Global Fintech innovators.* Report 2015. Retrieved August 24, 2016, from http://www.fintechinnovators.com/

Fujitsu EMEIA. (2016). *Banking on change: Consumers drive digital charge in financial services.* Retrieved July 31, 2016, from http://www.fujitsu.com/fts/about/resources/news/press-releases/2016/emeai-160504-banking-on-change-consumers-drive-digital.html

Hutter, K., & Hoffmann, S. (2011). Guerrilla marketing: The nature of the concept and propositions for further research. *Asian Journal of Marketing, 5*(2), 39–54.

[38] http://www.insurancenetworking.com/news/innovation/insurtech-companies-are-the-new-fintech-leaders-37470-1.html, Accessed 23 August 2016.

Kearney, A. T. (2014). *The Internet of things: Opportunity for insurers*. Retrieved July 31, 2016, from https://www.atkearney.com/documents/10192/5320720/Internet+of+Things+-+Opportunity+for+Insurers.pdf/4654e400-958a-40d5-bb65-1cc7ae64bc72

Kipling, R. (2013). *Just so stories*. CreateSpace Independent Publishing Platform.

Klahr, R. (2016). *Cyber security breaches survey*. Doctoral dissertation, University of Portsmouth.

Koller, M. (2012). Unit-linked policies. In *Stochastic models in life insurance* (pp. 93–113). Berlin, Germany: Springer.

McKinsey. (2016). *Transforming life insurance with design thinking*. Retrieved July 31, 2016, from https://www.mckinsey.it/idee/transforming-life-insurance-with-design-thinking

Nicoletti, B. (2016). *Digital insurance*. London, UK: Palgrave Macmillan.

Oliynyk, H., & Sabirova, A. (2013). Insurance company and bank partnership as a distribution channel of insurance products. *Economics & Economy, 1*(2), 131–141.

PwC. (2016). Blurred lines. How Fintech is shaping financial services. Retrieved February 22, 2017, from https://www.pwc.com/il/en/home/assets/pwc_fintech%20global_report.pdf

Saunders, A. (2004). Bank-insurance model–Pros and cons. Keynote Speech. In *17th Australasian Finance and Banking Conference*, Sydney, Australia.

Zhu, N. Q. (2013). *Data visualization with D3. js cookbook*. Birmingham, UK: Packt.

9

A Case

Introduction

This chapter analyzes through a real case the business model introduced in this book. The company is active in advanced technology. Robotica is an Italian B2B company that performs its business at the top of the fintech value chain by providing software solutions to organizations operating in the financial services industry.

This book has repeatedly stated that the definition of fintech initiatives does not encompass only startups, but also traditional organizations and companies that have passed the embryonic and initial hurdles and have eventually reached the competitive or mature phase. The case discussed in this chapter deals with a company that has achieved competitive success in the very first period of its life cycle. The company has followed a conservative strategy from the very beginning. Robotica has pursued growth not as a primary objective, but in favor of specialization and ever-increasing margins.

B. Nicoletti, *The Future of FinTech*,
DOI 10.1007/978-3-319-51415-4_9

Robotica

Robotica was born from the meetings of professional managers, technicians, and high-level web designers with a sound work experience and high professional standing. The company provides assistance through well-trained consultants and experts of the logics and business issues. The target market ranges from large multinational companies to SMEs of any economic sector that monitor and are keen to synchronize with the new rules of the market.

The company's mission is to create and deliver to customers

- online management applications;
- web design; and
- consulting and technological support to optimize costs, thus increasing the customers' success while increasing Robotica's profitability.

The vision is to be the number one choice in any sector they operate in.

Business Model Canvas

This section provides further details on some macro-areas in the Robotica business model (Fig. 9.1).

The Value Proposition

Robotica, over the years, has shown its innovative and forward-looking attitude especially in value proposition. In particular, it has been providing the market with various innovative products and services, adding value to its customers, some of which are as follows:

- Management software
- Neural technologies and virtual robots
- Risk management products
- Algorithms
- Accounting software solutions

Business Model Canvas

<table>
<tr>
<td rowspan="2">Partnership and Collaboration
• Traditional Financial Institutions
• Consultancy companies</td>
<td>Processes and Activities
• R&D
• Software development</td>
<td rowspan="2">Products and Services
• Management software
• Virtual Robots
• Risk management
• Algorithms
• Accounting software</td>
<td>Customer Experience
• Support 24*7
• International coverage
• Customizations
• Flexibility</td>
<td rowspan="2">Market:
• Customer
• Competitors
• Regulators
• Financial institu.
• Insurers
• Telco
• Broers
• International companies
• SME
• Competition from large system integrators</td>
</tr>
<tr>
<td>Resources and Systems
• R&D team
• Partnerships
• Market position
• Java Framework</td>
<td>Channels
• Word of Mouth
• Website (under construction)</td>
</tr>
<tr>
<td colspan="3">Costs and Investments
• Platforms/software solutions/Algorithms development and maintenance
• Customer acquisition costs
• Light assets</td>
<td colspan="2">Revenue Streams
• Traditional pricing
• Also success fees</td>
</tr>
</table>

Fig. 9.1 Robotica's business model canvas

Traditional organizations typically request management software solutions, within the context of both small and large projects. Among other things, Robotica has developed products for the management of human resource (HR), solutions linked to POS programming and management, and support to risk management.

One of the most interesting things with regard to virtual robots is their extensive use in stock markets.[1] In the United States, automatic trading manages around 60% of the whole volume of shares traded in the market. This percentage is increasing.

This figure should make companies reflect on the impact of technology on the financial services industry. It should encourage and induce companies into researching new ways of doing business. Robotica has been riding the wave of "technological opportunities" since the beginning, selling algorithms and managements systems to its target markets,

[1] Carlini, V. (2015), Borsa, processo ai robot-investitori. Accusa e difesa degli algoritmi, Il sole 24 Ore, Oct. http://www.ilsole24ore.com/art/finanza-e-mercati/2015-10-28/borsa-processo-robot-investitori-accusa-e-difesa-algoritmi-205631.shtml?uuid=ACJxrwOB, Accessed 31 July 2016.

leveraging on the significant value that such solutions bring in. According to its General Manager, Daniele Monteleone, Robotica's virtual robots provide values that no company should ignore:

- Creativity: Even though robots are not creative, Robotica has developed machine-learning algorithms that are able to learn effectively even from other operators' results.
- No emotional involvement: Algorithms, thanks to the use of neural technologies, have no emotional involvement during their decision-making process, which is widely considered as one of the main threats.
- Time coverage: An algorithm may be programmed for supporting decisions for different stock markets, performing its operations at whichever hour of the day in different time zones.
- Geographical coverage: An algorithm may be programmed for supporting decisions for geographically dispersed stock markets, performing its operations in different countries.
- Fewer costs: Except the initial investment, the cost of managing and running software is significantly lower than that required in consulting an equivalent expert analyst.

Robotica adds a real value to its customers since it provides solutions to the jobs to be done (Christensen et al. 2016).

Thanks to the pricing strategies that Robotica promotes to its customers, these solutions may be extremely convenient for a large number of businesses.

Robotica is actively involved in the development of risk management products. In particular, these products aim to provide customers with a tool that allows them to manage different typologies of risks, mainly assessed through simulation sessions.

In this case, as much as in most of its solutions, Robotica has adopted a pull-push approach. A large pharmaceutical company requested the development of a software for managing insurance policies—also from third parties—for its internal insurance division. The company asked Robotica to develop a risk management platform able to detect both the frequency and the profitability of a possible investment, which when combined identify the company's risk index. After having successfully delivered this solution, Robotica has actually changed its approach, pushing a generalized solution to the market by making the necessary adaptations and refinements.

Robotica plans to extend over time to serve other market segments. In particular, some organizations have the need of computing, and verifying financial plans, or even of getting an expert report on the documents that comprise these plans. Robotica provides audit software solutions able to detect all the possible anomalies. If, for instance, a company wants to verify whether the loan of a bank has exceeded even slightly the usury threshold, Robotica's products can alert the customer.

The values for the customers of Robotica's solutions are substantial. By way of example, one of Robotica's software solutions for risk management has allowed many companies to save 30–35% of the overall insurance costs.

Customer Experience

Robotica is a B2B company that provides organizations with cutting-edge propositions. The model is customer centric. It aims to deliver value to its customers (see Table 9.1). Dealing with customer experience in a B2B organization is not as easy. It is not possible to use several components normally used for raising up the perceived value for the consumer, since they could not be effective or not suitable in the case of business customers. For instance, leveraging on the design of the whole value proposition's ecosystem in order to increase the overall marginality is a lever that may not be a choice for Robotica, as well as the possibility to play on physical or online shops to better convey its brand image.

Robotica has only a few tools to leverage on the perceived value for its business customers. Robotica is paying much attention toward the

Table 9.1 Robotica and its customer experience

Tangible value	Perceived value
Costs of the investment	Online website
Success fee on generated savings	Software design
Savings	Technological innovation

key elements capable of having a drastic impact on customer experience (Table 9.1). It especially stresses the fact that it is a technological partner aiming to grow "together" by supporting companies all along their evolution.

Robotica's products have proved to satisfy many relevant aspects that add value to its customers in many sectors, especially in terms of the costs of the investment, the software design, and the extent to which a company is innovating.

Channels

Robotica's target markets are several. The main ones are as follows:

- Utilities
- Financial services
- Health care

Robotica seems not to effectively leverage digital channels. Its "conservative" strategic choice of not pursuing growth through the enlargement of the customer base is because of this deliberate choice. Furthermore, more projects imply more resources. Over the years, its "sustainable growth" has paid in terms of economic solidity. In addition, the reallocation of exceeding resources scares the top management. On the other hand, growth is not always the right choice to pursue.

Eventually, Robotica has recently decided to update its website, designing it in a way that could better fit its innovative way of working. This decision takes into consideration the importance of improving its brand image in the eyes of its customers.

Processes and Activities

One of the main pillars of the model presented in this book is the increased attention toward marketing. In fintech initiatives, marketing should not use traditional campaigns or channels such as radio or television. These initiatives may be highly effective for B2C companies. B2B companies need other forms of activities for promoting their products or the set of services delivered.

Robotica management has had always put emphasis on the concept of sustainable growth: without relevant economic efforts. It considers its rate of growth as optimal. This is the main reason why in the past it has not pushed toward marketing. Robotica has run some traditional marketing campaigns in the past. Robotica has not relied very much on advertising. Its main source of prospects is via "word-of-mouth", along with demonstrations and other relationship techniques.

The "production" of a software is a layered process. There is a core functionality, but several layers to add on additional functionalities. Mainly working in a Java environment, Robotica operates in specific layers, designing modules that have the advantage to be "attached" via API (application programming interface) to the main core, without being completely part of it.

Resources and Systems

One of the main strengths of Robotica is its research and development (R&D) team. They are responsible for generating expertise, new algorithms, and software solutions in specific areas:

- Neural technologies and robotics
- Building automation;
- IoT
- Three-dimensional (3D) printing.

Furthermore, Robotica's R&D team collaborates with important organizations such as National Aeronautics and Space Administration (NASA), European Space Agency (ESA), and Confindustria with the aim of continuously updating and reviewing their products and services.

A key activity of Robotica is the development of software solutions and algorithms. Robotica allocates resources usually on a flexible basis: whenever a project is finished, available resources are re-allocated to other customer projects or to some R&D activity.

Partnership and Collaborations

The position of Robotica at the top of the value chain implies the loss of certain forms of vertical cooperation. Nevertheless, this is not an issue for this company. It is able to leverage on technology and to build trust-based relationships with customers and consultancy companies.

The business model of Robotica focuses on collaboration with customers. This is normally of pivotal importance, especially in the early phases of fintech companies' life cycles. Traditional financial organizations have embraced the innovation challenge in different ways. Some financial institutions have become venture capitalists, while some other have set up innovation labs, actively participating in business incubators and accelerators with the aim of narrowing their technological gap. They are therefore adopting different solutions to simplify their processes and foster a digital transformation. It is exactly in this framework that Robotica has managed to achieve a competitive advantage.

In the very first phases of a company's life cycle, fintech startups may gain access to funding and resources along with financial institutions acquiring innovative knowledge to narrow the technological gap. Mature organizations normally establish this cooperation in other forms. This is the case of Robotica, which works with financial institutions in two ways: either directly or indirectly.

Along the years, indeed, Robotica has managed to build trust-based relationships with financial institutions, which have mainly acted as customers, directly commissioning projects and allowing Robotica to become their technological partners. An example is a recent project for a local bank, dealing with POS programming and management.

Robotica's indirect relationships with customers are an interesting aspect. The end-customers usually assign big projects to large vendors, and not to small companies, for a number of reasons. The large vendors subcontract or outsource part of their work to partners. The large vendors normally provide directly around 50% of the total amount of resources needed for the completion of a project, while they assign the remaining part to smaller and more flexible companies, such as Robotica. Big corporations thoroughly assess their partners. The solid professional experience and the extensive range of tools provided by Robotica is one of their main levers for successful cooperation and established partnerships.

Revenues

The focus, here, is on how Robotica makes money, and in particular the pricing structure of its products and services.

Robotica gets revenues from three main areas:

- Technological consultancies
- Software licenses
- Success fees on the revenue of its customers

The first two points are in common with the practices of the industry. The third one is very infrequent. Robotica proposes to SMEs or individual brokers the possibility to implement one of its portfolio management solutions without charging them the entire cost. Instead, it offers a success fee model. Customers pay a fee based on the revenues gained by them using the tool. Many stock market brokers have decided to adopt Robotica's Virtual Robot with a success fee. This approach relies on the optimism of both the parties regarding the success of the solutions. It creates a true partnership between the vendor and customer.

The main competitor in the Italian market is the Italian system integration company, Engineering. However, other smaller companies may be, in the future, a threat.

Costs and Investments

In terms of costs and, especially, of investments, Robotica has adopted a very lean approach. The "headquarters" and the main offices are in a relatively small apartment in a popular suburb of Rome. In this office, meeting rooms occupy most of the space in order to be able to meet and demonstrate products and services to the prospects and customers or for performing internal teamwork.

The main servers are outsourced and only backup servers are located in the offices in order to be able to assure internal business continuity even if there are networking issues.

Wherever possible, Robotica uses open-source software in PCs and servers running on Linux.

Conclusions

This chapter has analyzed an Italian B2B company, Robotica, also active in fintech initiatives, by applying the model developed in Chap. 3.

That provides business solutions, in particular algorithms and software products, to the financial services industry or to its customers.

The overall process of matching and adapting the model presented in this book to a real company has certified the validity of the model's main pillars.

References

Carlini, V. (2015). Borsa, processo ai robot-investitori. Accusa e difesa degli algoritmi, Il Sole 24 Ore, Oct. Retrieved February 21, 2017, from http://www.ilsole24ore.com/art/finanza-e-mercati/2015-10-28/borsa-processo-robot-investitori-accusa-e-difesa-algoritmi-205631.shtml?uuid=ACJxrwOB

Christensen, C. M., Hall, T., & Duncan, D. S. (2016, September). Know your customers' "Jobs to Be Done". *Harvard Business Review*, 54–62.

10

The Future: Financial Services as Platforms

Introduction

In discussing strategy and the future, it is important to focus more on the nature of the disruption one could expect to occur in the financial services industry rather than on who the disruptors are today. It is relevant to develop a view of the deeper forces behind disruption. An understanding of those forces, combined with solid analysis, can help explain not so much as which companies will disrupt a business as why. This chapter analyzes the nature of the transformation and disruption that the financial services sector faces rather than just the specific parties that might initiate them.

This approach helps reveal the two primary sources of digital transformation and disruption:

- The making of new models, where supply and demand change less
- The dynamics of hyperscaling platforms

These opportunities and threats are not mutually exclusive; new entrants, disruptive attackers, and aggressive incumbents typically exploit

B. Nicoletti, *The Future of FinTech*,
DOI 10.1007/978-3-319-51415-4_10

digital dislocations in combination (Dawson et al. 2016). Indicators of disruption in this zone include:

- Redundant value-chain activities, such as a high number of handovers or repetitive manual work
- Well-entrenched physical distribution or retail networks
- Overall industry margins that are higher than those of other industries

High margins invite entry by new participants. Value-chain redundancies set the stage for removing intermediaries and going directly to customers. Digital channels and virtualized services can substitute for or reshape physical and retail networks. This is exactly the situation in financial services.

This chapter deals with the hypothesis on the future for fintech. Before doing that, this chapter defines the service concept for a financial company. An organization's definition of its service concept is necessary at the strategic level of planning. It underlines how the service concept drives design decisions for new and redesigned services (Goldstein et al. 2002). The thesis is that the service concept in the case of financial service is to consider them as a platform. Second, this chapter describes how the service concept is useful at the operational level during service design planning. It is useful in particular in integrating service strategy into the service delivery system and in determining appropriate performance measures for evaluating service design. Finally, service recovery, one component of service design, shows the usefulness of applying the service concept in designing and enhancing service encounter interactions.

Platform Concept

Some authors have written about the decreasing importance of traditional financial services offered by financial institutions. This is certainly true. Financial institutions might decrease in importance but banking will not. Banking is the interaction between providers of funds and users of those funds. The same would also apply to other sectors of financial services. Insurance companies might decrease in importance but insurance will not.

In order to go deeper into this statement, it is important to consider financial institutions as platforms rather than as providers of services. A platform is a business based on enabling value-creating interactions between external producers and consumers (van Alstyne et al. 2016). In more details, it is possible to conceptualize a platform as an evolving organization or meta-organization that (Gawer 2014)

- federates and coordinates constitutive agents that can innovate and compete;
- creates value by generating and harnessing economies of scope in supply or/and in demand; and
- entails a modular technological solution composed of a core and a periphery.

The platform provides an open, participative infrastructure for these interactions and sets governance conditions for them. The platform's main purpose is to create and operate interfaces among participants. In this way, platforms facilitate the exchange of goods, services, or social relationships. In addition, they enable value creation for all participants. A platform is particularly effective in the exchange of information, as exactly happens in the financial world.

A platform provides the infrastructure and rules for a marketplace, bringing together producers and consumers. The participants in a platform ecosystem fill four main roles, but may shift rapidly over time from one role to another. Understanding the relationships both within and outside the ecosystem is central to defining a platform strategy. It is even more important to understand the critical success factors of a platform.

The players in a platform ecosystem are the 4 P's (see Fig. 10.1):

- The Proprietors, or Owners, are the controllers of the platform intellectual property and arbiters of who may participate and in which ways. The proprietors work on the innovation of the platform either modifying the business model or aggregating other business models (Moser and Gassmann 2016).

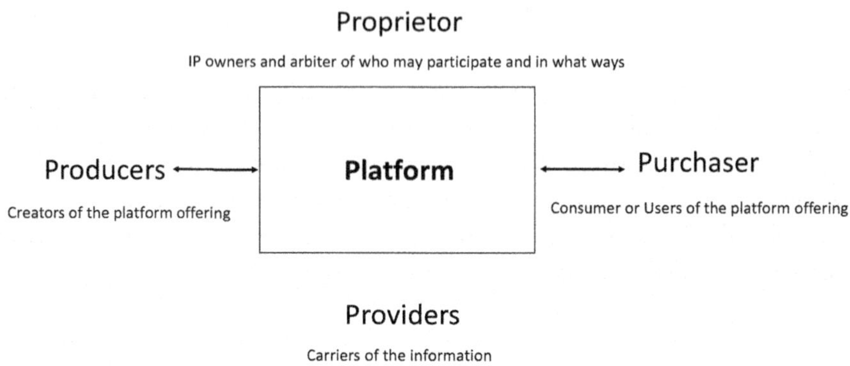

Fig. 10.1 The 4 Ps: the players in a platform ecosystem

- The Providers make available the platform, from an infrastructural point of view.
- The Producers are the creators of the platform's offerings.
- The Purchasers, or Consumers, are the buyers or users of those offerings.

The operations of a platform are not easy. Today's platforms, empowered by digital technology, are able to eliminate time and space barriers:

- They employ sophisticated solutions that connect producers and consumers more precisely, speedily, and easily than ever before.
- A platform can produce results not even imaginable some years ago.

The previous chapters explored at length the first aspect. This chapter explores platforms. With them, there is an exchange of value, information, and feedback between the producers and consumers. Though they come in many varieties, platforms all have an ecosystem with the same basic structure, including the four types of participants.

A financial institution is a platform. In the case of a bank:

- The proprietor is the bank organization.
- The (traditional) providers are the branches or, more generally, the channels.
- The producers are the depositors of funds.
- The purchasers are the users of those funds.

Platform businesses bring together producers and consumers in high-value exchanges. Their chief assets are information and interactions. Apple launched the iPhone and its operating system as more than a product, as a conduit for services. It imagined them as a way to connect participants in two-sided markets—app developers on one side and app users on the other—generating value for both groups (and of course to produce value for the providers and the owner). As the number of participants on each side grew, that value increased. This is the network effect (Moser and Gassmann 2016).

A typical example of a platform in the case of fintech initiatives is marketplace lending. Credit is a fundamental franchise of the banking industry. In the last few years, a growing number of fintech startups have taken a sledgehammer to that pillar (Orem 2016). Today, there are generally three ways through which financial institutions get into marketplace lending:

- build a proprietary platform in-house;
- form a referral partnership with a marketplace lender, or
- license a marketplace lender's platform.

The in-house option is usually the most expensive and time-consuming. It offers ultimate control over underwriting and customer experience. Referral partnerships, whereby financial institutions send potential borrowers to a marketplace lender's site and either buy the resulting loans or receive referral fees, generate income and quickly fill product gaps. They often come with underwriting and user-experience risks. Platform licensing allows financial institutions to capitalize on white-labeled plug-and-play technology and non-traditional credit criteria. It is not free and the integration requires effort.

From Banking to Fintech

It is important to understand the strategic steps to a successful platform (Van Alstyne et al. 2016). Platforms have existed for years. Financial institutions and insurance companies link consumers and producers of funds. ICT makes building and scaling up platforms much simpler and cheaper.

It allows participation nearly without friction that strengthens network effects. It enhances the ability to capture, analyze, and exchange large amounts of information that increase the platform's value for everybody. Examples of platform business have grown in an almost unbelievable way in many sectors, as happened to Uber, Alibaba, and Airbnb.

To understand how the rise of platforms is transforming competition, it is interesting to examine how platforms differ from conventional financial services that have dominated the industry for centuries. Traditional financial services create value by controlling a linear series of activities: the classic value-chain model that is essentially a pipeline. Inputs at one end of the chain undergo a series of steps. These steps transform the inputs into an output that is worth more: the finished product. Apple's handset business is essentially a pipeline. Combine it with the App Store, the marketplace that connects app developers and iPhone owners, and you get a platform.

Companies need not be only a pipeline or a platform; they can be both. While plenty of pure pipeline businesses are still highly competitive, when platforms enter the same marketplace, the platforms always win in the long term.

The move from a traditional financial institution to a financial platform involves three key shifts (van Alstyne 2016):

- From resource control to resource orchestration: The resource-based view of competition holds that companies gain an advantage by controlling scarce and valuable assets. In a traditional financial services world, those include tangible assets such as branches, funds, and intangible assets such as brands, intellectual property, or similar. With platforms, the assets that are hard to copy are the community and the resources its members own and contribute, be they funds or policies or ideas and information. In other words, the network of producers and consumers is the main asset.
- From internal optimization to external interaction: Traditional financial services companies organize their internal labor and resources to create value by optimizing an entire chain of product activities, from materials sourcing to sales and service. Platforms create value by facilitating interactions between external producers and consumers. Because of this external orientation, they often allow cutting even the variable

costs of production. The emphasis shifts from dictating processes to getting participants into the platform. The governance of the ecosystem is fundamental to the success of the platform.

- From a focus on customer value to a focus on the ecosystem or shared value: Traditional financial services companies seek to maximize the lifetime value of individual customers of products and services, who, in effect, sit at the start or at the end of a linear process. Platforms seek to maximize the total value of an expanding ecosystem in a circular, iterative, feedback-driven process. Sometimes that requires even providing some of the services for free. On the other side, producers can enjoy the information on what consumers do or use. Consumers become an audience of marketing ads. This, in some cases, is more than rewarding the platform players of their costs.

These three shifts make clear that competition is more complicated and dynamic in a platform world. The competitive forces described by Michael Porter (the threat of new entrants and substitute products or services, the bargaining power of customers and vendors, and the intensity of competitive rivalry) still apply (Porter 1990). On platforms, these forces behave differently. New factors come into play. To manage them, executives must pay close attention to the interactions on the platform, participants' access, and new performance metrics.

The Power of Network Effects

The engine of the industrial economy was, and remains, supply-side economies of scale. Massive fixed costs and low marginal costs mean that companies achieving higher sales volume than their competitors have a lower average cost of doing business. That allows them to reduce prices, which increases volume further, which permits more price cuts: a virtuous feedback loop that tends to produce monopolies.[1]

[1] That was the philosophy of Jack Welch in GE: He had GE cut all businesses in which the company could not dominate the market in first or second positions. http://www.investopedia.com/ask/answers/09/neutron-jack-welch-ceo-general-electric-ge.asp#ixzz4IeWz7LB7, Accessed 28 August 2016.

In supply-side economies, financial institutions achieve market power by controlling resources, continuously increasing efficiency, and resisting challenges from any of the five Porter model's forces. The objective of this strategy is to build sustainable competitive advantages that protect the organization from competition and channels competition toward other companies.

The platform should incentivize users and innovators to use and contribute to the platform. The result is ecosystem growth and the release of network effects. Strong network effects are an important value driver for platforms as they might create "winner-take-all" situations among competing platforms. There are two types of network effects:

- Direct network effects describe the increased value for platform users when more users join the ecosystem.
- Indirect network effects emerge when new applications for the platform get introduced. They increase the value for users to join the platform.

Both types of network effects have positive feedback loops. Each time the ecosystem grows by new users or applications, the value to be part of the ecosystem gets increased, which is what attracts new users and developers for new applications. However, a good governance of the ecosystem through the platform owner is essential as network effects can also turn negative and ruin a platform and its ecosystem.

Greater scale generates more value, which attracts more participants, which creates more value. This is a virtuous feedback loop. The bad side is that it can also produce monopolies. Network effects gave us Alibaba, which accounts for over 75% of Chinese e-commerce transactions; Google, which accounts for 82% of mobile operating systems and 94% of mobile search; and Facebook, the world's dominant social platform (for the time being).[2]

The five Porter model's forces do not factor in network effects and the value they create. The Porter model regards external forces as "depletive"

[2] https://hbr.org/2016/04/pipelines-platforms-and-the-new-rules-of-strategy, Accessed 30 July 2016.

or extracting value from a firm, and so argues for building barriers against them. In demand-side economies, however, external forces can be "accretive" (Van Alstyne et al. 2016). In other words, they can add value to the platform business. The power of vendors and customers, which is threatening in a supply-side world, is actually an asset in the case of platforms. Understanding when external forces may either add or extract value in an ecosystem is central to the platform strategy.

Cofunds

"The acquisition of Cofunds is a unique opportunity to further accelerate the execution of our UK strategy. It enables us to create substantial value as the number one provider in the fast-growing UK platform market. I am proud that the number of customers we are helping in the United Kingdom to achieve a lifetime of financial security now exceeds three million."—Alex Wynaendts, CEO of Aegon[3]

The case of Aegon buying Cofunds shows the relevance and the value for financial services of platforms. Legal & General has sold Cofunds, the main investment platform in the United Kingdom for financial advisors, to Aegon for £140 million but the British insurer will incur a net loss of about £65 million on the disposal.[4] Aegon, the Dutch insurer, receives also the Investor Portfolio Service platform—which is a similar offering for banks and building societies—as well as the retail and institutional businesses of Cofunds. Cofunds was established in 2001. It does not deal directly with private investors but provides financial advisors with access to more than 2100 funds as well as administration services to manage portfolios on behalf of clients.

How Platforms Change Strategy

In pipeline businesses, the five Porter model's forces are relatively defined and stable. A traditional finance institution knows pretty well the customers and the competitors. The boundaries separating vendors, customers,

[3] http://finance.yahoo.com/news/aegon-acquires-cofunds-becomes-leading-053000038.html, Accessed 26 August 2016.

[4] http://www.ft.com/fastft/tag/companies/, Accessed 22 August 2016.

and competitors are reasonably clear. In platform businesses, those boundaries can move rapidly over time, geographical locations, and even technologies.

The forces to consider are essentially the following ones (Van Alstyne et al. 2016):

- Forces within the ecosystem: Platform participants—consumers, producers, and providers—typically create value for a business. They may fail if they believe that other companies can better meet their needs. They could even turn on the platform and compete directly with it. The new roles that participants assume can be either accretive or depletive. For example, consumers and producers can swap roles in ways that generate value for the platform. Users can use the services of a fintech company today. The day after, they could switch their funds to a different crowdfunding fintech company. In contrast, providers on a platform may become depletive, especially if they decide to compete with the platform owner. Networks invert the companies. Platform companies must constantly encourage accretive activity within their ecosystems while monitoring participants' activity that may prove depletive.
- Forces exerted by ecosystems. Managers of traditional financial institutions can fail to anticipate platform competition from seemingly unrelated industries. Successful platform businesses tend to move aggressively into new fields and into completely separate industries with little warning. Because of such shape shifting, a platform can abruptly transform an incumbent's set of competitors. First, competitors may come from an established platform with superior network effects that uses its relationships with customers to enter the industry. Products have features; platforms have communities. It is important to leverage those communities. The final pattern, in which platforms collect the same type of data that a company does, suddenly goes after your market. When a dataset is valuable but different parties control different parts of it, it is possible that competition arrives from unlikely camps.
- Focus: Managers of traditional financial institutions focus on growing sales. For them, products and services delivered (and the revenues and profits from them) are the units of analysis. For platforms, the focus shifts to interactions: exchanges of value between producers and

consumers on the platform. The unit of exchange can be so small that little or no money changes hands. The number of interactions and the associated network effects is the ultimate source of competitive advantage. A critical strategic aim in platforms is a strong upfront design that can attract the desired participants, enable the right interactions (so-called core interactions), and encourage ever-more-powerful network effects. Most successful platforms tend to launch with a single type of interaction that generates high value even if, at first, low volume.

- Access and governance: In a traditional financial institutions world, strategy revolves around erecting barriers. With platforms, while guarding against threats remains critical, the focus of strategy shifts to eliminating barriers to production and consumption in order to maximize value creation. For this objective, platform executives must make smart choices about governance and access.
- Metrics: Leaders of financial institutions have long focused on a narrow set of metrics that capture the health of their platforms.[5] For example, financial institutions grow by optimizing processes and opening bottlenecks; one standard metric, net banking income, tracks the flow of inward and outward funds margins. If a company pushes enough services through and gets margins high enough, it will get a reasonable rate of return. In a fintech world, it is necessary to consider other metrics. Monitoring and boosting the performance of core interactions becomes critical. In the case of fintech initiatives, the metrics which should be considered are the following ones:
  - Interaction failure: If a borrower opens a marketing lender site and sees that no funds are available, the platform was not able to match the intent of a consumer. Failures like these directly diminish network effects.
  - Engagement: Healthy platforms track the participation of ecosystem members that enhances network effects with activities such as information sharing and repeat visits.
  - Match quality: Poor matches between the needs of users and producers weaken network effects.

[5] Interesting enough only recently regulators have come up and forced financial services to use new, but essential, metrics (see the case of Basel or Solvency).

- Negative network effects: Badly managed platforms often suffer from other types of problems that create negative feedback loops and reduce value for the participants. For example, congestion caused by unconstrained network growth can discourage participation (as could happen with Bitcoin due to the limitations of blockchain technology).

Finally, platforms must understand the financial value of their communities and their network effects.

Four Steps to Success

Not every initiative to leap from the traditional financial institutions model to launch a fintech venture is successful. To understand why some enterprises pull it off and others do not, it is interesting to refer to the work of Zhu and Furr (2016). After studying more than 20 companies that have tried to move from the product approach to platforms, the authors point to four practices that can separate winners from losers:

- Start with a defensible product and a critical mass of users: A strong product and a loyal customer base can attract third parties to your platform.
- Apply a hybrid business model: Instead of operating with a "product mindset" or a "platform mindset" alone, combine the two in order to discover the best opportunities for creating value.
- Drive rapid conversion to the platform: Existing customers are likely to use a platform if it provides enough new value. This requires that the additional products and services offered are consistent with the brand and the users have opportunities to improve both the products and the platform.
- Deter competitive imitation: Make it tough for rivals to copy the strategy of moving from product to platform. Consider creating proprietary standards, using exclusivity contracts, and erecting other barriers to competition.

Conclusions

There are many benefits gained by financial institutions that transform themselves into platform-based, digital banking ecosystems. Customers could have an easy access to several personalized products and services, including those of external providers. The ICT environment can be more secure. Customers could also make interactive contributions on the financial platform in a variety of useful ways.

A financial services platform offers a flexible architecture that can enable as-yet-unimagined solutions or products or services or technologies to interface with one's own infrastructure in a timely fashion and at an acceptable cost.

Platforms require new approaches to strategy and new leadership styles. The skill it takes to tightly control internal resources just does not apply to the job of nurturing external ecosystems.

Several solutions can add value to platforms[6]:

- Open programming interfaces (API) and the use of advanced key technologies: Besides using compatible and interoperable technologies, both structured and unstructured data must be recognized (processable), evaluated, and processed.[7]
- The combination of automation and self-learning algorithms can provide a powerful support to the customer's own information consumption in order to generate new products, services, and processes (Siciliano and Khalib 2008).
- AI can provide support for valuable services in the financial services platforms (Shrier et al. 2016).[8]

Platform startups naturally launch with an external orientation. Traditional financial institutions must develop new core competencies

[6] http://www.dbresearch.com/PROD/DBR_INTERNET_DE-PROD/PROD0000000000356835/Fintech+reloaded+%E2%80%93+Traditional+banks+as+digital+ec.PDF, Accessed 09 August 2016.

[7] https://www.gartner.com/doc/2967517?ref=SiteSearch&sthkw=%22Application%20Programming%20Interfaces%22&fnl=search&srcId=1-3478922254, Accessed 09 August 2016.

[8] http://fsroundtable.org/cto-corner-artificial-intelligence-use-in-financial-services/, Accessed 20 August 2016.

and a new mindset to design, govern, and expand platforms on top of their existing businesses. The inability to make this leap explains why some traditional business leaders with impressive records of accomplishment falter in platforms.

The failure to transition to a new approach contributes toward explaining the precarious situation that traditional financial institutions find themselves in at this moment. For them, the most important rule is to learn the new rules of strategy for a platform world or begin planning the exit.

References

Dawson, A., Hirt, M., & Scanlan, J. (2016, July). The economic essentials of digital strategy. *McKinsey Quarterly*. Retrieved August 24, 2016, from http://www.mckinsey.com/business-functions/strategy-and-corporate-finance/our-insights/the-economic-essentials-of-digital-strategy

Gawer, A. (2014). Bridging differing perspectives on technological platforms: Toward an integrative framework. *Research Policy, 43*(7), 1239–1249.

Goldstein, S. M., Johnston, R., Duffy, J., & Rao, J. (2002). The service concept: The missing link in service design research? *Journal of Operations Management, 20*(2), 121–134.

Moser, D., & Gassmann, O. (2016). Innovating platform business models. *Proceedings of ISPIM—International Society for Professional Innovation Management* (pp. 1–14). Porto, Portugal.

Orem, T. (2016). Platforms and partners. *ABA Banking Journal, 108*(4), 32.

Porter, M. E. (1990). The competitive advantage of nations. *Harvard Business Review, 68*(2), 73–91.

Shrier, D., Canale, G., & Pentland, A. (2016). Mobile money & payments: Technology trends. *MIT Connection Science's series on financial technology*, Cambridge, MA.

Siciliano, B., & Khalib, O. (2008). *Handbook of robotics*. Berlin, Germany: Springer.

Van Alstyne, M. W., Parker, G. G., & Choudary, S. P. (2016). Pipelines, platforms, and the new rules of strategy, *Harvard Business Review*, 1–18.

Zhu, F., & Furr, N. (2016). Products to platforms: Making the leap. *Harvard Business Review, 94*(4), 72–78.

11

Conclusions

This book illustrates the status of the fintech sector. It defines a business model framework that allows companies to gain insights into the innovations that, along the years, have characterized the ongoing process of disintermediation in which startups and financial institutions are involved.

By analyzing the main regions and ecosystems of the fintech industry from a global perspective, both traditional organizations and fintech companies may better understand the path of the industry altogether, founding further evidence of the current main economic trends. Fintech initiatives are a "hot-spot": in terms of market size and investments. The United States (combining Silicon Valley and New York ecosystems, although acting as separate hubs) and the United Kingdom are currently holding a position of undisputed leadership. On the horizon, China and Japan can play a very interesting role. Unfortunately, continental Europe is lagging.

This book reports a conceptual business model, derived from the economics literature. The model is based on nine components, whose improvement should lead and support fintech startups in their path toward competitive success, as well as in their continuous pursuit of a

B. Nicoletti, *The Future of FinTech*,
DOI 10.1007/978-3-319-51415-4_11

competitive advantage while lumping together their main challenges. In particular, the approach in this book considers three macro-areas: technology, customer centricity, and strategic partnerships. Technology and customer centricity encompass a set of processes, resources, and measures that fintech companies should address with an innovative, effective, efficient, economical, and forward-looking framework.

This book underlines the intrinsic innovative attitude of fintech initiatives. Fintech initiatives are a global phenomenon aiming to provide innovations in the financial services industry. Fintech initiatives leverage on innovation with the aim of disrupting the industry, especially by disintermediating traditional organizations such as financial institutions and insurance companies through different business models.

Innovations—both pure and marginal—have played a vital role throughout the whole process of disintermediation. The innovative attitude of the fintech initiative is the catalyst for their growth. In particular, four categories are important for the innovation: products, processes, organizations, and business models. Cloud computing provides a flexible and cheap infrastructure channel to support the success of fintech initiatives.

The book has thoroughly analyzed these innovations in Chap. 3, therefore providing additional insights on several game-changing technologies:

- Currently, customers see mobility apps as payment "facilitators", especially since payment is a "mobile" function itself and normally is not related to a specific place. Nevertheless, innovative solutions are going to turn mobile devices into full financial services platforms. The suggestion is to leverage on mobility as soon as possible.
- Big Data analytics is allowing relevant cost savings not only by contributing cost benefits but, first and especially, by identifying new paths and ways of doing business. This technology is bringing in better decision-making processes, with reference to time, quality, and costs. Decision-makers have the opportunity to analyze new sources of data in a faster way that could lead to the discovery of completely "uncharted oceans", such as new markets, products, or services.
- Robots and neural technologies have been allowing the enlargement of the customer base, achieved through a significant cost reduction in the internal processes of organizations while making possible mass private financial services.

- Traditional financial institutions should consider either internally nurturing fintech companies or collaborating with the most interesting ones available in the market.
- Financial institutions should thoroughly take into consideration innovations in their business models while developing their business plans. This is even more important for traditional institutions. Implementing an innovative culture and being inspired, not feared, by innovation is their key to growth.
- Blockchain technology has the potential to revolutionize many fields, not only the financial services industry, by ensuring the traceability of transactions and generating trust between users of the same network.
- IoT affects especially insurtech initiatives.

Stay tuned. The future is, as always, very interesting and full of opportunities to grab. Dare to try!

Glossary

Accelerator: It is a center or program to incubate fintech startups through mentorship, workspace, and, sometimes, the provision of finance. They are similar to incubators in achieving the same overall goal of helping to improve the odds of success for startups. Accelerators generally make an investment in the companies enrolled in their programs. In addition, accelerators differ from incubators in the duration of time companies spend in the program: normally three to four months to complete. Like incubators, accelerators exist for all different industries and interests. Some of the biggest and best in Europe include Startup Bootcamp, Barclays Accelerator, Fintech Innovation Lab, Seedcamp, Level 39, Anthemis, Bright Bridge Ventures, Unicredit Group EU, 3ds, and Holland FinTech.

Adoption Rate: It is a metric to measure how quickly it takes for the public at large to adopt new technologies.

Advertising-Based Pricing Model: It is a pricing model with services to customers at low or no cost. The vendor obtains most of its revenues from delivering ads to the customer along with the service.

These definitions are synthetic; therefore, they are not necessarily precise. The main objective is to provide a quick reference during the reading of this book. The sources of most of the definitions are websites with definitions related to fintech initiatives, modified and simplified to adapt to this book. Please consult the text or sources on the internet for a complete presentation of the terms.

B. Nicoletti, *The Future of FinTech*,
DOI 10.1007/978-3-319-51415-4

Agility: It is a metric to measure how quickly a solution responds as the customer's resource load scales, allocating additional resources to the activity.

Algorithms: They are an essential part of modern advanced applications. They are used for a range of tasks, from recommending books, movies, and music to automating investments online. In stock markets, algorithms are plugged directly into an electronic market and trading happens without human intervention. Algorithms suggest where the most money can be made, faster and more accurately than any human being, according to the BBC.[1] In his book *The Master Algorithm*, Pedro Domingos (2015) offers a simple definition: "An algorithm is a sequence of instructions telling a computer what to do." He goes on to explain, algorithms are reducible to three logical operations: AND, OR, and NOT. While these operations can chain together in extraordinarily complex ways, at core, algorithms are built out of a simple rationale.

Alternative Finance (Altfi): It is the set of financial channels and tools that have emerged outside of the traditional finance system, such as regulated financial institutions and capital markets.[2] It encompasses several fintech innovations, from online investing and peer-to-peer lending to mobile banking and low-cost foreign exchange apps. The altfi market grew by £3.2 billion in 2015 according to Nesta, with debt- and equity-based funding for real estate amounting to almost £700 million.[3]

Android: It is an open mobile phone platform developed by Google and, later, by the Open Handset Alliance. It consists of the operating system and the middleware.

Anonymity: It is any interaction a user has on the internet that protects his or her identity from being shared with another user or with a third party. Different levels of anonymity exist.

Anti-Money Laundering (AML): It refers to a set of existing laws or procedures or systems meant to reduce illegally obtained income. In most cases, illegal money launderers hide their actions through a series of steps that make it look like legitimate money.

App: It is short for application. It is a program or piece of software, especially one downloaded by a user on a mobile device.

Application Programming Interface (API): It is a specification for the interfaces used by software components to communicate with each other. The specifications include a set of requirements that define how two pieces of software

---

[1] http://www.bbc.com/news/technology-14841018, Accessed 30 July 2016.

[2] https://www.jbs.cam.ac.uk/fileadmin/user_upload/research/centres/alternative-finance/downloads/2016-americas-alternative-finance-benchmarking-report.pdf, Accessed 30 July 2016.

[3] https://www.nesta.org.uk/sites/default/files/pushing_boundaries_0.pdf, Accessed 30 July 2016.

can interact with each other. It allows moving data between applications. An API may include specifications for routines, data structures, object classes, and variables. These are important because they enable other programmers to use components of existing software, allowing for faster and more reliable software development. API is a major component of the fintech movement.

Application/App Store: It is the virtual location for the distribution of digital applications. It is available on mobile devices.

Application: It is a software program that uses the basic software, middleware, and network environments to achieve a specific function related to the purposes of the organization.

Audit and Compliance: It is the ability to collect, audit, and verify compliance information.

Augmented Reality (AR): It is the overlaying of digital data on the real world, for instance, through special visors.

Authentication: It is the verification of the identity of a user by a system or service.

Authorization: It is the procedure to check whether a customer or another person inside or outside the organization has the right to do a certain action, for instance, to transfer funds or access sensitive data.

Automation: It is the automated handling of services or goods. It is also the percentage of requests to the vendor handled without human intervention.

Availability: It is the metric which measures the percentage, usually calculated over a periodical (such as a month) basis, or the net, of planned or unplanned service downtimes of service coverage.

Bad Actor: It is a mean, ill-tempered, trouble-making, or evil person.

Bank Grade ID Verification: It is a term used to describe identity verification that meets the high standards of financial institutions for reliability, accuracy, and security.

Basel 2 and 3: The second and third Basel Accords were signed in 2004 by the G10 central bank governors (Basel 1 was signed in 1998). Basel 2 is a package of measures designed to introduce new rules for prudent credit risk management. Financial institutions are required to put aside equity capital to reduce the risks of their lending and investment activities, thereby bringing greater transparency and reliability to financial institutions' solvency. In 2010, the central bank governors introduced further proposals for international banking regulation in the Basel 3 reforms.

Basic Software: It is the set of software programs enabling a user to perform basic operations such as building and running a program or managing a database. Typical examples of basic software are the operating systems, the editors, the compilers, and the management systems of databases.

Benchmarking: It is the comparison of processes and/or measures with other processes and/or measures implemented by well-organized entities or a large number of them.

Big Data: It is an all-encompassing term for any collection of data sets so relatively large and complex that it becomes difficult to process them using traditional data processing applications. Big Data have the 5 Vs characteristics: Volume, Velocity, Variety, Veracity, and Value.

Biometrics: It is the process to detect and possibly record a person's unique physical and other traits using an electronic device or system as a way of confirming identity.

Bitcoin (BTC): It is the most popular cryptocurrency, generally considered the first of its kind. Bitcoin is a consensus network that enables a new payment system and a digital money. It is the first decentralized peer-to-peer payment network powered by its users and with no central authority or intermediaries. The open-source software comes with a mysterious history. Only recently, the press believes it has identified its innovator. In the past few years, Bitcoin has evolved from being a murky money of the digital underworld to an increasingly mainstream digital currency, though not without some problems. Bitcoin mining is the process of adding transaction records to Bitcoin's public ledger: the blockchain. From a user perspective, Bitcoin is like cash on the internet.

Bleeding Edge: It is a showy way of saying to be on the vanguard.[4]

Blockchain as a Service (BaaS): It is a relatively new term in 2016, coined by William Mougayar of Virtual Capital Ventures in early 2015.[5] It means "Blockchain as a Service". Equivalent terms include "Ethereum Blockchain as a Service" (EthBaaS) and "Blockchain as a Platform" (BaaP). BaaS refers to the growing landscape of services based on blockchain technology available in cloud computing. One example is Microsoft EthBaaS on the Microsoft Azure cloud platform. This platform allows companies to begin working with blockchain technology without having to make significant investments in hardware.

Blockchain: It is the technology used by Bitcoin transactions. It can record cryptocurrency transactions. It operates like a distributed public ledger where information, once entered, cannot be altered. Blockchain technology has

[4] https://blog.lendinvest.com/2016/04/what-is-alternative-finance-blockchain-bitcoin-explained/, Accessed 30 July 2016.

[5] http://www.slideshare.net/wmougayar/blockchain-2015-analyzing-the-blockchain-in-financial-services, Accessed 30 July 2016.

several non-cryptocurrency applications, including smart contracts and the recording of digital assets. It is a method of recording data—a digital ledger of transactions, agreements, contracts—anything that needs to be independently recorded and verified as having happened. The blockchain runs across several, hundreds, or even thousands of computers. Every time a new batch of transactions is encrypted, it is added to the ledger "chain" as a "block". Blockchain's appeal stretches beyond fintech into government and other fields. It is the technology that underpins Bitcoin transactions. The simplest definition is that blockchain is a decentralized digital ledger which records all digital transactions as a string of data stored on a global network of computers. Every time the network encrypts a new batch of transactions, it is added to the string (or chain) as a "block".

Blog: It is a contraction of the term "weblog". It is a type of website, usually maintained by an individual, with regular entries of commentary, descriptions of events, or other material such as graphics or videos.

Bootstrapping: It is a slang for using "friends and family" cash to get going.

Broad Network Access: It facilitates network capabilities and their access through standard mechanisms. Different types of thin or thick client platforms support the access to the network. Notebooks, tablets, personal computers (PCs), personal digital assistants (PDAs), smartphones, and so on are the devices that can access the network.

Business Intelligence (BI): It is a broad category of applications and technologies for gathering, storing, analyzing, retrieving, and providing access to data to help users make better organization decisions. BI applications include the activities of decision support systems, querying and reporting, online analytical processing, statistical analysis, forecasting, and data mining. Analytics has generalized and extended BI.

Business Model Canvas: It is a strategic management and entrepreneurial tool. It allows one to describe, design, challenge, invent, and pivot one's business model.

Business Process Management (BPM): It is the management of processes in order to improve them substantially.

Business-to-Business (B2B): It refers to organizations that relate to other organizations, rather than to customers.

Canada's Anti-Spam Legislation (CASL): It is the unofficial name of a Canadian law intended to help protect Canadians while ensuring that businesses can continue to compete in the global marketplace. It prohibits the sending of unsolicited commercial electronic messages by e-mails, social media, or text messages.

Cash-in: It refers to exchanging cash for e-money.

Cash-out: It refers to exchanging e-money for cash.

Churn: It refers to customers moving from a service provider within one specific product category to another, based on price, value, or some other factors.

Client: In this book, it refers to the customer. It could be either external or internal to the organization. In some cases, the word "client" indicates the access device. In this latter meaning, there is always, in this book, a specification (such as a thin client).

Cloning: It refers to copying the identity of one mobile phone to another, thereby allowing the perpetrator to masquerade as the victim. The intent normally is to use the phone for calls and other services billed to the victim's cell account. In the case of mobile banking, cloning could give the hacker access to the victim's financial accounts.

Cloud Computing: It is a computing capability that provides convenient and on-demand network access to a shared pool of configurable computing resources. These resources can be rapidly provisioned and released with minimal management effort or vendor interaction. Cloud computing has six essential characteristics: pay-per-use, self-service, broad network access, resource pooling, rapid elasticity, and measured service. In general terms, cloud computing enables three possible modes: Infrastructure as a Service (IaaS), Platform as a Service (PaaS), Software as a Service, and Business Process as a Service (BPaaS). It can be public, private, or hybrid.

Cloud: A metaphor for a global network or synthetic for cloud computing. Initially, it referred to the telephone network. It now refers to the internet.

Cloud-Based Payments: Cloud-based payments enable users to perform contactless payment transactions using NFC card emulation without using a hardware Secure Element (SE) in mobile handsets. Cloud-based payments store credentials remotely. An end user, who wishes to make a cloud-based payment, must use software and connections to remote servers.

Cockroach: It is similar to the term Unicorn, to define a startup that reaches a valuation of a billion or more. It underpins a venture capital (VC) investment strategy for investing in billion-dollar startups focused on resiliency. While a Unicorn achieves rapid growth, a Cockroach achieves slow, steady, sustainable growth.

Collaboration Risks: These are the risks arising from the legal structure of a joint venture; for example, while the finances of each partner in a joint venture might be robust, the joint venture vehicle itself may be poorly capitalized and carry a real risk of insolvency.

Collaborative Consumption: It is an economic model based on the sharing, swapping, and renting of services. Uber, Airbnb, and Kickstarter are examples of the "sharing economy" or "collaborative economy". It is growing in fintech solutions via solutions such as peer-to-peer lending.

Collaborative Economy: It is an economy built on distributed networks of connected individuals and communities versus centralized institutions, transforming how we can produce, consume, finance, and learn.

Collective Wallet: It is a virtual wallet designed by a group of credential issuers so that payment credentials from only this group of credential issuers may be used for payment.

Combating the Financing of Terrorism (CFT) or Counter-Terrorist Financing (CTF): These are policies introduced by many jurisdictions as a means to prevent, trace, and recover illicitly acquired assets that are the proceeds of crime, and to disrupt and dismantle global terrorist financial and criminal laundering operations. CFT/CTF is often associated with AML when dealing with compliance issues.

Companion Application: It is an application associated with a payment application to increase functionality (e.g., personal code management or transaction log).

Compliance: It is the respect for the internal and external compulsory rules of an organization.

Computer Security Incident: It is an event that involves a violation or imminent threat of violation of the rules and business practices in the field of information security. It refers, for instance, to computer frauds, attacks through the internet, malfunctions, and faults.

Configuration Management: It refers to the ability to federate configuration data, systems, or devices for services.

Consumer Risks: These are the risks that the use of service directly exposes the consumers to, for example, fraud, breaches of privacy, or the accumulation of debts that the consumer is unable to service.

Consumption-Based Pricing Model: This is a pricing model in which the vendor charges its customers based on the number of services they consume, rather than a time- and material-based fee. For example, a cloud storage vendor might charge per gigabyte of information stored.

Controlling Authority (CA): The CA manages key exchanges in an "open wallet model". This is a model recognized but not mandated in the near-field communications (NFC) mobile payments reference model. This document is an alternative to many-to-many relationships between a payment credential issuer's Telecommunication Management System (TSM) and a secure domain manager (SDM)'s TSM.

Credential: It is the secure, encrypted information associated with a specific payment product.

Credentials Information: It refers to information used by a user for authentication to a system or service. It is included in the definition of the physical tools that provide or store information (for instance, password generators of a non-reusable smart card) or something that reminds the user (for instance, a password) or represents him/her (for instance, biometric characteristics).

Crisis: It is a situation formally declared as a service interruption or the deterioration of one or more critical processes or as systemically important because of incidents or disasters.

Cross-Selling: It is a method of targeting and selling additional products or services to an existing customer.

Crowdfunding: It is the practice of funding a project or venture by raising money from a large number of people. This takes place most often via online platforms. It can also happen through mail-order subscriptions, benefit events, and other methods. Equity crowdfunding is the process whereby people (the "crowd") invest in an early-stage unlisted company or initiative in exchange for shares in that company. A shareholder has partial ownership of a company and stands to profit should the company do well. The opposite is also true; so if the company fails, investors can lose some, or all, of their investment. Seedrs is an example of an equity-based crowdfunding platform in the United Kingdom. Debt-based crowdfunding is when people lend to a company. The lenders earn a rate of return based on the interest charged on the loan. Typically, loans are secured against an asset, which provides the investors with some protections should the borrower fail to repay. Donation-based crowdfunding is when people donate money to a project. In return, backers may receive token rewards that increase in prestige as the size of the donation increases; for small sums, the funder may receive nothing at all.

Cryptocurrencies aka Altcoins/Cryptocoins: It is another word for digital currencies using cryptography for regulation and security. It is a decentralized system, meaning no central entity exists to oversee the processes. Instead, it uses a blockchain. Bitcoin was the first cryptocurrency created in 2008. Since then, numerous cryptocurrencies have been created, such as Ethereum, Litecoin, Namecoin, Stellar, and Dogecoin. Encryption techniques regulate the generation of units of cryptocurrency and verify the transfer of funds. Central banks do not issue cryptocurrencies, making them theoretically immune to not only government interference or manipulation but indeed also protection.

Cryptocurrency Exchange: It is a way to buy (and sell) Bitcoin and sometimes other digital currencies. Buying Bitcoin today is simple as a growing number of businesses facilitate the buying and selling of Bitcoins. Bitstamp, Coinbase,

Coinfloor, and Coincorner are a few options. An interested person can also invest through peer-to-peer platforms and Bitcoin brokerages.

Customer Knowledge Management (CKM): It is a strategic initiative employed by organizations to get intelligence from their customers as it relates to their organization. Organizations using CKM will effect organizational and behavioral changes based on knowledge obtained from their customers.

Customer Lifetime Value (CLV): It is a metric for customer selection and marketing resource allocation by developing a dynamic framework that enables managers to maintain or improve customer relationships proactively through marketing contacts across various channels and to maximize CLV at the same time.

Customer Relationship Management (CRM): It is an information system for managing relationships with customers. It helps to manage the whole customer life cycle, from the acquisition of a new customer to the growing of relationships with the most relevant ones to loyalty building with customers who have more relations with the organization. It allows the optimization of relationships with customers by increasing loyalty, selling more products and services, and so on.

Customer Service Representative (CSR): It is the staff working in a call or service center to assist customers with inquiries.

Customer Value Propositions: They are the benefits a product or service holds for a customer, the reasons why a customer might buy that product or service.

Customer: It is the contracting authority of the contract.

Cyber Identity: It is a set of information taken from a person's activity on the internet. This information is aggregated and resolved to a single identity from sources, which include social media, ad networks, mobile applications, and/or e-commerce websites.

Cyberbullying: It is the use of cell phones, instant messaging, e-mail, chat rooms, or social networks to harass, threaten, or intimidate someone. The problem is complicated since a bully can hide behind an electronic veil, disguising his or her identity. This secrecy makes it difficult to trace the source and encourages bullies to behave more aggressively than they might face to face.

Data Breach: It is the intentional or unintentional release of secure information to an untrusted environment.

Data Exchange: It is a platform available to select global data partners and clients interested in providing access to customer data for instance for electronic identity verification (eIDV) purposes. It enables clients and partners to set bid/ask prices for eIDV on a regional basis.

Data Governance and Compliance: It defines who is responsible for what, and the policies and procedures that persons or groups need to follow. Data governance requires governing the organization's own infrastructure and the infrastructure that the organization does not totally control. Data governance has two key components: understanding compliance and risk, and fulfilling the organization's performance goals.

Data Source: It is a database of personal information used by identity verification/identity-proofing services to validate an identity. Examples of data sources include credit bureau records, government records, property files, consumer marketing data, and telephone/utility records.

Database: It is a set of data, organized in a computer, in such a way as to allow a quick access.

Debt Investment: It is when an investor loans money to a business or individual that borrows the funds for a defined period at a fixed interest rate.

Debt-Based lending platform: It is a way to organize marketplace lending platforms. Models vary. In general, debt-based lending platforms allow people to invest in loans secured against an asset. In exchange for their money, investors get a fixed return per loan for a defined period from the borrower.

Default: It is an action or dataset used unless another specific application or credential is selected.

Detection and Forensics: It is mining and separating legitimate from illegitimate activity, before or after a breach in security.

Digital Challenger Bank: It is a broad term that refers to any new bank that has been granted a banking license since 2010. The latest innovators are using technology to help customers get maximum benefit from and even enjoy their relationship with such a bank. Four leading digital startup financial institutions are Atom Bank, Mondo, Starling, and Tandem.

Digital Financial Services: They are the financial services provided via digital remote access, including e-money or mobile money, which is in contrast to traditional financial services accessed through physical means, such as visiting a bank branch.

Digital Native: It refers to a person who has grown up with the availability, and use of, digital technology. This group includes millennials and post-millennials (aka Generation Y and Generation Z, respectively), or the younger users of technology. This demographics is vital to the growth of fintech initiatives as they are more likely to expect their banking services to be technologically advanced and always online.

Digital Wallet: It refers to any electronic device or application that allows an individual to make payment through electronic transactions, normally of small amounts. This can be done either using cryptocurrency or real money pre-loaded onto a digital account.

Disruptive Innovation: It is an innovation that completely changes the way people do something (Amazon vs. in-store shopping). It describes innovations that improve products or services in unexpected ways and change both the way things are done and the market. The smartphone is an example of a disruptive technology. It has the potential to change completely the way in which users connect to information and communications technology (ICT) services.

Durability: It is a measure of how likely it is that the data are lost.

Ecosystem Participants: They are a set of organizations or individuals that can work together in order to gain synergies.

Electronic Communications Network (ECN): It is an electronic network that facilitates trading between stock or commodities exchanges.

Electronic Receipt: It is a receipt that is presented and stored as data only. No hard copy of this type of receipt is issued. The recipient can print it wherever the local fiscal laws so require.

Emergency Situation: It is a situation caused by accidents or disasters affecting the operator, and is characterized by the need to take appropriate technical and managerial exceptional actions aimed at the early restoration of normal operations.

Emerging Market: It is a country or region or market segment that has some characteristics of a developed market but does not meet the standards to be a developed market. This includes countries that may be developed markets in the future or were in the past.

E-money: It is a monetary value electronically recorded with the following attributes: (i) issued upon receipt of funds in an amount no lesser in value than the value of the e-money issued; (ii) stored on an electronic device (for instance, a chip, prepaid card, mobile phone, or computer system); (iii) accepted as a means of payment by parties other than the issuer; and (iv) convertible into cash.

Enabling Regulator: It is an agency that creates a regulatory environment conducive to the secure growth of fintech initiatives.

Encryption: It is the process of encoding messages or coding to protect the customer's information assets. Encryption is vital to fintech, the blockchain, and anything else that needs to be secure. Documents or data, such as names and numbers, are turned into a code using algorithms (mathematical formulas). A key is required to turn that code back into useful data (decryption).

End User: It is the end or final user of an application.

Enterprise Content Management (ECM): It is the management of all contents (data, unstructured documents, e-mail, voice, video, and so on).

Enterprise Resource Planning (ERP): It is the extension of manufacturing resource planning II to the remaining functions in the organization, such as engineering, finance, and personnel administration and management. It consists of a software package with a single data model that facilitates the horizontal and vertical integration of all interorganizational processes, improves process efficiency, and monitors processes through special key performance indicators (KPIs) according to quality, economic values, service levels, and timeliness. Some components of an ERP are accounting, industrial accounting, payrolls, sourcing, warehouse management, production, project control, sales, distribution, and facility maintenance.

Equity Investment: It refers to an investor buying an equity stake in a business. The value of that stake depends on the performance of the business. It can also be negotiated on stock exchanges for listed companies. It is a higher risk on respect to other investments.

Ethereum: It is a blockchain-based cryptocurrency platform that runs smart contracts. It was originally authored by Vitalik Buterin and Gavin Wood. Ether is the currency unit of Ethereum. It is used to pay for computational services on the Ethereum network.

Europay, Mastercard, and Visa (EMV): It is an international standard for smart credit cards that have a built-in CPU chip. It is branded with names such as "Chip and PIN". The smart card provides greater safety than a magnetic strip since it can support sophisticated security methods and make decisions on its own. It stands for Europay, MasterCard, and Visa, a global standard for inter-operation of integrated circuit cards (IC cards or "chip cards") and IC card–capable point of sale (POS) terminals and automated teller machines (ATMs) for authenticating credit and debit card transactions. It represents the global standard for credit and debit cards.

Facebook: It is a hugely popular online social network founded in 2004 for helping students to stay in touch and share information.

Federation: It is the act of combining organizations, data, or identities across multiple systems or companies.

Financial Inclusion or Inclusive Financing: It is the delivery of financial services at affordable costs to sections of disadvantaged and low-income segments of the society.

Financial Institutions: These are the institutions that handle financial transactions and are normally the place where people deposit their money or get credit.

FinServ: It is an abbreviation that appears largely on Twitter, referring to anything in the financial services industry.

Fintech: It is a contraction of the words "financial" and "technology", an industry known for championing software and technology in the financial sector.

It is also popular for generally challenging traditional banking and incumbent institutions. Fintech has become a ubiquitous term for any technology applied to financial services, typically where financial institutions use a technology for front- and back-office functions in support of their customers. According to *Fintech Weekly*, it is "a line of business based on using software to provide financial services. Fintech companies companies are generally startups founded with the purpose of disrupting incumbent financial systems and corporations that rely less on software such as financial institutions".[6]

First-Mover Advantage (FMA): It is the competitive advantage gained by being first in the market. Not every startup is the first in the market. If it is, it is useful to signal to potential investors. First to market also means educating your market as you go, which is more costly than it would be in a market with clearly established demand.

Foreign Exchange, Forex (FX): In the context of fintech initiatives, it is a dynamic subsector where companies are offering ordinary people and businesses ways of saving considerable amounts on foreign exchange rates when they travel or move abroad. Revolut, Curve, Currency Fair, and TransferWise are some of the forerunners. Startup digital financial institutions such as Mondo also offer low exchange rates.

Generation Y (Gen Y): It is a term commonly used by marketing professionals to describe the segment of the population born between 1977 and 1994, especially in the United States.

Generation Z (Gen Z): It is a term commonly used by marketing professionals to describe the segment of the population born between 1995 and 2000, especially in the United States. This generation is sometimes also called m-generation, due to their extensive use of mobile devices.

Geolocation: It is the process or technique of identifying the geographical location of a person or device by means of digital information processed via the internet or GSM (global system for mobile communications).

Global Gateway: It is an online eIDV service developed for the international market. This product was created specifically to help businesses comply with AML and know your customer (KYC) rules, and has since evolved to support a diverse range of international eIDV requirements. Global Gateway is used by e-commerce, finance, insurance, gaming, and social media clients worldwide for all their compliance, risk mitigation, and age verification needs.

Global System for Mobile Communications (GSM): It is a standard for digital mobile phones. It is used by 80% of the global mobile market.

[6] https://www.finextra.com/blogposting/12890/what-is-fintech-and-where-does-it-live?utm_medium=rss&utm_source=finextrafeed, Accessed 31 July 2016.

Governance: It refers to the controls and processes that make sure the effectiveness, efficiency, and economics of a sector. The sector might refer to the entire organization or to an organizational unit, a process, or data.

High Risk: It is a payment or a loan that meets the risk criteria established by payment networks or credential issuers.

High Value: It is a payment or a loan exceeding certain payment network or credential issuer value criteria or a combination of value and spend category criteria.

Hijacking: It refers to when an attacker takes control of a communication between two entities, masquerading as one of them. As with cloning, hijacking could give the hacker access to the victim's financial accounts.

Hybrid Payments: These are the solutions that can handle both proximity and remote payments. This category contains solutions that extend existing behaviors. It can be card payments done in mobility with a smartphone card reader, for instance, iZettle.

Identerati: It is an informal collective of individuals, organizations, and companies with a common interest in identity and identity management in a digital and online context. This group is among the top influencers and thought leaders in the sphere of identity and access management. The term refers to the future of the industry usually, without naming any specific member of the group.

Identity Management: It is the management of personal identity information so that access to computer resources, applications, data, and services is controlled properly.

Identity Proofing: It is the process of providing sufficient information (for instance, identity history, credentials, and documents) to a service provider for proving that a person is the same person he/she declares to be.

Identity Theft: It is the illegal use of someone else's personal information (as a Social Security number), especially in order to obtain money or credit.

Identity Verification: It is the identification of individuals by using their physiological and behavioral characteristics to establish a mapping from a person's online identity to their real-life identity.

Incident: It is any event that is not part of the standard operations of a service and that causes or may cause an interruption to, or a reduction in the quality of that service.

Incubator: It is an institution or process that accelerates the successful development of startups by providing entrepreneurs with a certain number of targeted resources and services. In short, these programs exist to help improve the odds of success for startups.

Information and Communications Technology (ICT): It is the combination of computers, storage, network, applications, and so on that provides integrated computer-based services.

Information Risk: It is the risk of incurring financial, reputational, and market share losses in relation to the use of information technology and communications. In the integrated view of the business risks for prudential purposes (ICAAP), this type of risk includes operational, reputational, and strategic risks.

Information Technology Infrastructure Library: It is a methodology for the management of ICT services.

Instant Messaging (IM): It is a protocol for communicating between two parties using text-based chat through IP (Internet protocol)-based clients.

Integration: It is the process of combining components or systems into an integrated entity.

Interaction Design (IxD): It is a customer-led design methodology for improving the interaction between customers and systems.

Interactive Voice Response Systems: These are the automated telephone support systems that people hear when they call a free phone helpline or customer support number. They use menus and responses via touch-tone and/or voice response for navigation.

Internet Bot: It is a software application that runs automated tasks over the internet. Typically, bots perform tasks that are both simple and structurally repetitive, at a much higher rate than would be possible for a person alone.

Internet of Things: It is a development of the internet in which everyday objects have network connectivity, allowing them to send and receive data. Internet of Things (IoT) has the ability to record, receive, and send data. This covers internet-connected vehicles, devices, switches, sensors, and everything in between.

Internet Protocol (IP): It is the primary protocol for transmitting data or information over the Internet.

Internet Service Provider (ISP): It is an organization providing internet access to customers.

Internet Troll: It is a person whose sole purpose in life is to seek out people to argue with on the internet over extremely trivial issues. Such arguments can happen on blogs, Facebook, Myspace, and others. The best thing to do to fight an internet troll is to not answer or report them.

Interoperability: It is concerned with the ability of systems to operate in multiple environments.

Invoice Trading: It is the process in which small- and medium-sized enterprises (SMEs; sellers) auction their invoices online as a way to unfreeze a credit that would otherwise be tied up. They can sell these invoices individually or in bundles to bidders (buyers) who offer the most competitive price to advance them the money. Invoice trading platforms include Market Invoice and Platform Black.

iOS: It is Apple's mobile operating system for its iPhone, iPod touch, iPad, Apple television, and similar devices.

Key Performance Indicators (KPIs): These are the metrics (or measures) used within corporations to measure the performance of one department against another with respect to revenue, sales lead conversion, costs, customer support, and so on.

Know Your Customer (KYC): It is an application used to collect information in order to know the customer better using the data in some application or site. In some countries, it is mandatory for AML or blacklisting verifications. It also refers to the process used by a business to verify the identity of its clients. The term could also refer to the bank regulation that governs these activities. Companies of all sizes employ KYC processes for ensuring their proposed agents', consultants', or distributors' anti-bribery compliance. Financial institutions, insurers, and export credit agencies are increasingly demanding that customers provide detailed anti-corruption due diligence information to verify their probity and integrity.

Knowledge-Based Authentication (KBA): It is a security measure that identifies end users by asking them to answer specific security questions in order to provide accurate authorization for online or digital activities. Knowledge-based authentication is used in many different types of network setups and across the internet, where companies often ask users to answer these questions in order to gain access to personal, password-protected areas of a site. It is used for fraud prevention. Consumers probably know this as the "secret question" users must answer before being granted access.

Lean and Digitize: It is the method used to make the processes at the same time lean and automated, wherever it is necessary.

Least Privilege: It is the principle that states that each user or system administrator has the qualifications strictly necessary for the performance of assigned duties.

LinkedIn: It is an online social network for business professionals.

Logical Security: It is a set of processes and activities aimed at obtaining confidentiality, integrity, and availability of data and information through the adoption of measures: techniques (system for access control, antivirus, firewalls, intrusion detection systems, and so on), organizational (definition of policies, safety standards, user profiling and related ratings, and so on), and procedural (process definition).

Loyalty Service Provider: It is an organization that provides the administration of loyalty and rewards programs.

Machine Learning: It comprises algorithms that modify themselves to better perform their assigned tasks. This makes them sound as if they are humans.

Machine Vision: It is where computers try to identify the elements of a picture.

Malicious Code: It is the software in the form of a virus, worm, or other malware that hackers load into the handset, the SMS gateway, or the financial institution's server. Its objective is to perform an unauthorized process that has an adverse impact on the confidentiality, integrity, or availability of financial information and transactions.

Malware: It is a contraction for "malicious software", inserted into a system, usually covertly, with the intent of compromising the confidentiality, integrity, or availability of the victim's data, applications, or operating system, or otherwise annoying or disrupting the victim.

Marketing: The American Marketing Association defines it as the activity, set of institutions, and processes for creating, communicating, delivering, and exchanging offerings that have value for customers, clients, partners, and society.

Marketplace Lending: It is the lending which occurs through an online platform. Funding Circle, Zopa, and LendInvest are all examples of this. Their business models vary very much. Sometimes, a borrower and an individual lender are directly connected, sometimes indirectly. To use LendInvest's business model as an example, LendInvest provides the borrower with a property loan and then places it onto its marketplace platform for investment. With £1000 or more, people can deposit into their LendInvest account and invest from £100 onward in the loans on the platform. After investing, they earn regular payments, from 5% up, as the borrower pays interest on the loan. They get their investment back when the borrower repays the loan. The platform is designed to offer simple, secure investment opportunities to both new and sophisticated investors while helping SMEs of, for instance, professionals.

Match Rate: It is, in identity verification, a measurement of how often queries on data sources yield sufficient information to confirm an identity. Higher match rates represent more reliable and effective identity verification.

Messaging Commerce: It is the type of commerce that lets users make purchases with something as simple as messaging apps. It is where messaging apps meet a POS. This trend is currently largest in Asia, but will likely continue growing.

Microcredit: It is the granting of small loans to entrepreneurs, professionals, or artisans who cannot access traditional financial institution loans, usually because they cannot offer adequate guarantees or collateral and/or do not have a credit history. It first emerged in developing countries. It enables micro-projects to be implemented. It encourages economic activity and wealth creation. It is now also practiced in developed countries and transition economies. Microcredit is part of a wider field that includes other financial tools such as saving, micro-insurance, and other products that together comprise microfinance.

Microfinance Institution (MFI): It is an alternate form of financial institutions found in developing countries that provides microcredit lending.

Microfinance: It is a range of financial tools (loans, savings, insurance, money transfers, and so on) designed for people who do not have access to traditional financial services.

Micro-SD Card: It is a memory card that is designed to integrate with mobile phones and other mobile devices.

Mini-bonds: These are a way for individuals to lend money directly to businesses. These are, in effect, IOUs (I owe you) which companies sell to investors. Typically, they have terms of three to five years, and investors earn regular interest payments during the life of the mini-bond.

Minimum Viable Product (MVP): It is the version of a new product which allows a team to collect the maximum amount of validated learning about customers with the least effort.

Mission: It is the way to proceed toward the vision of the company.

Mobile Banking: It comprises platforms that enable customers to access financial services such as transfers, bill payments, balance information, and investment options. It also encompasses SMS (short message service or text messaging alerts) using a smartphone to access a bank's website as well as services provided directly through a bank's app on a smartphone.

Mobile Device: It includes smartphones, feature phones, and tablet computers. The term "mobile device" is also used interchangeably with "mobile handset" or "handset".

Mobile Money: It comprises services delivered over mobile devices to enable payments between two parties. Examples of successful providers include M-Pesa, Edy, G-CASH, MTN Money, T-money, and Suica.

Mobile Network Operator (MNO): It is the provider of mobile device connectivity services. For the purposes of this book, this role also refers to the original equipment manufacturer (OEM) and SDM.

Mobile Payment: It is a payment service that includes digital money, either transferred or placed in a mobile wallet. The transaction is performed on a mobile device. Mobile payments are defined as either proximity payments or remote payments. It is also known as "mobile money, mobile money transfer, and mobile wallet". Mobile payment refers to "payment services operated under financial regulation and performed from or via a mobile device". Most major financial institutions facilitate some form of mobile payments, including e-transfers and credit card payments.

Mobile Portal: It is a website designed specifically for mobile phone interfaces and mini-browsers.

Mobile Wallet: It is an electronic account, denominated in a currency, held on a mobile phone that can be used to store and transfer value. Examples of mobile wallets that exist today include Google Wallet, Obopay, PayPal, and the Visa digital wallet. A mobile or digital wallet is a way to carry your credit card or debit card information in a digital form on your mobile device. Instead of using a physical plastic card to make purchases, it is possible to pay with smartphones, tablets, or smartwatches. In theory, it is safer to use a mobile wallet rather than a physical credit or debit card, as the owner does not need to reveal their account number at a point of purchase. Even if someone was able to intercept the transmitted encrypted information, he/she could not reuse it to authorize further payments. Android Pay and Apple Pay are two of the big players. Google Wallet has a tap-to-pay feature similar to Android Pay. Gizmodo reports that it is a way of transferring money between friends over the internet.

National Institute of Standards and Technology (NIST): It is a US Department of Commerce agency that, among other responsibilities, promotes the effective and secure use of cloud computing within organizations.

Near-Field Communications (NFC): It is the technology behind digital wallets, tap-to-pay cards, and other similar items. It is a set of communication protocols that enable two electronic devices, one of which is usually a portable device such as a smartphone, to establish a contactless communication by bringing them no more than 4 centimeters (2 inches) of each other. It allows for instance for simplified transactions, data exchange, and wireless connections between two devices. NFC transactions for mobile payments are transmitted using ISO 14443 A/B standard.

Network Software: It is the set of specialized programs for the management of communications. Typical examples of network software are the mailers and products management and sharing of distributed resources.

Network Virtualization: It is a form of virtualization with a method for combining the available resources in a network by splitting up the available bandwidth into channels. Each channel is independent of the others. Each one can be assigned (or reassigned) to a particular server or device in real time.

Non-Blocking Failure or Malfunction: These are system malfunctions which do not substantially compromise the operations of the system. The services for which the system is used can continue to operate.

Norm: It is an alternative word for standardization.

Omnichannel: It is a multichannel approach to sales that seeks to provide the customer with a seamless shopping experience, whichever channel the customer uses. It could be online either from a desktop or mobile device or by telephone or in a branch/agency.

Onboarding: It includes all the steps to get a new customer integrated into a new program. Exactly what counts as onboarding varies from company to company. Streamlined onboarding processes are one of fintech's advantages over traditional financial institutions.

Online Investment: It is an investment in initiatives in online solutions. Fintech entrepreneurs have brought down the barriers to investment. As savings account interest rates stagnate, technology is fast making it easier for more people to benefit from the higher returns investment can offer. Online investment may contain a certain amount of risks.

Open Wallet: It is a mobile wallet that is designed so that payment credentials from multiple credential issuers can be bound and used for a payment. Although "open", this type of wallet requires agreements and business relationships between credential issuers and wallet providers before a wallet may be bound to credentials.

Organization: In this book, this term indicates a company, a public institution, either central or local, or a non-profit entity.

Original Equipment Manufacturer (OEM): It refers to a producer of devices or components used by the end user or by other manufacturers. For the purposes of this book, this role is interchangeably with the MNO and the SDM.

Output: It is the result produced by a system or process. The final output is normally a product, a service, or an initiative.

Over the Counter (OTC): It refers to physical transactions or trades done on behalf of a customer by a trader or customer representative who has access to a specific closed financial system or network.

P2P Lending: It is short for peer-to-peer lending, or social lending. It involves lenders loaning money directly to borrowers without the traditional institutions' processes and structures, typically put in place by traditional financial institutions. Online platforms match lenders and borrowers, providing the services at a lower cost than traditional institutions. P2P lending refers to anything that is decentralized and direct. Digital platforms handle the transactions using an algorithm to manage transactions between parties. Examples include Lending Club and Lending Loop.

Pass Code: It is an authentication method for end users' devices.

Payment Application: It is an application providing the security requirements for making a payment and storing the payment credentials.

Payment Card Industry Compliance (PCI Compliance): It is the respect of a set of specific security standards that were developed to protect card information during and after a financial transaction by the payment card industry. There are six main requirements for PCI compliance. All card brands are required to comply with these industry standards, and, though not always explicitly required, many fintech initiatives start using PCI compliance in order to assure a good security standard.

Payment Credential Issuer (PCI) : It is an organization responsible for the encryption, safety, and security of payment credentials. The relationship between the end user and the credential issuer is based on financial services offerings and products.

Payment Gateway: It is a service provider that authorizes card payments. It acts as an intermediary between a payment portal, such as a website, and a bank. It is a service that for example automates the payment transaction between the shopper and the merchant. It is usually a third-party service that processes, verifies, and accepts, or declines card transactions on behalf of the merchant through secure Internet connections. Examples include PayPal and Moneris.

Payment Network: (or the Payment Application Creator) It is a network that creates the non-user facing payment application software (for instance, Visa, MasterCard, CUP, etc.).

Payment Service: It is a provider-independent organization that develops a payment solution. It could be entrepreneurs, online payments services, or technology organizations.

Payment Task Force: It was a working group formed by the Canadian government in 2011 to evaluate the future of payments in Canada.

PayPal: It is a leading P2P payment provider; others include Square, iZettle, ClearXchange, Dwolla, PingIt, PopMoney, QuickPay, Vermo, and ZashPaY.

Pay-per-Click (PPC): It is a method of paying that appears in search engine results by bidding and paying for specific keywords. You then pay at the successful bid rate every time a user/visitor clicks on your link.

Peer-to-Peer Economy: It is a person-to-person/peer-to-peer marketplace that facilitates the sharing and direct trade of assets built on peer trust.

Peer-to-Peer Lending (P2P Lending) aka Crowdlending: Some marketplace lending platforms are P2P. P2P lending is the practice of lending money to individuals or businesses using online platforms that match lenders directly with borrowers. Since P2P lending companies offering these services operate entirely online, they can often run with lower overhead and provide the service more cheaply than traditional financial institutions.

Peer-to-Peer or Person-to-Person (P2P): It is a method of passing information or data via IP-based communication methods between two individuals connected to the internet via a computer or mobile device.

Peer-to-Peer Payments: These are payments that occur directly between end users. A schema is not involved in this transaction.

Personal Productivity Software: It is a software used for processing individual tasks (for instance, WinZip, Adobe, MS Office, Google Apps, MS Project, and so on).

Person-to-Person Payment: It is a payment from a customer to another customer or to a small business.

Plan-Do-Check-Act (PDCA): It is the improvement cycle introduced by Deming. It is based on the sequence of actions: plan, do, check, and act.

Point of Sale (POS): It is the device that a merchant uses to capture payment credential information. It can be physical or virtual (via a mobile device). It refers to the capturing of data and customer payment information at a physical location for buying or selling goods or services. A variety of devices, which include computers, cash registers, optical and bar code scanners, magnetic card readers, or any combination of these devices, capture the POS transaction. The POS is the location where a retail transaction occurs. A POS terminal refers more generally to the hardware and software used at checkout stations. POS is that important step where customer payment information is taken at a physical location when making a purchase. Several popular fintech startups have created apps and services to expedite this process and keep it safe.

Policy: It is a general term for an operating procedure.

Portability: It is the ability to run applications, components, or systems running on one implementation and to deploy them on another implementation, for instance, of another vendor.

Primary Account Number (PAN): It is a 16-digit Issuer Identification Number (IIN), the first digit of which is the Major Industry Identifier (MII), followed by a variable-length (up to 12 digits) individual account identifier and then a single check digit.

Problem: It is the cause that creates an incident. Incidents that cannot be resolved due to the lack of an available solution, as well as repeated incidents related to a known issue ("known problem/error"), pass to the process of problem management. A workaround could remediate the problem, before finding the root causes and resolving them.

Process Improvement: It is a continuous effort to learn from the causes and effects in a process, aiming at reducing the complexity, the variation, and the cycle time. Eliminating or reducing the effects of the root causes improves the processes.

Process Management: It is a methodology used to optimize the organization as a system, determine which processes need to be improved and/or controlled, define priorities, and encourage the leadership to initiate and sustain process improvement efforts. It manages the information obtained because of these processes.

Process of Continuous Improvement: It is a structured approach that improves the overall performance of the organization by using methods appropriate to its problems. Its scope may be the quality or social responsibility of the business.

Process: It is a set of interconnected activities that transforms a set of inputs in one or more results.

Proprietary Wallet: It is a mobile wallet that is designed so that only the payment credentials from the wallet provider may be bound and used to make an NFC mobile payment.

Proximity Payment: It is the type of payment done at the merchant's POS using a contactless device.

Quality: There are many variations of the concept of quality, sometimes determined by an adjective or specifications. In general, quality is customer satisfaction in a way that is profitable for the organization.

Relationship Manager (RM): It is a dedicated customer service manager assigned to look after specific customers, usually high-net-worth customers.

Reliability: It is a metric on how often or the percentage of time the service is available.

Remote Payment: It is the opposite of proximity payment. Remote payment can be done remotely without requiring a physical contact between the actors in the payment process. It is done either between persons or to a merchant over the wireless network or through SMS.

Reporting: It consists of supplying and updating representative data and indicators, whose degree of details tends to vary depending on the person or organization for whom or for which they are intended. For the purposes of sustainable development, tools such as the GRI (Global Reporting Initiative) enable a standardized methodology to be agreed on at the international level. In a certain number of countries, there are laws that require that all organizations beyond a certain size publish a corporate social responsibility (or "sustainability") report.

Robo-Advisor: It is an online, automated advisor that provides financial advice or portfolio management, providing answers based on data and algorithms. Examples include Betterment and WealthSimple. These robo-advisors automate investment advice. Though they sound like metal robots in ties, they are primarily rooted in algorithms. Robo-advisor comes from online platforms and limits the need for human interaction when managing financial services, such as a portfolio.

Search Engine Optimization (SEO): It is the science of optimizing websites so that they appear in the top results for search engine inquiries.

Seed Capital: It is the initial capital used to start a business. It usually comes from VCs, friends, and family, and is relatively small.

Series A: It is a company's first round of VC financing.

Series B: It is a company's second round of VC financing.

Service Provider: It is an organization, such as a bank, a telecommunication organization, a merchant, and so on, that provides services to be integrated, for instance, with NFC mobile payments.

Sharing Economy: It is an economic model based on sharing, borrowing, swapping, trading, or renting temporarily products and services, enabling access or use over ownership. It is reinventing not just what is consumed but how it is consumed. The sharing economy model is becoming popular when the price of a particular asset is high and the asset is not fully utilized all the time.

Short Message Service (SMS): It is a system of communicating by short messages over the mobile telephone network. It can be rather secure if encrypted.

Siri: It is an application on the iPhone that recognizes the voice to send messages, make calls, set reminders, and more.

Six Sigma: It is a philosophy and a performance objective. It is a structured method for the continuous improvement of processes. The objective is a measure of process performance defined in terms of defects, with 3.4 defective parts per million opportunities.

Skype: It is a computer and mobile application company providing web, video, and phone chats. There is also a version for businesses (Skype for Business). Skype is now part of Microsoft.

Smart Contracts: These refer to computer programs that automatically execute a contract or part of it. These are automated and often blockchain-based contracts. They could save time and reduce costs in common transactions. Smart contracts are computer protocols that facilitate, verify, or enforce a digital contract. The idea is that these programs will potentially replace, in the future, notaries, lawyers, and financial institutions when handling common legal and financial transactions.

Smartphonatics: These are people who are fanatic about mobile phones. Aci Worldwide and Aite Group introduced this term.

SMiShing: It is a contraction of "SMS phishing". This attack uses SMS to facilitate bogus requests for personal information.

Social Data: It refers to the collective data produced by individuals as they actively participate in online social activities (including mobile).

Social Login: Also known as social sign-in, it is a form of single sign-in using existing login information from a social networking service such as Facebook, Twitter, or Google+ to sign into a third-party website in lieu of creating a new login account specifically for that website. It reduces website registration barriers, allowing users to authenticate using their existing social media identities and pre-verified user accounts.

Social Verification (or Consensus Verification): It refers to using a "Wisdom of Crowds" methodology to confirm identity. The wisdom of the crowd is the collective opinion of a group of persons rather than that of a single expert.

Software as a Service (SaaS): It is a software distribution model in which applications are hosted by a vendor or service provider and made available to customers over a network, typically the internet. Many fintech startups use this software distribution model. SaaS refers to applications hosted by a vendor on the cloud. Users can access them online for a subscription fee, as opposed to users buying the license of a software outright in a hard format such as a tape or a CD. SaaS is a common tool utilized by startups. A vendor sells the service of hosting applications on a cloud for users to access online.

Software Development Kit (SDK): It is a package provided by a mainstream software or operating system provider to the developer community to assist them in application construction.

Solvency II: It is a European Union (EU) legislative program compulsory in all 27 member states, including the United Kingdom. It introduces a new, harmonized EU-wide insurance regulatory regime. The legislation replaces 14 EU insurance directives.

Stakeholder: It is an individual, group, or organization that is likely to be affected, directly or indirectly, by an activity, a program, or a particular arrangement of an organization. Stakeholders include all those groups that participate or are otherwise involved in an organization's economic life (employees, customers, vendors, shareholders), those who observe it (unions, non-governmental organizations), and those it affects either directly or indirectly (civil society, local authorities, and so on).

Startup: It is a company that is in the first stage of its operations. Entrepreneurial founders of startups roll them initially as they attempt to capitalize on developing a product or service for which they believe there is a demand.

Stored-Value Card: It is a monetary value stored on a card, not in an externally recorded account. Examples are the Octopus, Oyster, and Suica systems used to replace public transport ticketing.

Straight-Through Processing (STP): It is the implementation of a system that requires no human intervention for the approval or processing of a customer application or transaction.

Subscriber Identity Module (SIM): It is the module that securely stores the service subscriber key International Mobile Subscriber Identity (IMSI) used to identify an individual subscriber on a mobile phone.

System: According to Deming, the system is a network of interacting components that cooperate to achieve the goals of the system. It can also represent the organization as a set of customers, vendors, a flow of materials, and information.

Tablet: It is a general-purpose computer contained in a single panel, with a touchscreen as the input device.

Technical Rules: These are compulsory indications for technical standardization or compliance.

Telematics: It is a synergy of telecommunications and informatics. In this book, it is synonymous with ICT.

The Financial Transactions and Reports Analysis Centre of Canada (FINTRAC): It is Canada's financial intelligence unit. It was founded in 2000. It is an independent agency, reporting to the Minister of Finance, who is accountable to the Parliament for the activities of the Centre. It was established and operates within the ambit of the Proceeds of Crime (Money Laundering) and Terrorist Financing Act (PCMLTFA) and its Regulations.

Thin File: It is a term used in credit scoring to describe a brief credit history. Traditionally, credit bureaus would not lend to people with thin files because they displayed too little experience in handling loans. More credit bureaus are considering alternate data—such as the history of utility payments or rent—in evaluating credit decisions.

Throughput: It is a metric on how quickly a service responds.

Token: It is a cryptographic value provided by a card issuer as proof that a delegated management operation has been properly authorized.

Tokenization: It protects sensitive data with unique physical or virtual devices. These "tokens" allow users to retain essential information about their financial transactions without compromising security. Tokenization can turn complex information into short, useful codes. It, when applied to data security, is the process of substituting a sensitive data element with a non-sensitive equivalent, referred to as a token that has no extrinsic or exploitable meaning or value.

Total Cost of Ownership (TCO): It is a metric taking into account the costs all along the life cycle of a solution. Typically, it includes procurement, installation, testing, maintenance, use, and disposal costs at the end of the useful life of a solution.

Touchpoint: It is any channel or mechanism by which a customer can have day-to-day interactions with a service organization, such as a bank, in order to transact or conduct business.

Trading and Robo-Advisors: It is an online advisory management service that provides automated, algorithm-based portfolio management advice without the use of (human) financial planners. Robo-advisors use the same software as traditional advisors, but usually only offer portfolio management. They are normally not involved in more personal aspects of wealth management, such as taxes and retirement or estate planning. They tend to be of a lower cost with lower account minimums.

Transaction Review: It is an administrative feature accessed through the Global Gateway portal that provides visibility into a customer's verifications regardless of integration. Global Gateway customers can repopulate entries automatically, review failed transactions for data optimization, add data sources to boost match rate, and create lists of historical transactions for audits or reports.

Transaction: It is the action of executing a function or an application. An example of a transaction is the execution of the purchase at the POS and the processing of authorization and clearing messages.

TruDetect: It is a SaaS identity verification product capable of scoring the authenticity of cyber identities. It evaluates global internet identity information and behavior by applying proprietary, machine learning algorithms to determine the authenticity of a profile in real time. TruDetect can be integrated via an API, Web-based User Interface (UI) or batch process. It requires only the user registration information currently collected. This SaaS process is invisible to the users. It can be used at any point in the validation workflow. In this way, it thereby enables seamless and effective authentication.

Trust: It is the ability of two parties to define a trust relationship with a formal authentication of themselves.

Twitter: It is a social media website that supports microblogging between participants in the network, similar to SMS but on the Web. It had an initial limitation of 140 characters.

Umbrella Application: It is an application that enables the communication between a wallet and all payment applications related to this wallet. The umbrella application is used only when a payment application is stored on the Universal Integrated Circuit Card (UICC). The relationship of the umbrella application to payment applications is a one-to-many relationship. For an embedded secure element, the device software plays this role.

Unbanked: These are persons who do not have a current account or a savings account with a financial institution. Unbanked persons transact with cash. Unbanked persons are often poor; lack of a bank account often renders one ineligible to buy a house or take advantage of some social services.

Underbanked: These are persons who have a financial institution account that is not used more than once per year. The underbanked are people or businesses that have poor access to mainstream financial services, normally offered by retail financial institutions. The underbanked are a distinct group from the unbanked, who do not have banking relationships at all. They might have a banking account but rely largely on alternative methods. The ability to serve the underbanked is one of the most important facets of fintech.

Unicorn: Cowboy Ventures founder Aileen Lee coined the term in 2013 to describe startups with billion-dollar valuations. "Decacorn" refers to startups with a valuation of +$10 billion.

Universal Product Code (UPC): It is the standard used to name products in a unique way.

Upselling: It is a system of selling an additional service of a higher margin or total revenue within the same product or asset class to a customer, typically upgrading from one class of product to another.

Usability Testing (UT): It is the science of testing how users interact with a system, product, or interface through observation.

User as Owner: Trulioo defines this concept as personal information aggregated or stored by an organization. This means that companies and governments can store an individual's information, but they cannot use the information or share it without the individual's consent. It enables standardized privacy policies that work across borders under the assumption that the individual owns their own personal identifying information (PII). User as Owner negates the need for governments to create individualized and quickly outdated regulations that govern the use of personal data. It ensures that policy-makers and businesses, such as Google, are not deciding how a person's information is used in any context. This will create an environment of accountability, which naturally leans in the favor of consumer privacy. The penalties for the mishandling of personal information spur data aggregators to proceed only with the individual's knowledge.

Validation: It is a method to provide specific personal information to prove ownership of the identity for the purpose of identity verification.

Value: It is a measure defined by the end customer. Conceptually, it is the relationship between benefits and cost/damage of a product or service. It is expressed in terms of a product/service that can meet the customer's demands at a given price and at a given moment. It is also possible to refer to value as perceived by the customer, and see all the product/service characteristics that the customer considers as necessary and valuable. Any activity that consumes resources (including time) and does not bring value to the customer or to the organization is waste (*Muda*, in Japanese).

Vendor: It is a person or organization that provides goods or services for use in a process.

Video Chat: From the English word "chat", meaning to converse or discuss informally. It is a web technology facilitating long-distance discussions in real time, combining video, sound, and text.

Virtual Currency: It is a form of currency, such as Bitcoin, Linden dollars, QQ coins, Project Entropia Dollars (PED), and so on, that exists in the virtual world and can be exchanged for real currency by users.

Vision: It is an expression of what would represent a success for the organization. The objective is to produce a mental image to aim at generating creative tensions between the current reality and the vision of the organization. In order to be valuable, the whole organization should share it. This requires many efforts and much patience. The mission is the way to proceed toward the vision.

Voice over Internet Protocol (VoIP): It is an internet-based protocol. It allows users to use voice communication, such as over a telephone system.

Wallet Application or Wallet: It is an end-user facing financial application. It installs on a mobile device. The application allows users to enter and manage account specific information used in an NFC mobile transaction. It may be possible for one or more mobile wallets to reside on a mobile device at any given time.

Wallet Provider: It provides the mobile wallet (for instance, Google Wallet, ISIS, Visa, MasterCard, FIs, or other third parties).

Web 2.0: It refers to web applications that facilitate interactive information sharing, interoperability, user-centered design, and collaboration on the World Wide Web.

Widget: It is a generic type of software application. It is usually portable, working across different operating systems and devices.

References

Accenture. (2014a). *Digital disruption: Bank revenues at risk*. Accenture Research, 1–61.

Accenture. (2015). *The future of Fintech and banking: Digitally disrupted or reimagined?* Accenture Research, 1–12.

Agrawal, A. K., Catalini, C., & Goldfarb, A. (2011). *The geography of crowdfunding* (NBER Working Papers 16820). National Bureau of Economic Research, Inc., 1–63.

Agrawal, A. K., Catalini, C., & Goldfarb, A. (2014). Some simple economics of crowdfunding. *Innovation Policy and the Economy, 14*(1), 63–97.

Ahamad, S., Nair, M., & Varghese, B. (2013). A survey on crypto currencies. *Proceedings of International Conference on advances in computer science*, AETACS, 42–48

Aksoy, L., Keiningham, T. L., & Bejou, D. (2007). Objectives of customer centric approaches in relationship marketing. *Journal of Relationship Marketing, 6*, 1–8.

Al-Fedaghi, S. S., & Taha, M. M. (2006). Personal information eWallet. *IEEE International Conference on Systems, Man, Cybernetics*, 2855–2862. doi:10.1109/ICSMC.2006.385307.

B. Nicoletti, *The Future of FinTech*,
DOI 10.1007/978-3-319-51415-4

Ali, R., Barrdear, J., Clews, R., & Southgate, J. (2014). Innovations in payment technologies and the emergence of digital currencies. *Bank of England Quarterly Bulletin, Q3*, 262–276.

Alt, R., & Puschmann, T. (2012). The rise of customer-oriented banking—Electronic markets are paving the way for change in the financial industry. *Electronic Markets, 22*, 203–215.

Arner, D. W., Barberis, J., & Buckley, R. P. (2015). The evolution of FinTech: A new post-crisis paradigm? Retrieved February 24, 2017, from http://holland-fintech.com/wp-content/uploads/2015/10/SSRN-id2676553.pdf

Arslanian, H. (2016). *Entrepreneurship in Finance*. London, UK: Palgrave Macmillan.

Barriball, K. L., & While, A. (1994). Collecting data using a semi-structured interview: A discussion paper. *Journal of Advanced Nursing, 19*(2), 328–335.

Batiz-Lazo, B., & Efthymiou, L. (Eds.). (2016). *The book of payments*. London, UK: Palgrave Macmillan.

BBVA. (2015a, September 21). Crowdfunding (Fintech Series) (English Edition). *BBVA Innovation Center.*

BBVA. (2015b, September 21). Mobile banking (Fintech Series) (English Edition). *BBVA Innovation Center.*

BBVA. (2015c, September 15). P2P Finance (Fintech Series) (English Edition). *BBVA Innovation Center.*

BBVA. (2015d, November 1). Personal financial management (Fintech Series by innovation edge) (English Edition). *BBVA Innovation Center.*

BBVA. (2015e, September 21). Social media banking (Fintech Series) (Spanish Edition). *BBVA Innovation Center.*

BBVA. (2016a, February 7). Blockchain technology (Fintech Series by innovation edge) (English Edition). *BBVA Innovation Center.*

BBVA. (2016b, March 15). Ebook: Biometric technology (Fintech Series by BBVA) (English Edition). *BBVA Innovation Center.*

Beijnen, C., & Bolt, W. (2009). Size matters: Economies of scale in European payments processing. *Journal of Banking and Finance, 33*(2), 203–210.

Bergek, A., & Norrman, C. (2008). Incubator best practice: A framework. *Technovation, 28*(1–2), 20–28.

Berger, A. N., & Udell, G. F. (2006). A more complete conceptual framework for SME finance. *Journal of Banking and Finance, 30*, 2945–2966.

Bholat, D. (2015). Big Data and central banks. *Bank of England Quarterly Bulletin, 55*(1), 86–93.

Birkinshaw, J. (1997). Entrepreneurship in multinational corporations: The characteristics of subsidiary initiatives. *Strategic Management Journal, 18*(3), 207–229.

Bisges, M. (2014). Ökonomische Analyse des Urheberrechts. *Zeitschrift für Urheber- und Medienrecht, 58*(12), 930–937.
Bonacchi, M., & Perego, P. (2011). Improving profitability with customer-centric strategies: The case of a mobile content provider. *Strategic Change, 20*, 253–267.
Boot, A. W. A. (2000). Relationship banking: What do we know? *Journal of Financial Intermediation, 9*, 7–25.
Boot, A. W. A., & Thakor, A. V. (2000). Can relationship banking survive competition? *Journal of Finance, 55*, 679–713.
Boschma, R. (2005). Proximity and innovation: A critical assessment. *Regional Studies, 39*(1), 61–74.
Boulding, W., Staelin, R., Ehret, M., & Johnston, W. T. (2005). A customer relationship management roadmap: What is known, potential pitfalls, and where to go. *Journal of Marketing, 69*(4), 155–166.
Bower, J. L., & Christensen, C. M. (1995). Disruptive technologies: Catching the wave. *Harvard Business Review, 73*(1), 43–53.
Bryman, A. (2012). *Social research methods* (4th ed.). New York, NY: Oxford University Press.
Caluwaerts, P. (2015). Social networks, game-changer for e-money? Will social networks (e-monetise the payments industry?). *Journal of Payments Strategy and Systems, 9*(1), 90–110.
Campbell, D., & Frei, F. (2010). Cost structure, customer profitability, and retention implications of self-service distribution channels: Evidence from customer behavior in an online banking channel. *Management Science, 56*(1), 4–24.
Casadesus-Masanell, R., & Tarziján, J. (2012). When one business model isn't enough. *Harvard Business Review, 90*, 132–137.
Castells, M. (2002). *The Internet galaxy: Reflections on the Internet, business, and society*. Oxford, UK: Oxford University Press on Demand.
Chan, J. O. (2005). Toward a unified view of customer relationship management. *The Journal of American Academy of Business, 6*, 32–38.
Chan, K. F., & Lau, T. (2005). Assessing technology incubator programs in the science park: The good, the bad and the ugly. *Technovation, 25*(10), 1215–1228.
Chishti, S., & Barberis, J. (2016). *The Fintech Book: The financial technology handbook for investors, entrepreneurs and visionaries*. Chichester, UK: Wiley.
Chouday, S. P., Van Alstyne, M. W., & Parker, G. G. (2016). *Platform revolution: How networked markets are transforming the economy and how to make them work for you*. New York, NY: W.W. Norton.
Christensen, C. M. (1997). *The innovator's dilemma. When new technologies cause great fims to fail.* Boston, MA: Harvard Business School Press.

Clarke, A. H., Rostgaard Evald, M., & Munksgaard, K. B. (2012). Combining open innovation with corporate venturing: A case of how to balance incremental and radical innovation. *International Journal of Entrepreneurship and Innovation Management, 15*(4), 253–274.

Cohen, S. L., & Bingham, C. B. (2013). How to accelerate learning: Entrepreneurial ventures participating in accelerator programs. *Academy of Management Proceedings, 2013*(1), 14803–14803.

Cohen, W., & Levinthal, D. (1990). Absorptive capacity: A new perspective on learning and innovation. *Administrative Science Quarterly, 35*(1), 128–152.

Corbin, J. M., & Strauss, A. (1990). Grounded theory research: Procedures, canons, and evaluative criteria. *Qualitative Sociology, 13*(1), 3–21.

Covin, J. G., & Miles, M. P. (2007). Strategic use of corporate venturing. *Entrepreneurship Theory and Practice, 31*(2), 183–207.

Crockett, D. R., McGee, J. E., & Payne, G. T. (2013). Employing new business divisions to exploit disruptive innovations: The interplay between characteristics of the corporation and those of the venture management team. *Journal of Product Innovation Management, 30*(5), 856–879.

Dahlander, L., Dodgson, D. M., Gann, D., & Salter, A. (2006). The role of technology in the shift towards open innovation: The case of procter & gamble. *R&D Management, 36*(3), 333–346.

Davenport, T. H., & Dyché, J. (2013). Big Data in big companies. *International Institute for Analytics*. Retrieved August 24, 2016, from http://www.sas.com/content/dam/SAS/en_us/doc/whitepaper2/bigdatabigcompanies-106461.pdf.

Day, G. S. (1999). *The market-driven organization*. New York, NY: Free Press.

Dempwolf, C. S., Auer, J., & D'Ippolito, M. (2014). *Innovation accelerators: Defining characteristics among startup assistance organizations*. SBAHQ-13-M-0197. Washington, DC: US Small Business Administration.

Dietz, M., Khanna, S., Olanrewaju, T., & Rajgopal, K. (2015). *Cutting through the fintech noise: Markers of success, imperatives for banks*. Practice, G. B. (Ed.), 1–18. McKinsey and Company. Retrieved from http://www.mckinsey.com/industries/financial-services/our-insights/cutting-through-the-noise-around-financial-technology.

Dodgson, M., Gann, D., Wladawsky-Berger, I., Sultan, N., & George, G. (2015). Managing digital money. *Academy of Management Journal, 58*, 325–333.

Dolan, K. (2005). *Critical success factors in information technology project management, book*. Montreal, Canada: Universite' de Montreal.

Domingos, P. (2015). *The master algorithm: How the quest for the ultimate learning machine will remake our world*. New York, NY: Basic Books.

Dörr, D., & Natt Suchmaschinen, A. (2014). und Meinungsvielfalt. Ein Beitrag zum Einfluss von Suchmaschinen auf die demokratische Willensbildung. *Zeitschrift für Urheber- und Medienrecht, 58*(11), 829–846.

Dubois, A., & Gadde, L. E. (2002). Systematic combining: An abductive approach to case research. *Journal of Business Research, 55*(7), 553–560.

Dwyer, G. (2015). The economics of Bitcoin and similar private digital currencies. *Journal of Financial Stability, 17*, 81–91.

Edmonds, T. (2011). The demise of the cheque. *House of the Commons Library*. London, UK.

Eisenhardt, K. M., & Martin, J. A. (2000). Dynamic capabilities: What are they? *Strategic Management Journal, 21*(10–11), 1105–1121.

Ernst and Young. (2013). *Insurance in a digital world: Time is now, Ernst and Young Report*. Retrieved July 31, 2016, from http://www.ey.com/Publication/vwLUAssets/EY_Insurance_in_a_digital_world:_The_time_is_now/$FILE/EY-Digital-Survey-1-October.pdf.

Europe Central Bank. (2012). *Virtual currency schemes*. Europe Central Bank 21. Frankfurt, Germany.

F6S. (2015). *Welcome home*. Retrieved July 31, 2016, from www.f6s.com.

F6S Rockstart. (2015). Welcome. *F6S*. Retrieved July 31, 2016, from https://www.f6s.com/rockstartdigitalhealth.

F6S Startupbootcamp. (2015). Welcome. *F6S*. Retrieved July 31, 2016, from https://www.f6s.com/startupbootcampfintechlondon2015#/apply.

Ferrari, R. (2016). *L'era del Fintech: La rivoluzione digitale nei servizi finanziari*. Milano, Italy: FrancoAngeli.

Fishback, B., Gulbranson, C. A., Litan, R. E., Mitchell, L., & Porzig, M. (2007, July). Finding business idols: A new model to accelerate startups. *Ewing Marion Kauffman Foundation*, 2–8.

Flick, U. (2009). *An introduction to qualitative research*. Los Angeles, CA: Sage.

Flynt, O. (2016). *Smart contracts: How to use blockchain smart contracts for cryptocurrency exchange*. Seattle, WA: Amazon Digital Services LLC.

Galbraith, J. R. (2005). *Designing the customer centric organization: A guide to strategy structure and process*. San Francisco, CA: Jossey-Bass.

Ganguli, S., & Roy, S. K. (2011). Generic technology-based service quality dimensions in banking. *International Journal of Bank Marketing, 29*(2), 168–189.

Garg, R., Rahman, Z., & Qureshi, M. N. (2014). Measuring customer experience in banks: Scale development and validation. *Journal of Modelling in Management, 9*(1), 87–117.

Gartner. (2015). *Gartner says 6.4 billion connected things will be in use in 2016, up 30 percent from 2015*. Retrieved July 31, 2016, from http://www.gartner.com/newsroom/id/3165317.

Gilje, E. P., Loutskina, E., & Strahan, P. E. (2013). Exporting liquidity: Branch banking and financial integration. *Journal of Finance*, 1–37. doi:10.1111/jofi.12387.

Grimaldi, R., & Grandi, A. (2005). Business incubators and new venture creation: An assessment of incubating models. *Technovation, 25*(2), 111–121.

Guangzhou, A. (2015). Innovation and economic growth in East Asia: An overview. *Asian Economic Policy Review, 10*(1), 19–37.

Gulati, R. (1998). Alliances and networks. *Strategic Management Journal, 19*(4), 293–317.

Gupta, S., & Zeithaml, V. (2006). Customer metrics and their impact on financial performance. *Marketing Science, 25*(6), 718–739.

Hancké, B. (2009). *Intelligent research design: A guide for beginning researchers in the social sciences*. New York, NY: Oxford University Press.

Hill, M. D. (1990). What is scalability? *ACM SIGARCH Computer Architecture News, 18*(4), 18.

Hill, S. A., & Birkinshaw, J. (2008). Strategy–organization configurations in corporate venture units: Impact on performance and survival. *Journal of Business Venturing, 23*(4), 423–444.

Hoelscher, J. L. (2014). Digital currency risks. *Intern Audit, 71*, 24–25.

Holland Fintech. (2014). Holland FinTech making the Netherlands the next hub for global financial innovation. *Holland Fintech*. Retrieved July 31, 2016, from http://hollandfintech.com/.

Huang, E. Y., & Lin, C. (2005). Customer-oriented financial service personalization. *Industrial Management and Data Systems, 105*, 26–44.

Huber, A. (2014). Vernetzter Kontinent oder überregulierte TK-Branche. *Die Debatte über den Verordnungsvorschlag der EU-Kommission zum TK-Binnenmarkt, Multimedia und Recht, 4*, 221–224.

IBM. (2013). Analytics: The real-world use of Big Data in financial services. *IBM Institute for Business Value*, 1–12.

Idealog. (2014). Start me up: The Idealog Guide to Incubators. *Idealog*. Retrieved July 31, 2016, from http://idealog.co.nz/venture/2014/08/start-me-idealog-guide-incubators.

Jagersma, P. K. (2006). Strategic marketing and the global banking industry: Elements of excellence. *Journal of Business Strategy, 27*(4), 50–59.

Jayachandran, S., Sharma, S., Kaufman, P., & Raman, P. (2005). The role of relational information processes and technology use in customer relationship management. *Journal of Marketing, 69*(4), 177–192.

Johnson, J. A., & Friesen, M. (1995). *The success paradigm: Creating organizational effectiveness through quality and strategy*. New York, NY: Quorum Books.

Jonetzki, A. (2010). *Rechtsrahmen innovativer Zahlungssysteme für das Internet. Am Beispiel von PayPal*, Peter Lang GmbH, Frankfurt am Main, Germany.

Kanzler, V. (2015). *How do Fintech startups and a changing consumer behavior reshape the financial services industry?* Thesis at the Frankfurt Finance and Management School.

Katz, J. A., & Green, R. P. (2009). *Entrepreneurial small business*. Boston, MA: McGraw-Hill.

Kennedy, C. (2016). *Ethereum investing: Everything you need to know about ethereum*. Luxembourg: Amazon Media EU s.a.r.l.

Kohli, A. K., & Jaworski, B. J. (1990). Market orientation: The construct, research propositions, and managerial implications. *Journal of Marketing, 54*, 1–18.

Körber, T. (2015). Analoges Kartellrecht für digitale Märkte? *Wirtschaft und Wettbewerb, 65*(2), 120–132.

Kuratko, D. F., Hornsby, J. S., & Hayton, J. (2015). Corporate entrepreneurship: The innovative challenge for a new global economic reality. *Small Business Economics, 45*(2), 245–253.

Lähteenmäki, I., & Nätti, S. (2013). Obstacles to upgrading customer value-in-use in retail banking. *International Journal of Bank Marketing, 31*(5), 334–347.

Lavie, D., Stettner, U., & Tushman, M. L. (2010). Exploration and exploitation within and across organisations. *The Academy of Management Annals, 4*(1), 109–155.

LearnLaunch. (2014). Accelerator program. *LearnLaunch*. Retrieved July 31, 2016, from http://learnlaunch.com/accelerator/program/.

Lee, Y., & O'Connor, G. C. (2003). New product launch strategy for network effects products. *Journal of the Academy of Marketing Science, 31*(3), 241–255.

Lewis, B. R., & Soureli, M. (2006). The antecedents of consumer loyalty in retail banking. *Journal of Consumer Behavior, 5*, 15–31.

Lohit, N. (2013, July 5). Big data. *Bigger Facts*. Retrieved October 4, 2016, from http://blogs.sap.com/innovation/big-data/big-data-bigger-facts-098520

Mainelli, M., & Smith, M. (2015). Sharing ledgers for sharing economies: An exploration of mutual distributed ledgers (aka blockchain technology). *Journal of Financial Perspectives, 3*(3), 1–47.

Malek, K., Maine, E., & McCarthy, I. P. (2014). A typology of clean technology commercialization accelerators. *Journal of Engineering and Technology Management, 32*, 26–39.

Manyika, J. M., Roberts, R. P., & Sprague, K. L. (2008). Eight business technology trends to watch. *McKinsey Quarterly, 1*, 60.

Marinč, M. (2013). Banks and information technology: Marketability vs. relationships. *Electronic Commerce Research, 13*(1), 71–101.

Martelo, S., Soureli, M., & Cepeda, G. (2011). Creating dynamic capabilities to increase customer value. *Management Decision, 49*(7), 1141–1159.

Mason, C., & Brown, R. (2014). Entrepreneurship, entrepreneurial ecosystems and growth oriented. *Background Paper Prepared for the Workshop Organised by the OECD LEED Programme and the Dutch Ministry of Economic Affairs on entrepreneurial ecosystems and growth oriented entrepreneurship*. The Hague, The Netherlands.

Mcdermott, C. M., & Connor, G. C. O. (2002). Managing radical innovation: An overview of emergent strategy issues. *Journal of Product Innovation Management, 19*(6), 424–438.

McDonald, M., & Rowsell-Jones, A. (2012). *The digital edge*. Stamford, CT: *Gartner ebook*.

Meyer, E. (2014). *The culture map: Breaking through the invisible boundaries of global business*. New York, NY: Public Affairs.

Mielach, D. (2013). *Business incubators and accelerators: Here's the big difference*. Retrieved July 31, 2016, from http://www.businessnewsdaily.com/4658-businessincubator-accelerator-difference.html.

Miles, M. P., & Covin, J. G. (2002). Exploring the practice of corporate venturing: Some common forms and their organizational implications. *Entrepreneurship Theory and Practice, 26*(3), 21–40.

Min, B. S., & Smyth, R. (2015). *Determinants of R&D intensity and its impact on firm value in an innovative economy in which family business groups are dominant: The case of South Korea* (No. 25-15). Monash University, Department of Economics, Monash, Australia.

Moon, B. (2012). *SparkLabs, a new startup accelerator, launches bringing silicon valley and the world's innovators to Korea: A new technology startup accelerator launches to further develop one of the world's leading innovation nations by energizing its Entrepreneurial Ec*. Thesis at the Universitat Autonoma de Barcelona, 8–9, Barcelona, Spain.

Nasr, Y. (2016, January 15). Is your data safe? Fintech security: Challenges and solutions, *Fintech*. Retrieved August 25, 2016, from https://centricdigital.com/blog/fintech/is-your-data-safe-fintech-security-challenges-and-solutions/.

NIST. (2014, Feburary 12). *Framework for improving critical infrastructure cybersecurity, Version 1.0*. National Institute of Standards and Technology.

Nooteboom, B., Van Haverbeke, W., Duysters, G., Gilsing, V., & Van den Oord, A. (2007). Optimal cognitive distance and absorptive capacity. *Research Policy, 36*(7), 1016–1034.

O'Reilly, C. A., & Tushma, M. I. (2008). Ambidexterity as a dynamic capability: Resolving the innovator's dilemma. *Research in Organizational Behavior, 28*, 185–206.

O'Riain, S., Curry, E., & Harth, A. (2012). XBRL and open data for global financial ecosystems: A linked data approach. *International Journal of Accounting Information Systems, 13*, 141–162.

OECD. (2011). *Bank competition and financial stability*. OECD Competition Committee.

Ouellette, L. L. (2014). The Google shortcut to trademark law. *California Law Review, 102*(2), 351–407.

Parker, A. (2015). The commercial viability of financial inclusion. *Journal of Payments Strategy and Systems, 9*(3), 294–204.

Parkes, D. C., & Wellman, M. P. (2015). Economic reasoning and artificial intelligence. *Science, 349*(6245), 267–272.

Paternoster, N., Giardino, C., Unterkalmsteiner, M., Gorschek, T., & Abrahamsson, P. (2014). Software development in startup companies: A systematic mapping study. *Information and Software Technology, 56*(10), 1200–1218.

Pauwels, C., Clarysse, B., Wright, M., & Van Hove, J. (2015). Understanding a new generation incubation model: The Accelerator. *Technovation, 50–51*, 13–24.

Phillips, R. G. (2002). Technology business incubators: How effective as technology transfer mechanisms? *Technology in Society, 24*(3), 299–316.

Portsmouth, U. K., Klaus, P., & Nguyen, B. (2013). Exploring the role of the online customer experience in firms' multichannel strategy: An empirical analysis of the retail banking services sector. *Journal of Strategic Marketing, 21*(5), 429–442.

Pricewaterhousecoopers. (2015). Consumer lending: Understanding today's empowered borrowers. Retrieved February 24, 2017, from https://www.pwc.com/us/en/consumer-finance/assets/pwc-consumer-lending-radar.pdf

Raval, S. (2016). *Decentralized applications, Harnessing Bitcoin's Blockchain technology*. Sebastopol, CA: O'Reilly Media.

Rhino, C. (2013). A strategic view of payments, transaction banking and seizing the new opportunities. *Journal of Payments Strategy and Systems, 7*(3).

Robert, J., & Gordon, R. J. (2012). *Is U.S. economic growth over? Faltering innovation confronts the six headwinds* (NBER Working Papers 18315). National Bureau of Economic Research, Inc, 1–13.

Rockart, J. F., & Bullen, C. V. (1981). A primer on critical success factors. In C. V. Bullen (Ed.), *The rise of managerial computing: The best of the center for information systems research*. Homewood, IL: Dow Jones-Irwin.

Rockstart. (2015). *Rockstart Web and Mobile Accelerator program*. Retrieved July 31, 2016, from http://www.rockstart.com/accelerator/web-mobile/.

Rohrbeck, R., Hölzle, K., & Gemünden, H. G. (2009). Opening up for competitive advantage—How Deutsche Telekom creates an open innovation ecosystem. *R&D Management, 39*(4), 420–430.

Ronald, D. D. (1961). Management information crisis. *Harvard Business Review, 39*, 111–121.

Rowley, J. (2002). Using case studies in research. *Management Research News, 25*(1), 16–27.

Samani, R. E. (2013). *Digital laundry: An analysis of online currencies, and their use in cybercrime*. Beaverton: McAfee Labs.

Schildt, H. A., Maula, M. V. J., & Keil, T. (2005). Explorative and exploitative learning from external corporate ventures. *Entrepreneurship Theory and Practice, 29*(4), 493–515.

Schivardi, F., & Schneider, M. (2008). Strategic experimentation and disruptive technological change. *Review of Economic Dynamics, 11*(2), 386–412.

Shane, S. (2001). Technological opportunities and new firm creation. *Management Science, 47*(2), 205–220.

Shapiro, A. (2013). The way forward for digital currencies. *Promontory Sightlines Infocus*, 1–12

Sironi, P. (2016). *Fintech innovation: From Robo-advisors to goal based investing and gamification*. New York, NY: Wiley.

Skinner, C. (2014). *Digital Bank. Strategies to launch or become a Digital Bank*. Singapore: Marshall Cavendish International (Asia) Pte Ltd.

Skowron, L., & Kristensen, K. (2012). The impact of the recent banking crisis on customer loyalty in the banking sector. *The TQM Journal, 24*(6), 480–497.

Sullivan, B., Garvey, J., Alcocer, J., & Eldridge, A. (2014). Retail banking 2020—Evolution or revolution? *PwC Report*, 1–44.

Tasca, P., Aste, T., Pelizzoni, L., & Perony, N. (Eds.). (2016). *Banking beyond banks and money: A guide to banking services in the twenty*. Heidelberg, Germany: Springer Verlag.

Tidd, J., & Bessant, J. (2009). *Managing innovation, intergrating technologica, market and organisational change* (4th ed.). Chichester, UK: Wiley.

Todeva, E., & Knoke, D. (2005). Strategic alliances and models of collaboration. *Management Decision, 43*(1), 123–148.

Tom, E., Aurum, A., & Vidgen, R. (2013). An exploration of technical debt. *Journal of Systems and Software, 86*(6), 1498–1516.

Tushman, M., Smith, W. K., Wood, R. C., Westerman, G., & O'Reilly, C. (2010). Organisational designs and innovation streams. *Industrial and Corporate Change, 19*(5), 1331–1366.

Verhoef, P. C., & Lemon, K. N. (2013). Successful customer value management: Key lessons and emerging trends. *European Management Journal, 31*, 1–15.

Viaene, S. (2015). Driving digital: Welcome to the ExConomy. *Journal of Financial Perspectives, 3*(3), 40–25.

Wadhwa, A., & Mackenzie Hall, M. (2006). Knowledge creation through external venturing: Evidence from the telecommunication equipment manufacturing industry. *Academy of Management Journal, 49*, 819–835.

Wagner, M. (2011). Acquisition as a means for external technology sourcing: Complementary, substitutive or both? *Journal of Engineering and Technology Management, 28*(4), 283–299.

Wahlers, K. (2013). *Die rechtliche und ökonomische Struktur von Zahlungssystemen inner-und ausserhalb des Bankensystems*. Heidelberg, Germany: Springer Verlag.

Wattenhofer, R. (2016). *The science of the Blockchain*. Charleston, SC: CreateSpace Independent Publishing Platform.

Weber, R. H., & Volz, S. (2015). Kartellrechtlicher Handlungsbedarf im Lichte potenzieller Meinungsmacht von Suchmaschinen. *Wirtschaft und Wettbewerb, 4*, 356–368.

West, J., & Bogers, M. (2014). Leveraging external sources of innovation: A review of research on open innovation. *Journal of Product Innovation Management, 31*(4), 814–831.

William, J. (2016a). *Blockchain: The simple guide to everything you need to know* (English ed.). Luxembourg: Amazon Media EU S.à r.l.

William, J. (2016b). *Fintech: The beginner's guide to financial technology*. Seattle, WA: Amazon Digital Services LLC.

Wise, S., & Valliere, D. (2014). The impact on management experience on the performance of startups within accelerators. *The Journal of Private Equity, 18*(1), 9–19.

Wolman, D. (2015). *The End of Money: Indagine sul futuro del denaro: avvento e sopravvento di un mondo senza contanti*. Laterza and Figli Spa, Bari, Italy: Gius.

Xue, M., Hitt, L. M., & Chen, P. (2011). Determinants and outcomes of internet banking adoption. *Management Science, 57*(2), 291–307.

Yin, R. K. (2014). *Case study research: Design and methods* (5th ed.). Thousand Oaks, NY: Sage.

Zhao, X. (2009). Technological innovation and acquisitions. *Management Science, 55*(7), 1170–1183.

Websites (Accessed 12 July 2016)

tendermint.com
blockchain.info
www.leandigitize.com
www.crunchbase.com
www.ey.com/Publication/vwLUAssets/EY_Insurance_in_a_digital_world:_The_time_is_now/$FILE/EY-Digital-Survey-1-October.pdf
www2.deloitte.com/content/dam/Deloitte/us/Documents/regulatory/us-advisory-bitcoin-regulation-dcrs.pdf
Youtube, The Transformation of Finance. Fintech @ Davos World Economic Forum Video YouTube, 5:30. Published by YouTube, January 21, 2016. https://www.youtube.com/watch?v=AsetntXCPRQ
Fusionwire interview, 10 September 2015, retrieved 2016. http://www.fusionwire.net/insiders/forget-disruption-collaboration-is-the-key-to-fintech-innovation/
nexchange.com/article/10202#sthash.ulDAiwWm.dpuf
CollaborativeConsumption.com
Webopedia

Index

Note: Page number followed by "n" denote notes.

B. Nicoletti, *The Future of FinTech*,
DOI 10.1007/978-3-319-51415-4

CPSIA information can be obtained
at www.ICGtesting.com
Printed in the USA
LVOW05*2108180617
538525LV00011BA/563/P

9 783319 514147